A HISTORY OF THE DICKER

Two Sussex Villages

by
Lez Smith

This book is
dedicated to my wife Susie,
Colin, Rose and grand-daughters
Nikki and Kirsty.

Published by Lez Smith
9 Falcon Way, Hailsham,
East Sussex, BN27 1HY

Lez Smith asserts his right to be identified as the author of this book.

ISBN 0 9546322 0 6

Typeset by David Brown, Maynards Green 01435 812506
Printed by Windmill Press, Hadlow Down 01825 830319

CONTENTS

List of Illustrations

ACKNOWLEDGEMENTS

The author is deeply grateful to the many people who had volunteered information and who had kindly allowed me to reproduce their postcards and photographs, adding greatly to the book's text. Special acknowledgement is due to the staff of East Sussex Record Office, where the majority of my research was carried out, I am particularly indebted to Mrs Elizabeth Hughes (archivist) and the two ladies in the Search Room, Pauline Colwell and Jennifer Nash. To Hugh Rowlings (Editor: Sussex Express) in permitting the use of photographs and newspaper reports. Also to press photographer Terry Connolly for permission to use 'South Down Trugs' photograph and also Molly Beswick for inclusion of the map siting Dicker brickyards. To Airplic Ltd of Harpenden who permitted the use of aerial photographs taken of Upper Dicker in 1988. Every effort has been made to trace and acknowledge copyright of photographs and material in this book, the author duly apologises for any omissions. To Mr Clive Hale, Headmaster of Park Mead School, allowing me to examine the school log books; and Mrs R Ross for additional information. To the Scout and Guide Associations, also to Mr P B Burgess of the Military Aviation Museum, Tangmere.

Thanks are due to Jenners of Hailsham and the expertise of Mike Daws for lazer copying many photographs in the book's manuscribed stages, also to artist Nicholas Trudgian for his superb drawings.

To those who assisted and endured my persistent quest for information.

Christine Armitage	Jack Allcorn	Alan Boniface
Colin Borrer	Glen and Phyl Carr	Roy Clarke
Ivy Cull	Stuart and Carole Cole	Bert Dudley
Hilda Dann	Aubrey Dann	Frank Finch
Percy Guy	Cyril Hall	Dudley Hide
George and Pam Harmer	John Hawkins	Stan Henty
Martyn Hollebon	Roy and Margaret Lancaster	Dorothy Mitchell
Richard Millar	Fred and Dot Medhurst	Ron Medhurst
Robert Manley	Len Medhurst	Tom and Sylvia O'Shea
Les and Audrey Page	Dorothy 'Dorrie' Page	Jean Page
Roger Perrin	Richard Parker	Ernest Pitcher
Lynne Rennie	John and Kathleen Sheddon	Ernest and Daisy Smith
Kathleen Saunders	Bill Vidler	Betty Wickens
Don Wheatley	Nancy Wright	Richard Wise
Benjamin Wise	Les Winchester	John Young

My grateful thanks to Dev Ludbrook for checking the manuscript, and Sue Woodrow, whose willingness and countless hours spent typing my longhand written text to a legible format. Finally to Steve Benz for guidance and advice, and to Peter Gillies and David Brown, who brought my book to it's conclusion!

I dreamt I was dead and to heaven did go
Where did you come from they wanted to know
I answered 'From Dicker!' St Peter did stare
Please step inside – you're the first one from there

Geo Oliver
1923

INTRODUCTION

My interest in history really began at Hailsham Secondary Modern School, when barely into long trousers and sharing a desk with Bob Jarvis in 'Polly' Foster's classroom, who would wave a ruler in a sword-like manner proclaiming the Normans had landed near Pevensey or the bloody encounters that ensued between the Roundheads and Cavaliers during the English Civil War. I am sure that because Polly took no prisoners during these lessons, her enthusiasm and interest in the subject insured that one pupil found some fulfilment to compensate failings in maths and science lessons.

But the real seeds for this book were sown when Tom and Sylvia O'Shea cajoled and press-ganged me into doing an illustrated talk in Upper Dicker's Village Hall in 1988. It would not end there, with countless talks given to other audiences, my fascination to learn more about Dicker's past, brought about endless visits to the Record Office at Lewes and seeking answers to countless questions to numerous Dickerites, past and present. (Sadly there were those who would not see the book come to fruition.)

This is by no means a comprehensive or concise account of the Dicker area, nevertheless I would like to share with you a small facet of local history!

The Dicker, regards to this study, seems to break nearly all the ground-rules, the name referred to an area of land rather than a village, the tangle of civil and ecclesiastic boundaries with neighbouring Arlington, Chiddingly and Hellingly, sharing history with these three older parishes, creates confusion and uncertainty, especially when Latin written documents come into the equation; far beyond my limitations! This tentative approach to a history of Lower and Upper Dicker, may stimulate others to turn back the pages of time. Since that, "first in a lifetime experience" in 1988 of promoting local history, I fervently believe it should be recorded. For the bystander who ponders the idiosyncratic Sussex folk, may also ponder why the book's text includes Golden Cross – the area known as 'the Dicker' encompassed Broad Oak (now Golden Cross), hence the old Bat and Ball was always referred as being 'on the Dicker'. Through the centuries both farming and brickmaking have shaped Dicker's landscape and dwellings, which embraced a rural populace in work and leisure hours. Numerous local history books have been penned in recent years, my aim and endeavour over the past five years was to consign research and explorations of two Sussex villages into this book.

LEZ SMITH 2003

Chapter One

THE DICKER

The Dicker can be found a few miles inland from the South Downs and just west of the Cuckmere River. The puzzled visitor may question the origin of its unusual name, but a hasty motorist, would give it only a brief glance. However the name differs from other early settlements inasmuch as the name DICKER referred to an area of land rather than a settlement or village. A previous study of Sussex placenames confirms dyker or dicora as Old English combined with Latin words for ten, and establishes the once thousand-acre Dicker Common as "ten hides of open common land" situated between "Boarship" (Boship Green) and "Broad Oak" (now Golden Cross) and south into the village of Upper Dicker. This suggests the possibility of an earlier pattern of farmed enclosures around the periphery of the Common. Although it must be said that, apart from Michelham Priory, evidence of earlier history has been lost in the mists of time and we are left with little but conjecture.

Considering evidence of earlier occupation, archaeologists identified a pottery kiln and a scatter of pot sherds at Polhills Farm, Arlington, as being Roman which indicates Roman industrial activity and settlement in the area. Regarding its close proximity, Wick Street may well be of Roman origin, as 'street' suggests a link to places on or near a Roman road. There is little doubt that the more navigable Cuckmere contributed considerably to early Saxon settlements at Alfriston and Arlington. Michelham being Anglo-Saxon, meaning 'a large piece of land within a river bend', suggests there was likely to have been a Saxon settlement here long before the Norman Conquest.

With the ready availability and exploitation of the intensive woodland of the Weald, it is reasonable to assume that le Dykera gave way to open scrubland and pasture, and that the parochial system of Saxon churches formed the parishes of Arlington, Chiddingly and Hellingly.

Twenty years after the Norman Conquest in 1066, the Doomsday survey ascertained what or how much each landowner held and taxation due under Norman rule. Based on this evidence both neighbouring Claverham and Sessingham were identified as valuable pre-conquest settlements. The fact no record had been entered for Dykera probably implies the land was regarded as of little value or importance.

It was when Gilbert de l'Aigle (Lord of Pevensey Castle) obtained permission from Henry III to pull down an existing chapel at Michelham and founded a priory in 1229, that we may have the first documented reference to the Dicker. The Royal Licence which gave approval for this convent of Augustinian canons at Michelham, also ascribes land and property to the priory:

> *"given to God and the church of the Holy Trinity of Michelham, and to the prior and convent of Canons serving God in that place: all my demesne of Michelham and my Park of Pevense with the bondsmen, rents and other appurtenances; and 80 acres of marsh at Heylesham; and 20 acres of meadow in Wilendune; and pasture in the Diker and in the Broyle of Legton and other woods in Sussex for 60 head of cattle; and pannage for a 100 pigs in my said woods, and timber for building and repair of the said church and buildings and for fences, to be taken under the view of my forestors; and the advowsons of the church of Legton and Heylesham."*

Gilbert de l'Aigle proceeded to build first the magnificent church and then chapter house, dormitory and other buildings, but in 1235 journeyed to Normandy without consent of the King, leaving the Priory unfinished, and consequently forfeited his lands to the Crown. It is possible at this point in time the de l'Aigle family, in a vain attempt to rid themselves of the stigma of the King's displeasure, adopted the name le Dykere, apportioned to associated land. (Both place and surname have continued together until the present day.)

The priory offered charity to the poor as well as accommodation and food for the weary traveller. In 1302, Edward I, journeying with his royal entourage from Lewes, and probably through Selmeston and Wick Street, stayed the night of September 14th at Michelham Priory before continuing his journey to Battle Abbey. (In light of this, the priory could have claimed royal patronage; today, blue plaque status.)

Due to the ravages of the Black Death in 1348, the country's population was decimated. The Priory at Michelham suffered grave losses amongst the canons and workers, the pestilence brought a great deal of suffering to the parishes of Alciston, Arlington and Hellingly, and compounded by fear of the plague, led to some settlements actually being relocated. Without binding evidence, it remains difficult to ascertain why or when the settlement at Michelham ceased or when the village which is now Upper Dicker came into being. The question remains, did the Black Death bear sinister overtures, or had a settlement been established at the crux of four tracks before the plague and evolved to suit agrarian requirements?

With the Priory at Michelham not more than half a mile from the King's highway which ran from Berwick, across the Dicker Common, the Peasants Revolt in 1381 and subsequent threat directed towards religious houses, caused the Prior to implement construction of the priory's gatehouse.

In 1445 and again in 1478, the brethren at the Priory were seen to be behaving badly. The bishop's visitations to Michelham revealed a decline of

circa 1904

Michelham Priory

circa 1906

god-fearing practices. Of the many misdemeanours was: the selling of oak trees; millstones from the priory mills; and oxen, cows and horses for private gain. Later the canons were charged with religious laxity and promiscuous living involving a woman! Although unfounded, perhaps this was Alice Foord whom the Prior forbade to come within four miles of Michelham.

The Priory at Michelham was located in the midst of the community it served. The Act for the Dissolution of Monasteries in 1536 witnessed the closure and abandonment of the priory and canons were dispersed to livings elsewhere. The Priory succumbed to plunder; robbed out masonry stone was used in farmhouses in the seventeenth century; dressed stone found at Starnash and Lamberts during renovation in the 1980s may well have come from the priory's structure. Although no longer a monastic site, the Priory reverted to the Crown, and later passed through several hands, until 1587 when Henry Pelham purchased the priory, intent to restore and make some of the building habitable, and became the first owner to take up residence. In 1601, the Priory and associated lands were sold to the then Lord Buckhurst, Thomas Sackville, for £4,700 and remained in the Sackville family until 1897. Although Land Tax records listed the property as Michelham Manor, it had been let and occupied by tenant farmers until bought by J A E Gwynne in 1897.

Over the centuries, Dicker has been spelt various ways: Dykere in 1279 and Dekerre in 1535; by 1610 John Speed in his map of Sussex was less appreciative of the place, and it was shown by a cluster of trees and defined Ye Dike; by 1748 it had become Diccar.

The area we refer to as the Dicker fell mainly within the bounds of the manors of Alciston, Laughton and Michelham Park Gate, the tenanted farms and cottages were let by the Pelham, Gage and Sackville families. It is to this copyhold system that land holdings on the Dicker were held, this can be observed in the Alciston manorial accounts for 1625:

> "John Bodle paid rent for one cottage and 3 crofts called Plenties, bond tenure 3s. 4d, George Dawes – a tenement and 5 acres called Sternasshe 3s. 2d.
>
> "29 October 1795 – admission of William Bourne of Hellingly (yeoman), on surrender of John Staffell, a messuage and 4 acres near Diccar Fair Place, late Tylers, rent 4 shillings."

With only minimal placenames, an area of such diverse manorial and ecclesiastic boundaries, even for someone walking within the confines of Dicker, there was no knowing where the boundaries were! (Indeed it is frustrating for anyone who delves into local history. Even the eminent historian Mark Lower declared that the greater part of the Dicker Common had been in the Parish of Chiddingly, instead of Hellingly, bearing witness to the complex nature of local history.) Nevertheless what must be unique to the Dicker was the demarcation of a dwelling or parcel of land, "as situated and being at the upper end of the Diccar near the Fair Place", suggesting a hamlet of scattered dwellings which did not have a placename until the eighteenth century. The name Fair Place does not describe a beautiful location but rights to hold a fair there. When the 1789 Ordnance Survey map was published the orthography of Diccar had been transmuted to Dicker, and the hamlet identified as Upper Dicker. But half a century would pass before it gained ecclesiastical status. There is little wonder Dicker's boundaries have always been a continual source

Pollards Cottage, Upper Dicker

Sharrards (now Knights Acre)   *circa 1950*

of debate, and the ceremony of beating the bounds was essential to maintaining ancient rights and property. In 1946 controversy ensued following Ernest Shoosmith's death, when the hearse and mourners arrived at Upper Dicker church, only to discover the grave had been dug in the wrong parish!

History has witnessed farmland and dwellings owned by absent manorial lords and administered by a Court Leet, although the greater part of the Dicker Common had been encompassed within the bounds of the Manor of Laughton, even with commoner's rights to graze livestock; and illicit squatting and encroachment were promptly brought before the Manorial Court. But right to land holding with a new cottage plot probably led to Warren House being built on "Dicker Waste-land".

Indenture dated 10th January 1693:

"Doth demise, grant, lease and to farm, let unto the said Richard Walker, all that cottage and one piece of waste land containing two acres more or less called Warren House(later known as Field House), situate, lying and being in Hellingly upon the Common called the Diccar near the Fair Place – at a rent of ten shillings annum."

The key to the location of manorial tenements in and on the periphery of Upper Dicker in the eighteenth and nineteenth centuries, is provided by evidence gained from court-rolls and later from the 1843 Enclosure map and schedule. Although research remains both tentative and incomplete, my visit to the Centre for Kentish Studies at Maidstone proved beneficial; at last I was able to confirm what the Sackville family owned within the bounds of the Manor of Michelham Park Gate! In fact there had been little in Upper Dicker they did not own, whereas most of the farms on the east side of the Common were the tenure of the Manor of Alciston. This pattern of manorial land ownership as opposed to a closed parish with one dominant landowner, remains conducive to the pattern of small farms rather than a large estate.

Denuded of modern hedgerows, it is difficult to visualise the Dicker Common as open common. To journey along one of the Common's many tracks at the time when smuggling was at its height was fraught with danger. These were regular routes for contraband from Cuckmere Haven. It was probably on a dark moonless night, smugglers crossed the common in 1781 with twelve horses laden with tea, and became embroiled in a fight with Preventive Officers, wounding several smugglers and customs men, one of whom died later of his injuries. Subsequently Robert Hitchcock of Arlington was jailed for the willful murder of Thomas Holloway.

The piecemeal enclosure of the common in the nineteenth century was transformed by planting the thorn hedging which is what is seen in today's landscape. The Radcliffe Lunatic Asylum, near Oxford, acquired by grant or purchase Mount House, Caldicots and Coldharbour Farms, extending their land holdings at The Broad, Hellingly, and thus providing revenue for the far-flung asylum.

Extract from the Radcliffe trustees' minute books:

"By recent arrangements entered into with the tenants such annual rental had been increased to the sum of £611, which considering the present cultivation of the Dicker land, and recent depreciation of agricultural produce, appeared to the Trustees, highly satisfactory."

But they were probably horrified when the 1844 audit showed that carpenter Pitcher and thatcher Meadows had been paid £40 15s. 9d, and straw to thatch Mount Cottage had cost a further seventeen shillings. Hackles rose even further in 1853 when they realised repairs by Edward Tingley on the cottage cost another £1 17s. 5d!

There would have been a great demand on Dicker's brickyards when brick became the principal building material, with tiles replacing the customary thatched roof. The brick tax imposed in 1787 did little to impede the Goldsmith, Guys and Wenham brickmaking operations. At a time when the awe-inspiring Zoar Chapel had been built in 1837 and the parish church in 1843 Upper Dicker, as with many other villages, aspired to both brick and timber-framed houses. An era of architecture has passed, another has taken its place; some had their characteristic timber frame structures encased in brick.

Sharrards Cottage where once a none-too-friendly sheepdog snarled a greeting to a terrified paper boy had, in 1817, been denied a new bread oven by the parish overseers who deemed five pounds had been far too expensive, particularly when the annual rent was only twelve pence! In the 1950s, the old timber-framed cottage was stripped of its architectural past and renovated by the Griffin brothers. In 1961 it was sold for £10,500 and later renamed Knight's Acre. Widow Hide and others believed her cottage to be haunted; Pollards Cottage remains the last of the thatched dwellings in Upper Dicker.

To graphically record every dwelling would despatch the mentally sound to seek sanctuary in the nearest public house. Some may question why the older houses are set back from the Dicker Road, (the same terminology used by a nineteenth century census enumerator. The road through Upper Dicker village was once flanked on either side by open common land, (see 1843 Tithe map, page 8). Pre-nineteenth century dwellings were built on enclosed common, giving an outward appearance of a village green.

At the same time that London's first public flushing 'loo' for gentlemen was opened in 1852, the remainder of Dicker Common was being enclosed, giving the villagers a much needed Pleasure Ground that would be central to village celebrations. Although it remains uncertain as to whether the village held celebrations for Queen Victoria's Silver Jubilee; it was reported that the whole parish enjoyed one long day's entertainment and that over four hundred had entered into the spirit of the occasion for the 1897 Diamond Jubilee celebrations funded by Horatio Bottomley. But the purchase of a coronation

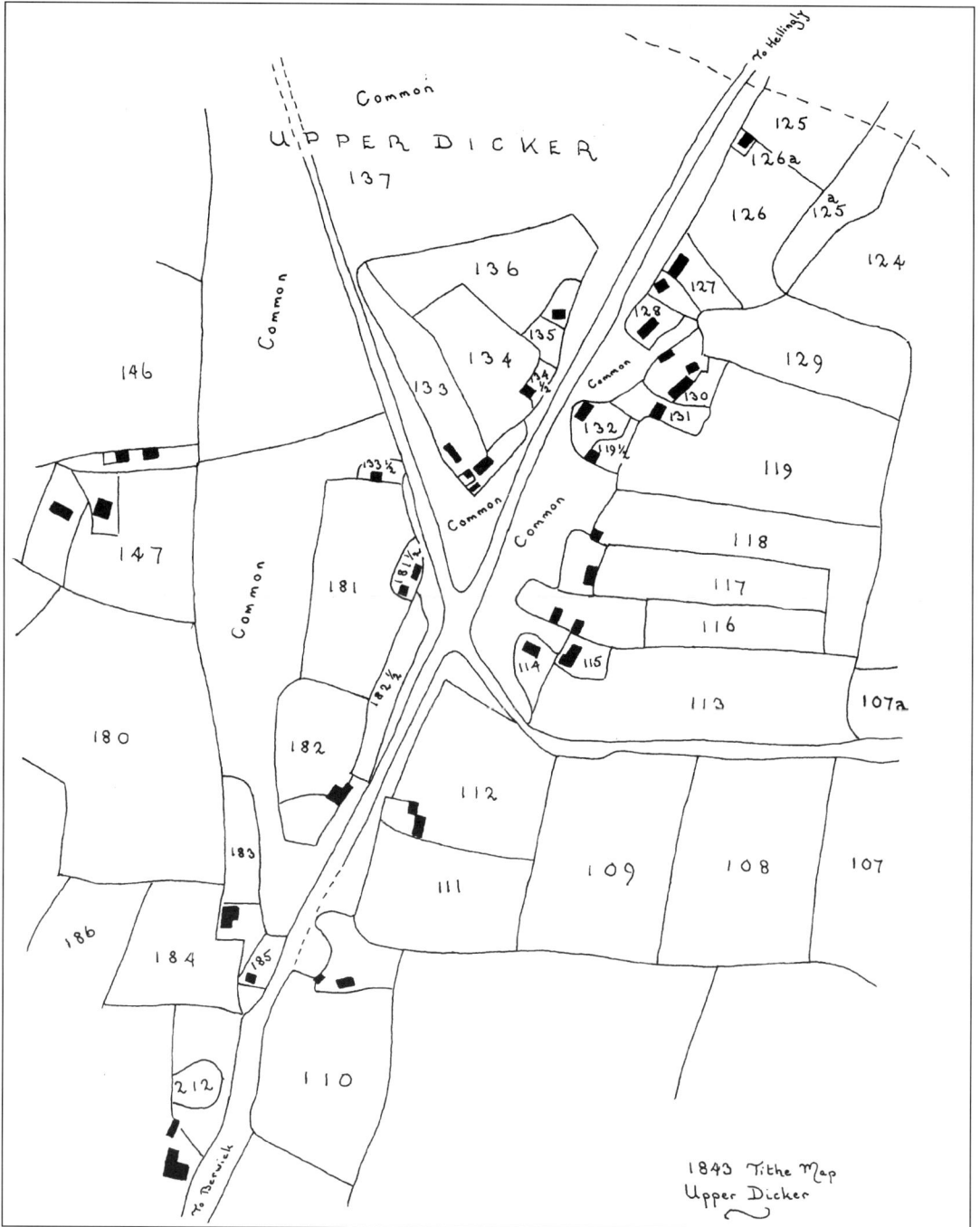

Segment of the 1843 Tithe Map which clearly shows Upper Dicker village as it was in the 19th century, and remaining common land which still isolated some dwellings

Field or dwelling		Occupier
107	Park Meadow (or Mead).	Thomas Child
107a	Pit (later called PETT)	
110	Cottage and garden (Osbournes).	John Osbourn
111	Field before the Door.	William Gutsell
112	House and field.	Levi Gutsell
114	Cottage and garden (White House).	William Gutsell
115	Cottage and garden – knocked down.	John Hamper
117	Cottage and garden – knocked down.	James Hide
119½	Cottage and garden (Ivy Cottage).	Jesse Savage
125	Dicker Field.	James Lambert
126	Chapel Field.	James Body
126a	Wesleyan Chapel (now premises of Huge Cheese Co.).	
127	House and garden – knocked down.	James Body
128	Cottage and garden (Cricket Field House, late Allander Lodge).	William Breach
130	Houses (owned by William Cowper – Providence House may have included Elm Cottages now part of Nos 1 to 8, and Cowper Cottages – knocked down.	William Cowper
131	Cottage and garden – knocked down.	John Page
132	Cottage and garden – knocked down and replaced by Firle and Carlton Houses	William Colman
133	House (Forge and Sideways Cottages).	William Balcombe
133½	Cottage and garden – knocked down.	James Crowhurst
134	Pollards Field.	Edward Huggett
134½	House and garden (Pollards Cottage).	Edward Huggett
135	Cottage (Plough Cottages).	William Gutsell
136	Plough Field.	William Gutsell
147	House (Clifton).	Eli Page
181½	Cottage and garden (Crossways).	Edward Huggett
182	House and field (Plough Inn).	William Gutsell
183	Cottage and garden (High Barn Cottage, late Ghylls Cotts).	Joseph Norman

Extracts from the 1843 Tithe Schedule and Map

Elm Cottages   *circa 1910-20*

Stud Cottages   *circa 1930s*

mug for four and a half pence from Mr Dunk's shop, held little solace after Upper Dicker's 1911 Coronation beacon (bonfire) ignited prematurely. The populace must have prayed for better luck at the next celebration!

Judging from such insights into Dicker's past from *Sussex Express* reports, one could wish to have been the proverbial fly on the wall. During 1869, reports stated the school had become dilapidated and in need of repair, and that the Reverend Drake had closed both the day and Sunday schools until the matter had been resolved. Letters submitted to the newspaper which claimed the school had displaced roof slates, cracked walls and broken windows, (although it was felt the latter may well be the handiwork of inept scholars whose young idea was of throwing stones, rather than learning the 3 R's!). Reports later confirmed the claims as being unsubstantiated, and had been the result of a clash between the reverend gentleman and certain aggrieved parishioners. One antagonist even signed himself as someone who had long gone to his maker! We shall therefore never know the real reason for this confrontation.

The village we now identify as Upper Dicker, differed from the village at the beginning of the last century. Horatio Bottomley's quest was to remove antiquated cottages and build others more favourable to his adopted village, and more recent building developments have left their own individual mark.

Valley of Achor may well be a name to conjure with, effectually a two-up/two-down dwelling with an outside privy, described in the 1901 census as Ravenscroft and home to a family with eight children, was the size of many

Camberlot Hall, Upper Dicker *circa 1922*

eighteenth century brick-built cottages with cramped living conditions. Those who made their way along the 'back road' to Lower Dicker in the late 1860s, would have been dumbfounded at the sheer opulence of Camberlot Hall, built by London-born architect Henry John Hammon.

Unfortunately, identifying most properties built before the twentieth century by name remains nearly impossible, although some have useful topographically-based names: The Mount, the highest point on the Dicker above sea-level; Oldways which suggests siting of a medieval road or footpath; several adopted a name allied to brickmaking and the pottery industry: Pot Kilns, the Crock House, Pottery Cottage or Brickyard Cottage; whereas others were linked to an earlier occupant, Caldicot, Sharrard, Foord or Gladman later Ghyll's Cottages; Stanley House and Livingstone Villa may well have been named after the Victorian explorers. In practice, place or property names, whether a byway, farm or field, remain an integral part of our local history. Here are just a few to stimulate the reader: Hanging Field near Park Wood may well refer to retribution for a criminal act, The Butts near Starnash was possibly where archery took place, Park Mead and Park Wood which fell within the perimeter of the large medieval deer park and Pit (Pett) Field where brick or fulling earth may have been extracted. Research into the history of land tax and rents relating to Arlington in the eighteenth century, corroborated evidence of a Fulling Mill near Sessingham, (which provided milled fullers earth used to cleanse oil from wool and fabrics). In 1798 William Child paid £2 16s. land tax for a fulling mill near Sessingham Lane, which was previously Fulling Mill Lane.

At the time when the well-defined Dicker roads were given improved surfacing, road users seemed hell bent on showing a clean pair of heels as they passed along the parish highways. Dicker's roads were to witness the advent of the horseless carriage with turns of speed well in excess of the 20mph speed limit. As early as 1903 motorists were ensnared in police speed traps along the Lower Dicker road and subsequently fined by a Hailsham magistrate. But a most unlikely speedy candidate was Frederick Manser of Arlington, who had been apprehended in 1906 by Police Constable Archer for furiously riding a horse to the common danger to the Dicker public! Ten years earlier, what may well have been the first cycling without lights by a Dicker person, occurred when Charles Clarke had the misfortune to be apprehended on July 18th 1896 at Lower Dicker. Today's modern globetrotter would fail to comprehend the problems which beset road users of earlier times.

At the time when the extended railway line ran northwards from Hailsham, rail travel had already become a considerable attraction. Therefore there was understandable excitement among the eighty school children from Upper Dicker who travelled by train in 1891 to Eastbourne for their annual

circa 1912

Boship Green, Lower Dicker
Zoar Villa, once the home of Uriah Clark is on the left;
the Forge and Dicker Pottery is in the centre.
The sign on the house reads 'G Stevens, Boot and Shoe Repairer'.

treat, deemed as both a novelty as well as educational. This excitement was experienced fifty four years later when Park Mead children journeyed by train to Mayfield, probably the longest trip they had taken in their young lives!

As already stated, boundaries had always been of importance in Dicker's history. Perhaps both Upper and Lower Dicker residents had always resigned themselves to the fact that their villages came under the civil jurisdiction of another parish, for what is a boundary other than an invisible demarcation line?

So with this thought in mind, we traverse the area that was known as the "lower end of the Diccar near that Fair Place in Hellingly Parish", now known as Lower Dicker. It has become a ribbon development along parts of the old turnpike road (now the A22). Apart from a brickyard situated near Boarship (Boship), the Zoar Chapel and two beer shops, only a scatter of dwellings were in evidence by 1843. However by 1875 we know many more houses had been built near the Dicker and Boship potteries; what remains uncertain is whether these were built by Uriah Clark. At the time when the old pair of Boship cottages were pulled down to accommodate the new A22 roundabout, they were always known as, the first and last houses on the Dicker! (depending on whether you're coming or going!)

The 1843 Tithe map confirms the field known as Croft was pasture land

Foord Cottages, Lower Dicker
(later pulled down and replaced by new dwellings Habitat and Freshfields)

Saga of the 26 buckets   *Oct 1934*

owned by James Wenham. At some time after that dwellings known as The Croft and Croft Cottages were built at the junction with Hackhurst Lane. Between 1875 and 1901 Egerton Cottages were built. The plan to build more houses and bungalows along The Croft at Lower Dicker, was undertaken during the 1930s, at a time when the road was concreted and widened. It now has considerable house-building development on it and is known as The Croft. The post-war enamelled roadsigns proclaimed Lower Dicker as a hamlet, and the name had also found its way onto Ordnance Survey maps!

This is a very brief attempt to record Dicker's early history, and probably more lies undetected, but it is hoped that this chapter, although fragmented, will give the reader an insight into the origins of two Sussex villages.

To conclude the chapter on a lighter note, history was made during October 1934, when Fred Medhurst and his sons Reuben and Fred endeavoured to retrieve a lost bucket from their well at Foord Cottages, Lower Dicker. Over a four-week period, the grapple recovered not one but twenty six buckets! The tale when told down at their local Potter Arms, must have been worth a free pint or two! (If this record can be improved upon, please contact the author!)

Chapter 2

CHURCH OF THE HOLY TRINITY

Long before the Dicker had become a parochial parish, with a church of its own, inhabitants who wished to pursue their faith were obliged to walk to Arlington church, probably by way of the footpath which skirts Park Wood towards Raylands Farm and Arlington village, (now part of Wealdway footpath), or by way of Sessingham Lane. During these early times, church-officiated functions i.e. baptisms, marriages and burials; would have taken place at St. Pancras Church, Arlington.

As early as 1740, the Pevensey Rural Deanery Council identified a need for a church within the confines of Dicker. This was followed by an agreement with the Church Commissioners for the building of a church and the creation of a new parish. In August 1745, the *London Gazette* reported that an area had been designated, known as the "Consolidated Chapelry District of the Holy Trinity". It was to be nearly a hundred years later before the Commissioners produced plans for the church; this was probably due to the complexity of Church and Civil jurisdictions within the same parish, coupled with the effect a newly created district would have on neighbouring parishes, which were parts of their own administration.

Extract – *Sussex Advertiser* 19th November 1842:

"PROPOSED NEW DISTRICT CHURCH ON THE DICKER
It is with feeling of gratification we notice the proposed erection of a Church in this scattered parish, and those who desire the extension of church instruction and accommodation, will rejoice to hear that the Rev D Warneford (Bishop of Gloucester) has promised £500 (upon its consecration) towards its endowment."

Extract – *Sussex Advertiser* 24th December 1842:

"THE NEW CHURCH ON THE DICKER.
We have the pleasure in announcing that her Majesty Queen Adelaide with her customary liberality, has graciously signified her intention to contribute £20 towards the erection of the new church on the Dicker Common, also A E Fuller Esq of Rose Hill, has made a very munificent offer in aid of its endowment."

In a conveyance dated the 1st June 1843, Lord Amherst and others had donated a piece of land as the site of a new 'chapel of ease' in the parish of Arlington. Reference to the 1813 Enclosure Map, indicates the land was part of the Dicker Common and had been given by Lord Amhurst. The building

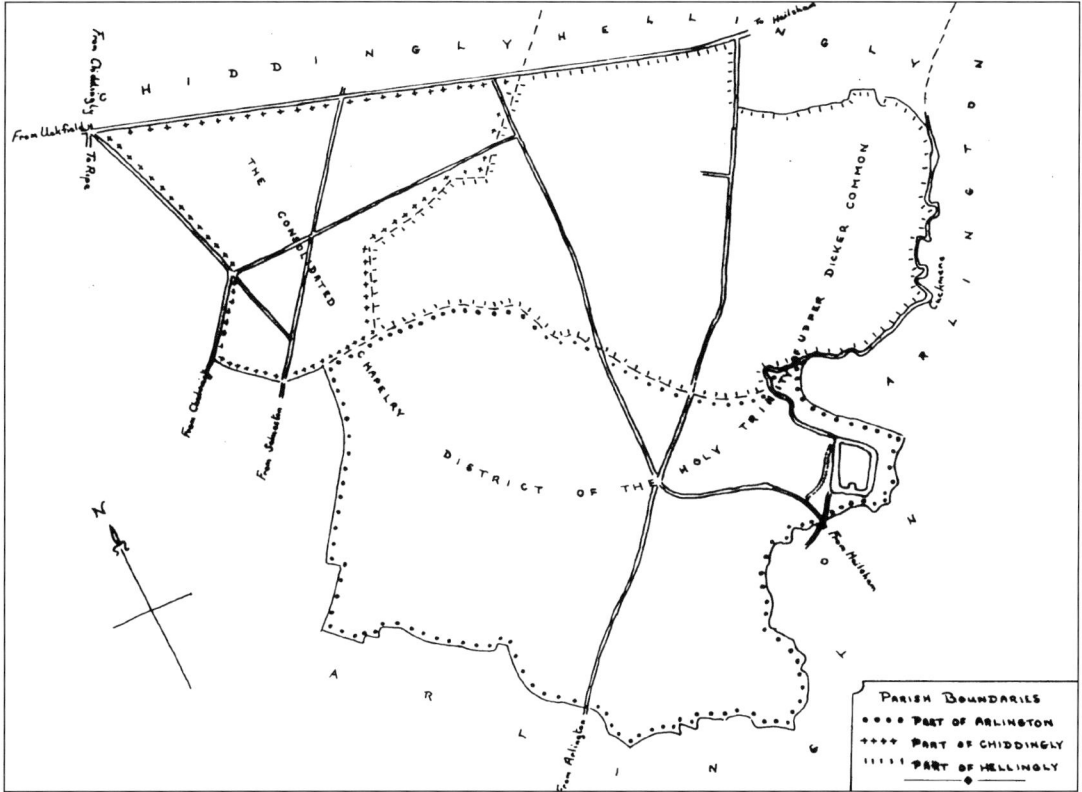

Map showing designated parish of Upper Dicker, August 1845

would be financed from three sources: by grants from the Incorporated Society for Church Building and the Chichester Diocesan Association, along with donations, (Lady Amherst being an outstanding benefactor, also Mrs Copper, widow of the late Vicar of Wilmington).

Mr Donthorn, a London architect, drew up plans for the new church, constructed of flint extracted from the South Downs and Caen stone. The materials were believed to have been conveyed by barge up the Cuckmere as far as Sessingham Bridge, and then hauled by waggons owned by Tranter Piper. The church was built in Norman style with high vaulted windows, and in the fullness of time, would cost £1,600 to build and seat 283 ("the whole of the sittings being free and unappropiated"). It was consecrated on the 12th December 1843, and dedicated to the Holy Trinity.

Extract from the *Sussex Advertiser*, dated 16th December 1843:

"CONSECRATION OF A NEW DISTRICT CHURCH ON THE UPPER DICKER

Great interest was excited in this parish and neighbourhood on Tuesday last, from the circumstance of its having been the day selected for the consecration of the new

Holy Trinity Church, Upper Dicker

Church on Dicker Common, and the number of persons present could not have been less than 600. The avenue to this pretty little Church was thronged with vehicles of all description. Fortunately the weather proved remarkably fine, to the gratification of those who had assembled to witness this solemn and highly interesting ceremony. The Right Rev. the Lord Bishop of Chichester arrived at the Church about quarter to eleven o'clock, accompanied by his Chaplain (the Rev. Henry Browne) and was received by the Ven. the Archdeacon Hare, George Hoper Esq. (the registrar), the committee, and a numerous body of the clergy. After his lordship had put on his robes in a tent near to the Church, he repaired to the Church, preceded by the churchwardens, and followed by the clergy in procession, who took their station on either side of the aisle immediately in front of the alter. The petition from the Vicar and Churchwardens of the parish of Arlington, wherein the Church stands, was then presented to the Bishop by the Rev. R Belaney, and read by the Registrar, which having been assented to, the office of consecration began by the Bishop, with his clergy, walking from east to the west end of the Church and back again, repeating in alternate verses of the 24th psalm. The deed of conveyance was presented to the Bishop, the Chancellor read the sentence of consecration, which was signed by the Bishop and commanded to be duly registered. At this part of the service, the Bishop withdrew from the Church, to consecrate the burial ground, which having been done, the morning service was read by the Rev. O E Vidal (the future incumbent).

"The Church was crowded in every part and probably contained no fewer than 400 to 500 persons, among whom we noticed A B Hope Esq MP, Laurie Esq (who presented the communion plate), Mr Donthorn, the architect, and most respectable inhabitants of the vicinity.

"This has been happily concluded a work undertaken and carried on with a most sincere desire to promote the glory of God and the welfare of the inhabitants of the Dicker. The 12th of December will be a day well remembered by those who were present, the blessed effects of which, it is earnestly hoped will be felt by generations yet unborn."

The new parish was made up from parts of the established neighbouring parishes of Arlington, Chiddingly and Hellingly, as endorsed in the 'Order of Council' dated August 1845. The Holy Trinity registers came into use in 1844 and records on 2nd June 1844 the baptism of Barbara, sibling of George and Caroline Colbran, residents at Week (Wick) Street; and on Tuesday 7th January 1845 the burial of Joseph Norman, age 75 years. It would be a further eleven years before the Rev Cooper officiated in the marriage between William Edwards (age 25) and Mary Ann Edwards (age 22) on the 10th April 1856, both of this parish.

Little of note remains from the Rev Owen Vidal's time spent as incumbent, except for an intrusion by burglars at the Vicarage on the night of the 20th September 1850. The details of this event are fully reported in the *Sussex Express* on 28th September:

"DARING BURGLARY AT THE REV. O. E. VIDAL'S – On the 20th inst., at a very early hour, a party of three men effected an entrance through the wash-house into

the dwelling-house of the Rev O. E. Vidal, on the Upper Dicker. They proceeded first to the servants' bed-room, where they got two common watches. One of them then went to the rev. gentleman's sleeping-apartment and awake him. This ruffian was about the middle height, and he appeared to be about thirty years old, but as he wore a blue mask, this certainly can only be regarded as an approximation. In one hand he held a tallow candle, and his right hand grasped a sword, which he brandished backwards and forwards, threatening Mr. Vidal he would use it, if he made any disturbance. He was dressed in a dark coat and trousers. In a few minutes, however, he left the room, and immediately a second ruffian, of shorter stature and stouter build than the first entered the apartment. Like the first he was masked, and had a lighted candle, and he carried for a weapon, the handle of an axe. Mr. Vidal asked him what he wanted? In reply the fellow demanded where the money was, and being told it was downstairs, he insisted on the rev. gentleman's getting out of bed, going down with him to get it. It was as he went down stairs that Mr. Vidal saw the third man, who appeared to be watching his aunt on the landing-place. On their reaching the study, Mr. Vidal showed them the drawers where the money was deposited, but they, finding they were locked, demanded the key, and he was forced to return up stairs, guarded by one of the fellows, to give it him. Having reached the sleeping room, Mr. Vidal gave up the key, and earnestly remonstrated with the ruffian, (the one armed with the sword) reminding him of the fate which must await him before God of justice hereafter, if he even escaped punishment in this world. The burglar, however, undeterred by fears of vengeance either here or hereafter, insisted with violence on the rev. gentleman's returning immediately to the study, though still undressed, and on his hesitating, dragged him down to the stairhead. Having once more reached the study, the fellow proceeded to rifle it, obtaining nearly £40. Mr. Vidal again remonstrated with him, on which, using violent threats, he placed the sword across the rev. gentleman's throat, saying if he made a noise, he would use it. One of the other men was then called in, and, finally, the rev. gentleman was locked up in the bedroom, we believe, whilst the daring scoundrels quietly went down stairs as they said to themselves, to get tea! In the meantime another villain had paid a visit to the room occupied by Miss Capper, who contrived with great presence of mind to secrete a handsome gold watch; and it is stated, that on demanding any valuables she had, the young lady courageously offered them the Bible, which was on the dressing table, as the most valuable thing she could give them. However, the house was industriously ransacked, and a quantity of silver plate carried off, including a teapot, gravy spoon, nearly two dozen forks, large and small, 10 table, 14 dessert, 15 tea, and six salt spoons, and two sauce ladles. The other articles stolen were two gold seals, with crest and mottoes, a silver hunter Geneva watch (Gillet, maker), a yellow-metal watch (Grant, maker), and a large-sized metal watch, a metal teapot, 12 plated dessert forks, a black summer overcoat, a silk hat, a blue window blind, and two aprons. £25 reward has been offered by the Rev. O.E. Vidal, for information leading to the apprehension and conviction of the offenders."

FOOTNOTE – Although no one was brought to book, supposition is that it had been perpetrated by members of a gang of violent, ruthless men armed with pistol, sword and cudgel, led by John Isaacs, who had laid Sussex and the borders of Surrey to a swathe of fearful burglaries. Targeting isolated houses set back off the beaten track and terrorizing anyone who confronted them. Such was their villainous infamy, they even cheated on one another when sharing out the booty! Other offences had been committed beforehand: the first reported burglary was on the 4th June 1850 at Kirdford near Petworth, and so their reign of felonies continued!

But as with most transgressors of the law, time runs out; a murder at Frimley sounded the demise of the Isaacs gang. James Hamilton decided to turn Queen's Evidence; John Isaacs and nine others were transported for life, three others were transported for 14 years, while Levi Harwood, and James Jones were hanged for the murder at Frimley. By the end of 1850 the Isaacs Gang were no more. (Reference – "Previous Offences" by W H Johnson).

After his incumbency at Upper Dicker, the Rev. Owen Vidal left England to pursue a missionary calling in West Africa; in the course of time, he was appointed in 1852 as the first Bishop of Sierra Leone. From that date, the missions were made over to the Church of Sierra Leone, with its own native pastorate. In 1854, apprehension over his wife's ill health, prompted their return to England. Within a few months Bishop Vidal boarded a ship for his return journey to Africa. This journey was to have tragic a overtone, for *en route* to Lagos the Bishop, after only a few hours illness, died on board ship on Christmas Eve 1854, at the age of 35. A plaque on the north wall of Upper Dicker Church commemorates the life of Bishop Owen Emeric Vidal.

The Rev Henry Law Cooper, the next incumbent, did not stay long. As a new parish it was reliant on limited tithe returns, as the greater apportionment were still claimed by the parishes of Arlington and Hellingly. However the Burial Register may bear reason as to why the Rev Cooper and his wife chose to leave Upper Dicker: deaths of three of their children, Myles Cooper aged 3 years in April 1856 and Amy aged 1 year 11 months in May 1856 and later Frank aged 13 days in 1862. A legacy of the Rev Cooper's brief alliance with the parish was that of a Free Church School established in the Parish Room.

At the time when the final enclosures of the Dicker Common and land apportionment was being settled, and land had been allocated as pleasure ground and allotments, James Thomas Drake was inducted on 17th July 1859, the event solemnized by the Bishop of Chichester and witnessed by Henry Bourne (church-warden), Samuel Gladman (schoolmaster) and William Body (builder). During Rev Drake's incumbency no recorded change occurred, the church's interior remained the same; the straight-backed forms were close to the altar rails; there were two pulpits, one for reading the lessons and one for preaching, the vestry was a curtained-off corner at the west end of the church. Unseen until now, Mrs Drake introduced boys and girls as choristers. (An old cliche had it that Sussex folk were more adept at whistling than singing!)

The above picture, a copy of a watercolour painted by W Crisford, was discovered and purchased by Mrs Stella Hardwick from a Chichester bookshop. It depicts the church before the addition of the porch and was painted in 1852 soon after the enclosure of the churchyard.

The Ecclesiastical Commissioners allotted £300 from a fund for the improvement of the Vicarage in 1877. Around this time, the Dicker Church was now detached from Arlington Parish and tithes were now apportioned to the Dicker District Chapelry, raising the dues paid to Rev Drake. At this time, instead of signing himself 'Incumbent', the bearer of this office now used the title 'Vicar' in the church registers.

After 35 years as vicar, the Rev James Drake died on the 1st May 1894. During his term in office he had officiated over 50 marriages and also married many of their siblings. Whilst exercising pastoral guidance to the inhabitants of his parish, the Rev Drake had been ably assisted by Charles Piper, James Stevens, and Henry Page (who had resided at Old Plough Cottage); all had served as Sexton.

The Rev George Munro Russell succeeded as Vicar in 1894, but might never have come to the parish if the Rev J H Cross had not died before his induction, the incumbency having already been accepted. The Rev Russell had been a missionary in the Orange Free State, South Africa, from 1873 to 1882. On his return to England he had clerical duties in various parishes, previously as curate at Firle, before moving to Upper Dicker.

At that time, it was reported that the Vicarage was in a wretched state and was in need of renovation and so he proceeded to spend his own money to provide a residence adequate for his large family. There were many alterations, an extension was added with a castellated parapet, attics converted into bedrooms, alterations to the kitchen and scullery, the rear entrance moved to face onto a paved courtyard. The Vicarage had been transformed from a draughty spartan abode to a more comfortable residence.

Although Sussex country folk treated newcomers with reserve, the Dicker populace warmed to their new vicar with his exuberance for change and improvement. Over a period of time, together with the help of his sexton and gardener Frank Stephens, (who resided at Firle House, in all probability the name deriving from the vicar's previous parish), the Rev Russell brought about an era of transformation.

The Rev Russell decided to enrich and alter the austere church interior. He removed the old black straight-backed benches and new polished pews were installed. The altar was raised and choir seating was placed behind a chancel screen crafted in the Rev Russell's workshop at the Vicarage. Likewise, using his carpentry skills he joined the two existing pulpits and set the new one in its present position. He went about merging two separate organs, one acquired from an Edenbridge Church in 1896 and an organ formerly used at St John's Church at Crowborough. The old vestry was enlarged and enclosed by a wooden partition and the original font was replaced by a smaller one in ornate marble.

The Rev Russell's fervour was also applied to the exterior of the church, with funds being raised by a tennis tournament in the Vicarage grounds, and by the efforts of the Park Mead school children. He prompted the building of the church porch, and was also instrumental in planting trees in the churchyard and asked Mr Tom French (blacksmith) to forge new gates and a fence.

The end of the Great War, as with other parishes who mourned those who had given their lives for King and Country, saw a memorial established in their honour. On Saturday 7th January 1922, Upper Dicker residents witnessed the dedication and unveiling of a stained glass window (the work of the eminent artist Mr G Kruger-Gray) in their parish church. Prior to this solemn occasion, headed by the Dicker Drum and Fife Band, about thirty ex-Servicemen of the village marched to the church and before entering were inspected by Lt Col Rowland Gwynne DSO. The Rev Russell conducted the service before a large congregation, who knelt in prayer for those who gave their lives and their thanks for those who had returned safely. After the service the vicar read the names of the men in whose memory the window had been installed. Afterwards at the chancel steps wreaths of holly and laurel from relatives and friends of the fallen were placed at the base of the altar. At this point, Lt Col Gwynne unveiled the window inscribed, "To the glorious memory of George Cottington, William Funnell, Thomas Kemp, C Milham, C W Pearman, F H W Shoesmith and Gordon W Russell, who gave their lives for their Country 1914-18". At the conclusion of the service, the last post and reveille was sounded by Sgt A F Nicholls RFA (Hailsham).

Initially the Rev Russell had been thought by Upper Dicker to be a reformer in a parish where people were contented to leave things as they were. But in time, they had grown to admire a vicar who not only had refurbished the Vicarage and church, but also the Parish Room, which had been in a derelict state, and was made fit to be used for the villagers' social events and Sunday School. At his retirement in October 1924, the Rev Russell was presented with a gold-mounted wallet containing £84 from his parishioners and friends; a gift as a token of thanks for his benevolence and unflagging service to Upper Dicker. (Much that can be seen in the Church today can be attributed to Rev George Munro Russell.)

Formerly Vicar of St Albans (Brighton), the Rev William Bassett-Smith's induction took place on the 31st October 1924, officiated by the Bishop of Lewes. Unlike his predecessor, the Rev and Mrs Bassett-Smith were greatly involved in the parish organisations, were involved in the resurgence of the Mother's Union, and also supported Miss Cornford's commitment in establishing the 1st Dicker Boy Scout Troop, and embraced the inauguration of the Women's Institute.

Vestry meetings, unknown until initiated by Rev Russell in 1924, introduced an administration involving the vicar and a Church Council, which sustained and amplified the work of the church. On Saturday 10th July 1926, a function to raise funds to provide roof guttering for the north and south sides of Holy Trinity Church was held: a Concert and Dance on the vicarage lawn. The major part of the entertainment was provided by the Rhoades Concert

Party from Brighton, and was followed by dancing to music furnished by a gramophone loaned by Mrs Cohn. Prior to this function, the Concert Party had held two previous concerts in the Parish Room which had resulted in raising money for the repair of the church organ, the final proceeds of £9 10s, bringing about the required total of £45. At the 1928 Holy Trinity parochial meeting the Sidesmen and Church Council were elected: Messrs J Finch, D Smith, F Thorpe, Balliston, F Stephens and E Butcher were elected as Sidesmen; the following were elected as Church Council, Mrs W R Bassett-Smith, Mrs D Smith, Miss Faulkner, Mrs Limburn, Miss J Haffenden, Miss Cornford, Mrs H Bramley, Mrs W G Wright, Mrs Carpenter, Messrs Balliston, D Smith, A H Clapp, H Bramley, F Stephens and J Finch. The accounts showed that £86 18s. 6d had been received for church expenses, and the yearly expenditure amounted to £50 0s.1d.

On 18th April 1928, a service was conducted by the Rev Bassett-Smith at which a memorial window was dedicated to the memory of the Rev George Munro Russell, Vicar of Holy Trinity Church for 30 years, from 1894 until October 1924. The window was designed by Mr G Kruger-Gray, friend of the late vicar.

There was sadness at the death of Mr Frank Stephens in 1932, who had officiated as verger and sexton for 36 years, and had retired two years earlier and had also, just recently, been presented the Supporter's Badge for sterling work connected with scouting in the village.

Functions continued to be held to raise funds for the church. In April 1933, a dance was held in the Village Hall with music provided by the Dicker Jazz Band. From this, funds were raised for further church repairs. On Saturday 27th August 1938, Michelham Priory became venue for the open-air spectacular "Midsummer Night's Dream", staged to aid the installation of electric lighting in the church. The scenes were produced by the Rev Filler and the costumes loaned by Mrs Godwin King.

The cast was:

      Theseas, Duke of Athens . . . . . . .Martin Manley
      Hippolyta, Queen of the AmazonsLouise Hunneysett
      Lysander . . . . .Maide Page
      Demetrius . . . . .Dorrie Page
      Philostrate . . . . .Lily Westley
      Puck .Emmie Douglas
      Quince . . . . .Robert Filler
      Bottom . . . . .Frank Westley
      Flute .Gordon Manley
      Snout .Stanley Page

Starvelling . . . . .Raymond Dinnis
Soldier .Sidney Brett
Court Ladies – Veronica Filler, Gwynneth Lewis, Minnie
Parry, Nora Bishop, Kathleen Dinnis, Daisy Hutchinson.

Cast of **A Midsummer Night's Dream**
Back row, left to right: ? , Daisy Hutchinson, Nora Bishop, Maidie Page,
Dorrie Guy, ? , Lily Westley, Louise Hunneysett, Martin Manley, ? , ? , Emmie Douglas
Front row: ? , Frank Westley, Gordon Manley, Stanley Page, Raymond Dinnis, Rev Robert Filler.

The Priory was also open to the public, and in addition, various stalls
and side-shows were set out in the grounds, such as bowling for a pig, bran tub,
electric rod, lucky spin, tipping the boat and so on. During the evening there
was an exhibition of folk dancing, with music provided by Mr John Davis of
Hailsham and teas were served in the Great Barn. The event raised over £25
after expenses had been accounted for.

Extract from the *Sussex Express* 2nd September 1938:

"LIGHTING DICKER CHURCH.

*Michelham Priory grounds on Saturday were placed by Mr and Mrs R B Wright at
the disposal of the Parochial Church Council of Holy Trinity Church, Upper Dicker,
for a fete. The function was in aid of the Sussex Church Builders Fund and the funds
of Holy Trinity Church, with the idea in mind of installing electric light in the
church.*

*"The Vicar (the Rev R C Filler) presided at the opening ceremony. Declaring the fete
open, Mrs J Godwin King of West Hoathly, said that in the olden days they used to
build churches, but now they constructed cinemas and aerodromes, and were making
war-like preparations. She looked on it as a great privilege that afternoon to be
associated with something that had for its object a peaceful and calmer outlook on life.*

"Cinemas were excellent in their way, but they also wanted their churches as well. Electricity was a modern thing and could be adapted for destruction, but they could also use it for lighting their churches. She paid a tribute to the enthusiasm of those who had organised the fete, and hoped they would get sufficient to pay for their electric light as well as help build new churches".

"Mrs W W Kerr thanked Mrs Godwin King for opening the fete and also for lending costumes for the Shakespearian scenes. A bunch of carnations was handed to Mrs Godwin King by Miss Betty Phillipson".

Unlike other functions to raise funds for repairs and improvements, in 1935 the Rev Bassett-Smith summoned a personal appeal for subscriptions in the hope that a liberal response from his parishioners would cover the immediate cost of £125 to repair the ceiling plaster which was in need of renovation.

Having presided over both the Silver Jubilee (1935) and the Coronation (1937) committees, and given his loyal support to the 1st Dicker Scout Troop, the Rev Bassett-Smith, throughout his incumbency, had been actively involved in village affairs. Each year he gave a Christmas party to the children who had attended the Sunday School, and held a social evening for those in the Parochial Council and churchwardens, who had assisted throughout each year.

At the celebrations for Empire Day in 1936, nearly 170 Scouts and Cubs of the Horam District Association paraded at Upper Dicker on Sunday 2nd May, which included groups from Hailsham, Hellingly, Heathfield, Polegate, Horam, Warbleton and Dicker. The Rev Bassett-Smith officiated at a service, with the Bishop of Lewes, the Rt Rev Hordern. In his address, the bishop reiterated the importance of the scouting brotherhood and the scouts and cubs re-affirmed their Scout Promise. On leaving Holy Trinity Church, with their troop flags unfurled, the parade marched to the recreation ground for inspection, followed by refreshments at the village hall.

On Armistice Day in 1936 the vicar integrated the morning service with the ceremony from London's Cenotaph, relayed by a wireless set.

Following his appointment as vicar of West Wittering, near Chichester, the Rev Bassett-Smith severed his thirteen-year association with Upper Dicker on Tuesday 26th October 1937, after which the Rev R C Filler from Bungalow Town, Shoreham, commenced his duties in November.

During April 1938, Rev Filler convened a Vestry and Parochial meeting in the Parish Room, at which he nominated Mr J Finch as his warden and Mr G F Manley as the people's warden. Those who were elected to the Church Council, were – Mrs F C Filler, Mrs D Smith, Mrs H Haffenden, Mrs T Henty, Mrs J Finch, Mrs J Hide, Miss E Rogers and Miss E Douglas, Messers F Barrow, D Smith, F L Page and Col Brook. At the meeting it was recorded that, as a result of a recent social event the sum of £5 10s had been raised to aid the recently inaugurated churchyard fund. The evening's agenda was

The Vicarage

1930s

brought to its conclusion once the church accounts had been approved and passed by those present.

When war broke out the vicar's parochial duties merged with those of Billeting Officer and sub-leader when firewatch patrols were augmented in the village.

On Sunday 26th Nov 1939, the annual church attendance prize-giving took place, when the Rev Filler distributed book prizes to: Leslie Page, Leslie Medhurst, Ivor Feakes, Len Medhurst, Ronald Medhurst, Victor Phillipson, Nelson Pelling, Maurice Pelling, Dorothy Moore, June Gray, Jean Page, Veronica Filler, Dennis Gray, Raymond Fowlie, Margaret Levett, Violet Shier, Christine Farley, Audrey Page and Phyllis Colman. Stalwart spirits prevailed, nothing would prevent the annual vestry meetings in the Parish Room, when church officials were elected and the church accounts were reviewed; at the 1940 meeting the accounts disclosed a balance in hand of £4 8s. 7d., the vicar confirming that the church electric light installation had been completed and paid for!

His commitment to his wartime parish led to Rev Filler's acceptance as officiating chaplain to soldiers billeted in the vicinity, with frequent services for army personnel being held in the parish church. The vicar's ecclesiastic and extra wartime assignments meant the Vicarage was unmanageable without domestic help. Added to this, the vicar was in ill health and an operation was necessary, so he and his wife vacated the vicarage and moved in 1943 to a smaller dwelling in Summerheath Road, Hailsham. This move meant that for the first time in the Dicker's parochial history, the parish was without a vicar in residence!

On Sunday 20th June 1943 the Church of the Holy Trinity, Upper Dicker, celebrated the centenary of its inauguration. Prior to the service officiated by Rev Filler, there was a music recital by the resident organist Miss Ruth Champion. The Bishop of Lewes conducted Confirmation as part of the morning service. The Evensong was attended by the Home Guard and local military personnel, who afterwards paraded behind the Hailsham Town Band (lead by Mr Shelley) past Major C S Gardner who took the salute before the delighted gaze of the whole village. Over the ensuing days, gifts totalling £81 were received by the church trustees as a centennial gift from the parish. The Rev Robert Filler was to write a history of his parish, *The Dicker Parish – Its First Hundred Years,* and in describing the period he wrote, "Such stirring events do not come often to our little village Church but after the repression of four years of war, how we blessed God for the elation that day!"

Having overseen his parish throughout the uncertain times of war, one can surmise that the Rev Filler's heart felt solace, when he conducted the service that gave thanksgiving for the cessation of the war in Europe. He had seen his parishioners endangered from bombing, possible invasion and doodlebugs – one of which had damaged the church in 1944. Early in 1946, after an incumbency of eight years, the Rev Robert Filler bade farewell to the Dicker for parochial pastures new at Tideswell, near Mayfield.

The Rev George Frederick Handel Elvey, following his appointment at Upper Dicker in February 1946, moved into the Vicarage. A quiet man who loved music and cricket, on a Saturday afternoon could be seen watching the game from the fringe of the out-field near the vicarage. In his inaugural year, the Rev Elvey became president of the recently formed Upper Dicker and Arlington Produce Association, and Mrs Elvey introduced a youth club which was held weekly in the vicarage, where snooker, billiards and table tennis were enjoyed by the village teenagers.

During a church service held on Sunday 4th August 1946, following his retirement from church duties, a presentation was made to Mr J Finch for his many years of sterling commitment to the church. The vicar also dedicated a new bible which had been purchased with part of the Peace Celebration Fund and presented it to the church. It replaced the large brass-bound bible, dated 1837, given by Horatio Bottomley, together with the lectern commemorating Queen Victoria's Golden Jubilee in 1897.

At the annual Vestry Meeting held in the Village Hall on Thursday 8th April 1948, Mr F Barrow was elected as the vicar's warden and Mr G Manley was re-elected as people's warden. During appraisal of the church accounts, it was agreed that £4 would be spent on tidying the churchyard. Sometime later, (date unknown) the burial mounds were levelled, this being a sign of the times, which would enable easier maintenance.

After only four years, the Rev Elvey resigned his incumbency at Upper Dicker in May 1950. From this point in time the parish would no longer have a 'vicar in residence', but as with many other rural parishes, a vicar from a neighbouring parish would officiate; the Parish of the Holy Trinity was now to forge a ministerial link with Hellingly. The Rev R W Shaw took charge in January 1951, followed by the Rev C W Fulljames (Chaplain of Hellingly Hospital) who could be seen doing his pastoral rounds on a 'high-stepping' bicycle.

The Vicarage had become vacant and was purchased by Mr Scott, who operated a light engineering business on the premises. In September 1994, the Rev David Swanepoel became assistant curate of Holy Trinity Church. After moving to Upper Dicker, he became an English teacher at St Bedes School in the village, thus bonding St Bedes and Church in devotional need and unity. Rev Swanepoel retired to Pretoria, South Africa.

The affiliation between the Holy Trinity Church and the St Bedes School was continued when the Rev Simon Morgan became priest-in-charge, and was licensed at Holy Trinity Church in September 1999. Mr Morgan combined his role as history teacher at the school with that of priest.

Chapter 3

NONCONFORMITY AND THE CHAPELS

T hroughout history, religious observance has changed direction many times. Since King Henry VIII's break with Rome after the Papal authority's predicament over the King's annulment from Catherine of Aragon, he asserted his right to head the clergy and the established church. Religious reformation took place in England, effecting the move away from Catholic orthodoxy to Protestantism, and the King's purge of religion brought with it bloodshed and dissension. There followed periods when religious unrest continued, opposing factions sought to eradicate Protestantism and revert back to Catholicism. The Act of Uniformity passed in 1662, required all clergy of the Church of England to accept the episcopal form of church government, to use the common prayer book and declare their compliance to everything therein. Those who did not conform were ejected from their livings – this act not only ejected ministers but many of the laity from churches as well. Such was their nonconformist ideology and because of interference with their religious liberty, many would pursue their belief at secret meeting places. The Conventicle Act of 1664, decreed that any person at a service other than was allowed by the practice of the Church of England, was liable to a fine and imprisonment, and on the third conviction, to transportation. The "Five Mile Act" of 1665, forbade Nonconformist ministers to go within 5 miles of any town where they had exercised their ministry as clergymen of the established church. In 1670 a new, and in some respects, a more severe Act was passed – a conventicle (assembly) of more than five persons in the same house, besides that of the family, would be fined five shillings, and the preacher £20. On 15th March 1672, King Charles II issued a Declaration of Indulgence, whereby dissenters were permitted to worship on condition that the ministers and meeting places were licensed. But this liberation did not last long – the King had given the declaration without consent of Parliament, and within a year the Declaration was annulled, forcing nonconformity back behind closed doors.

There had been many turbulent times for those who did not conform to the religious teaching of the day when they were persecuted and had to meet in secret. Those who preferred nonconformity and chose a religious path away from their village church door, would travel miles to hear their favoured minister preach.

The Toleration Acts of 1705 and 1715, enabled licences to be granted so meetings could be held in private houses and other buildings. East Sussex continued as a seat and stronghold of non-conformity.

Towards the close of the 18th century, George Gilbert, was much acclaimed for his preaching in East Sussex; Jenkin Jenkins was popular around the Lewes area, and the Vinalls, father and son, were equal at advocating their spiritual preaching in towns and villages alike. Early nonconformist meetings which took place on the Dicker were those held in Henry Bourne's barn (before its demise many years later), and in the front parlour of Providence House in Upper Dicker. Another place of worship is believed to have been a room above the old Ironmongery Store at the Dicker Potteries. Other locations recorded, are that of Henry Miller, and at the house of William Faulkner.

To improve administration and structuring, the Lewes and Brighton circuit was formed in 1807. This encompassed Ringmer, Dicker, Chiddingly and Hellingly, with others gradually included up to 1825.

As endorsement of the Protestant movement intensified, the need for purpose-built chapels became apparent, none more so than on the Dicker.

With meetings having been previously held in a barn at Golden Cross, a licence was granted to James Dunk and others, for a building to be erected on the Dicker, in the parish of Chiddingly. Built in 1813/14, it was probably the first chapel to be built on the Dicker. The Dunk family had lived in the immediate area for several generations, and Isaac Dunk, around 1844, resided at Providence House, Upper Dicker. The property at that time was owned by Mr William Cowper, this probably explains how Providence House became important to nonconformity in the immediate area. Around 1976 alterations were being made, when workmen discovered papers concealed in a fireplace recess relating to that of a register of early Baptists in the Dicker area. The register consisted of 16 folios of paper wrapped in a brown paper cover, on which was written "1785 Register Book of James and Ann Reed – Chiddingly, Sussex". One can only assume that he was the Mr Reed whose early preaching had been a cornerstone of the Baptist movement at the turn of the 18th century.

Those who preached the gospel at many of the chapels, travelled the length and breadth of England. Mr John Grace records in his diary that on 26th March 1822, he "travelled thirteen miles from Eastbourne to the Dicker to hear Mr Vinall; on the following Thursday went to Five Ash Down to accord Mr Vinall again". It would be 22 years later that Mr Grace would preach at Lower Dicker for the first time. As with the names of Messers Vinall, Pitcher, Crouch, Gadsby and Grace, people would travel considerable distances to hear the gospel preached by favoured ministers. Dunks Chapel at Golden Cross later became Little Dicker Chapel.

Zoar Baptist Chapel at Lower Dicker

Little Dicker Chapel at Golden Cross

1990

The increase in members and space being at a premium, a committee was formed to oversee the building of a new Chapel at Lower Dicker. Initially it was agreed to purchase the building then in use, but its dilapidated state and the cost of repair at the time made it unsuitable; for this reason, land adjacent to the brickyard owned by George Goldsmith, was procured for £20. Following Mr Cowper's and the trustees' steadfast endeavours, the Zoar Chapel was completed at a cost of £422, and was officially opened by Mr William Gadsby in 1838, with William Cowper becoming the chapel's first appointed minister. The chapel having gained ordinance for baptism, sixty members were baptised within the first year. Following William Cowper's death, Mr George Drake succeeded as minister in 1860, but within a few years the chapel would also mourn his death in August 1868.

William Vine was born in 1831 at the Dicker, and later moved with his parents to Wilmington, where he lived until being apprenticed to a draper in Hailsham, where he frequented a Baptist Chapel in the town. Through a meeting with Uriah Clark, William Vine became a worshipper at the Zoar Chapel and in the fullness of time became minister. His ministry extended to over 25 years, until his death in December 1896.

Extract from the *Sussex Express* 27th Sept 1887
"ZOAR CHAPEL, THE DICKER – JUBILEE SERVICES.
On Thursday last, the 22nd inst, the members and friends met at this place of worship to commemorate the Jubilee of the same, the chapel having been open for 50 years. At first it was only a very small place of worship, but under the ministry of the late Mr William Cowper a larger building soon sprang up, and which has several times been added to. The chapel (with the spacious schoolroom) now having seating accommodation for nearly 800, the present minister being Mr William Vine (of Whitesmith). Three services were held during the day, that in the morning commencing at 11am, the preacher being Mr E Ashdown of London, the place being crowded. The afternoon service at 2.30, when Mr E Page preached a very impressive sermon, also giving a brief history, nearly 1000 people were packed in the large building. The evening service was taken by Mr W Knight, the place was full again. (Dinner at 1 shilling and tea at 6 pence, was provided in a very large marquee – nearly 500 sat down.)"

The Chapel was built to accommodate around 400 but it was soon apparent, with extended numbers, that the chapel was too small and in 1874 was enlarged at a cost of £600, and in 1880 the burial ground area was increased. It was customary in rural chapels, where the mode of transport over any appreciable distance was by horse drawn conveyance, for a building to be provided to lodge chapel worshippers' horses and traps. A long brick-and-tile bulding was erected sometime prior to 1875 when nearby Chapel Cottages were built for Mr Uriah Clarke.

Following the death of Mr William Vine, the chapel's ministry had been met by supply preachers until Mr Botten was offered the pastorate in 1899, a businessman from Uckfield. His appointed ministerial position with the Zoar Chapel continued until 1912, when ill health cut short his devoted years to the chapel. Mr William Botten, who had resided at Harbour Villa, Lower Dicker passed away on 7th May 1916.

Again the vacant pulpit was sustained by supply preachers until 1919 when Mr William Hickman was appointed resident pastor. For over 50 years he had worked at the Dicker Potteries, and had been preaching at the chapel for many years and therefore became the obvious choice as minister and continued throughout to give spiritual guidance. His untimely death in 1936, came a year prior to the Zoar Chapel's centenary.

Since the chapel's inception it had not only expanded in dimensions but had become aligned to the Strict Baptist movement. A plaque affixed to the front of the Zoar Chapel celebrates dates (1837 and 1874) important in its history; the clipped hedge and avenue of yew, gave an atmosphere of grandeur.

In 1939, Mr John Sperling-Tyler became pastor at the Zoar; and not only became its devout mentor for fifty years but also was held in high esteem in the Gospel Standard Body of Churches. He was a qualified chiropodist practising in Hailsham. His musicianship meant they were never short of an organist. The chapel had become his whole life and he preached the gospel to full congregations. In January 1990, after over 50 years of sterling ministry, Mr Tyler died deriving the chapel of its revered pastor.

At present, a series of supply preachers administer at the chapel; the Zoar Chapel continues predominant in the Strict Baptist movement.

The now defunct Wesleyan Chapel at Upper Dicker, was one of the three chapels that catered for the nonconformist populace in the area but its life as a chapel was short lived. Apart from being recorded as a chapel on the Arlington 1843 Tithe Map, there seems to be a void in its early chronicled history and those associated with the chapel. (William Cowper was instrumental in its formation when the Zoar Chapel was built at Lower Dicker and may have contributed to its decline.) An adjacent field, known as Chapel Field, forms part of Lamberts Farm and remains a reminder of the non-conformist movement in the village. In all probability the chapel failed due to decreased attendance but for whatever reason, the chapel closed to further meetings. At some time (date unknown) the chapel became glebe property and was overseen by the resident clergy. In 1844 it was reported that 90 children were under tuition and the *Kelly Directory* declared a Church School had been established at Upper Dicker, (see page 51), so it is possible that the old chapel had become a schoolroom, and remained so until 1881 when Parkmead Council School was opened. The building and adjacent land continued as a glebe holding: the 1899 OS map shows it as the village Reading Room, which in the 1920s became known as the Parish Room; both church and village functions were held there, (e.g. Mothers Union, Womens Institute, Scout meetings, along with entertainment by the "Dandies" and the "Dicker Ducks", also village fund-raising events.)

Standing in the road, the photographer risked life and limb when capturing this wedding picture of Cecil and Mary Parsons in front of the Parish Room.

circa 1925

As soon as the Village Hall was built in 1931, the Parish Room became virtually redundant, apart from being used as a boys' club in the 1950s. In 1970 the building was taken over by Mr Michael Day, which suited the needs of his company for the distribution of cheese and dairy products in Sussex, Surrey and Kent. He purchased the property in 1980 and extended it five years later to accommodate his expanding business, the Huge Cheese Company.

Chapter Four

ROADS

Through the centuries, man's need to travel from one place to another, had induced him to use a regular trodden path or track, and in time, improvements were made to many of his chosen routes. The earliest paved roads were constructed during the Roman occupation of Britain, but as the era of Roman rule came to an end, further construction possibly ceased. After nearly four centuries of Roman influence, the Saxons, first as marauding raiders and then as settlers in the Sussex coastal regions, and colonization of forest clearings, used an intricate network of tracks, many remaining today.

The poor state of Sussex roads before methodical repair led to their being deemed the worst in England. Local roads suffered greatly because of the Wealden clay, making them almost impassable in winter. Because of this, an application was submitted in 1791 to construct a canal linking the River Ouse to the Cuckmere at Horsebridge, crossing the Dicker at a point near The Mount. Using shallow draught boats, the proposed canal was intended to avoid the adverse road conditions. For whatever reason, the venture never materialized.

The 1789 O.S. map gives an indication of the many byways and tracks that crossed and encompassed the area of the old Dicker Common. Some now only remain as lanes to farms and private residential properties. The oldest is believed to be an old Roman road, now known as Back Lane, which ran from Horsebridge, skirting north of Caldicott's Wood before joining Hackhurst Lane near the modern industrial estate, and then headed towards Chiddingly. Another ancient track is Mansers Lane, recorded in the 1881 Census as Mount Lane but has since derived its name from Richard Manser, who resided there. In 1789, the lane forked near 'Little Mount', one exiting on the Coldharbour Road near Starnash Farm and the other in Camberlot Road. Two other tracks that remain only as bridleways, are that of Twenty Foot Lane and Forty Foot Lane, both were important as they gave a shorter route from Dicker to Chalvington.

The roads which predominate today are those of the main London to Eastbourne road, Camberlot Road and Coldharbour Road; they form a triangle of roads around the area known as The Mount. Roads have seen changes, both in their composite structure and siting. Sometime prior to 1789

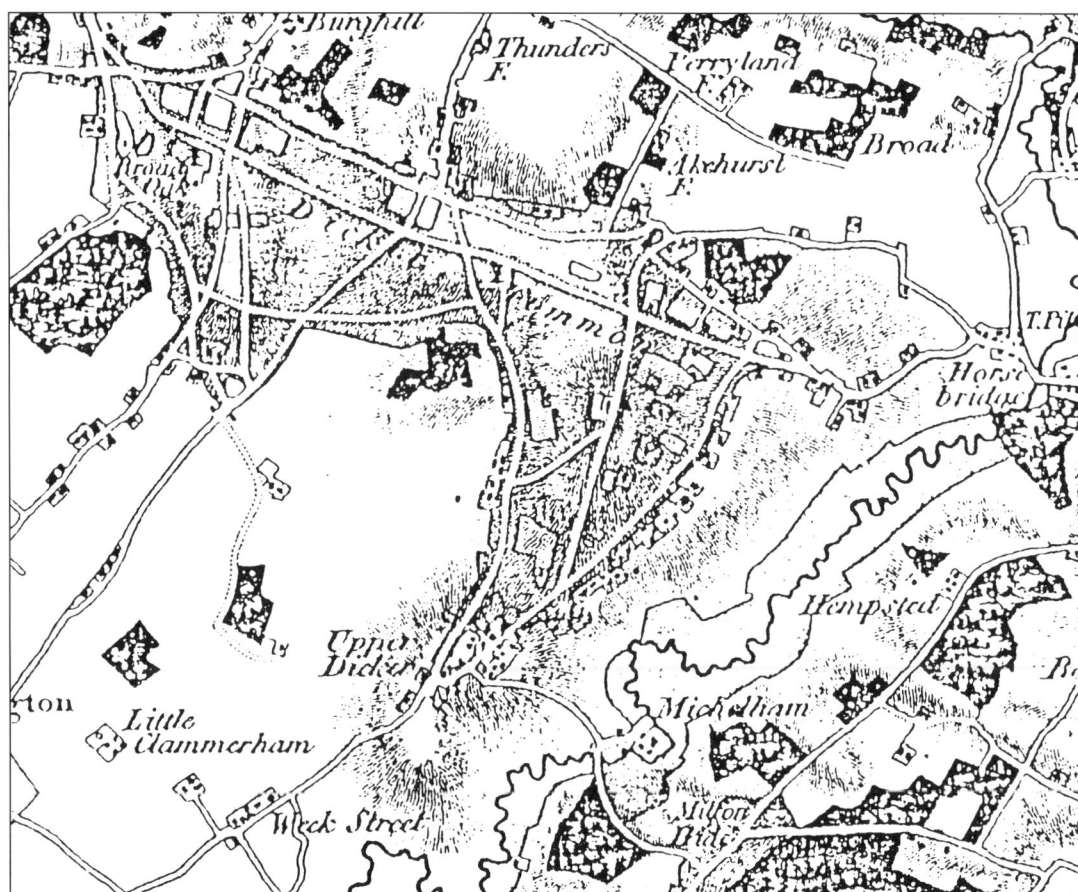

1789 OS map. Shading indicates area of the Dicker Common showing network of byways and roads

Coldharbour Road was re-routed and straightened. Originally the old road passed Penson's Grove near the Potter's Arms pub, crossing the brow of Coldharbour Hill close to the farmhouse, before skirting the dwellings of Hatches, Sharrards (now Knights Acre), Starnash, Plenties, Bourne and Lamberts Farms, before joining Shop Lane in Upper Dicker. The only visual evidence is the distance these properties are from Coldharbour Road. The possible origins of the name 'Coldharbour' are many: it could be a corruption of *col d'arbres*, (a hill with trees) but other evidence suggests 'Cold Harbour,' formerly a common name for a place of shelter from the weather for the wayfarer. Place names are an integral part of our history's past, a previously recorded account indicates 'Camberlot' has its origin in the Manor of Cromerlott.

Floods at Michelham

March 1967

Coldharbour and Camberlot Roads join two other ancient byways within the confines of Upper Dicker, forming the village's crossroads, one passing over High Barn hill towards Wick Street, while the other forks left at the crossroads before it skirts Michelham Priory and crosses the bridge to Arlington and Hailsham. Until more recent times, this was always liable to flooding until the road level was raised.

In 1854, Michelham bridge was deemed to be in a dangerous state, compelling the Ratepayers' Committee to resolve the problem. Following a meeting held at the George Inn in Hailsham, a tender of £145 was accepted from Mr Jason Thompson to rebuild the bridge; Lord Amherst agreed to contribute two-thirds of the cost. This ancient by-way was always an important direct route to the market town of Hailsham.

From 1841, Arlington Ratepayers minute books frequently recorded concern relating to the state of local roads within the parish. An overseer was duly elected to deal with matters concerning roads, bridges, bridleways and footpaths, and to administer the collecting of the highway rates. Further to a meeting held on the 28th Oct. 1854, it was resolved that the surveyor employ William Gosden to collect the rates at 9 shillings a week, "provided that he earns it"! By 1880, Arlington Parish Council elected Mr William Barber, who would be paid a yearly sum of £10 to keep accounts and collect the rates; twelve months later the committee resolved that Mr Barber's resignation be accepted! Following his departure, Mr Hugh Woodhams was appointed to superintend the accounts.

Repairs to secondary roads were fundamentally a local affair, with parish councils in control: for the road alteration and improvement at Chilverbridge in 1869, Mr George Woodhams agreed to bring 6 waggons of chalk free of charge, Mr Joseph Levett 3 waggon loads and the Rev. Farebrother one load. Such were the powers of local councils, they could deem what classified as a bridleway or a cart road, and the repairs that were necessary. Summonses were brought for non-repair of roads.

The Turnpike System

Even when the turnpike system came into being, the majority of road maintenance still came under the jurisdiction of the parish it traversed. An Act passed in 1585 compelled ironmasters to contribute to the repair of the roads they used. Under the parish repair system, owners or occupiers of lands rated at £50 per annum, were obliged to provide a cart, horse and two men for six days' work each year. Even so, roads in Sussex continued to be notoriously bad for the wayfarer.

The first Turnpike Act was passed in 1663, when thirteen main routes leading from London, were brought under the Act. The first Act referring to Sussex was passed in 1696; in all, 152 Acts were approved for turnpiked roads for the county) The only turnpike road in the Dicker, followed the old road (now the A22) from Uckfield to Langney Bridge, the relevant Act being passed in 1754. It came under the Horsebridge and Horeham Turnpike Trust, linking two sections of turnpiked road under the control of the Broyle Park Gate and Battle Trust. Although early development of the Turnpike Trusts had seen a scattered management of unconnected roads, capital for construction came from private investors and loans, with tolls levied to meet the cost of repairs.

Extract from the *Sussex Advertiser* 25th July 1791:

> *"With pleasure we announce that the turnpike road over the Dicker Common, in the parishes of Chiddingly and Hellingly is now quite completed; an object for long the wish and desire of the Public, that their interest and convenience cannot fail to be highly gratified in travelling one of the best roads in this County; excelled by but a few in the kingdom, that from Lewes to Hailsham; and we hear, every improvement in is intended in the several roads leading from Horsebridge to Eastbourne, Battle and Uckfield."*

By 1750, an Act had been passed that gave trustees powers to lease the collecting of tolls, with meetings being held at the Kings Head at Horsebridge, the Woolpack at Gardner Street and probably at the Roebuck hostelry at

Laughton. Notices were posted declaring the collecting of tolls that would be let by auction on a given date, the desirability of certain toll gates depended on the revenue collected the previous year.

Extract from a Turnpike Meeting Notice, 22nd Aug 1789:

"Notice Is Hereby Given".

That the Tolls arising at several Toll Gates upon the Turnpike Roads leading from Union Point near the Town of Uckfield, to Langney Bridge in the Parish of Westham, in the County of Sussex; and from the Side Gate on the Horsebridge Turnpike Road in the Parish of Hellingly, to the Turnpike Road leading from Cross in Hand to Burwash, known by the several names of Mount Ephraim Gate, Horsebridge Gate, Hailsham Common Gate, Stone Cross Gate, Langney Gate and Horeham Gate, will be let by auction to the best bidder, separately for the term of three years from Christmas next, at the house of James Bray, bearing the sign of the Kings Head at Horsebridge, on Tuesday the 22nd day of September next,

for the regulating of the Turnpike Roads,' which produced the last year, after the expenses of collecting them,

viz Mount Ephraim Gate	*£67 13s. 9½d*	
Horsebridge Gate	*£142 4s. 4d*	
Hailsham Common Gate	*£47 19s. 3d*	
Stone Cross Gate	*£4 10s. 10d*	
Langney Gate	*£90 12s. 4d*	
Horeham Gate	*£78 10s. 0d*	

There were no toll gates on the Dicker; the turnpike road was controlled and administered by gates at Horsebridge, Laughton and Uckfield. The tolls levelled varied, depending on whether a coach or waggon, drawn by six or four horses, width of wheels etc.; drovers paid per score of oxen or sheep.

In a county report of 1857 on the Turnpike Trusts, 640 miles of roads were controlled by 238 toll gates. Some reports implied the concept of the system was commendable in theory but was fragmented in its structure and costly to enforce. Consternation was shown in 1853, that Arlington Ratepayers' committee had agreed to meet other parishes for the purpose of inquiring into the management of the turnpike road that crossed the Dicker.

Travellers of any distance preferred to use the turnpiked roads because journey times were considerably shortened. One reported journey was an entourage in about twenty carriages of Alexander, the Emperor of Russia, the King of Prussia and his two sons, and many others of regal patronage, which passed along the Dicker Common road on Sunday 26th June 1814, *en route* to Dover. Reports of the event indicate they drove very fast, "some said at a rate of fourteen miles in the hour or more"!

Turnpike trustees brought great improvement to roads under their control; legislation required the trustees to measure their roads and place posts, stones or markers denoting distance between towns and villages. The three milestones that flanked the old turnpike road from Dicker to Golden Cross are unique in design: the stones show five bells decreasing in size surmounted by a bow, and above numbers indicate miles to London (Bow Bells), culminating in the Pelham buckle, in deference to the family who were large landowners and turnpike trustees.

The demise of the turnpike system was probably inevitable, many trusts struggling to remain cost effective in the face of competition posed by the railways. By 1870 most turnpike trusts had been wound up. The roads controlled by the Horsebridge and Horeham Trust were finally disturnpiked in 1872.

Bowbell milestone at Lower Dicker, 1998

Road at Lower Dicker approaching the old Dicker Potteries

1910-20

The Lower Dicker Road at the junction with Caldicott Lane

1910-20

The road near Golden Cross

Ultrmodern Road — the A22

The 1888 Parliamentary Act stipulated that county councils would be responsible for all main roads, superseding the turnpike trusts and eliminating the fragmentation of control and maintenance. Powers were further extended by the Local Government Act in 1929, which transferred all highway powers from a county responsibility to a national one.

In 1873 concrete was first used in road construction, bringing with it a new era of modern roadbuilding. Sixty years later concrete road surfacing was adopted by Mr H.E. Lunn, the County Surveyor for East Sussex County Council, and plans were implemented for the reconstruction of roads, notably the A22 from Uckfield to Polegate, the coastal road from Pevensey to Bexhill, and the Kitchenham road towards Battle.

During the early 1930s, the ESCC Roads and Bridges Committee embarked upon the greatest road improvement scheme seen since the turnpikes; the frequency of committee meetings indicates the complexity of planning and costing involved. The start of one such road was the road from Golden Cross to Lower Dicker; apart from being turnpiked it had seen little change over the previous hundred years.

A committee meeting held on Tuesday 5th July 1932, indicated plans had been submitted for a five-year improvement programme of the A22 road, with drafts submitted by the Clerk for the compulsory purchase of land; a further meeting found that no objections had been received. Notable was the compulsory purchase of Boship Cottages and land from Mrs Pratt, who received £1,500 in compensation. Boship Cottages were demolished to facilitate the construction of the roundabout, the Rodemark and Vine families, being the last to reside there.

Although no date so far has been found, it is probable that the construction of a concrete carriageway commenced in 1933, starting at Golden Cross from the junction of the Lewes road (A273) eastwards to near Willow Hyrst Farm. A recorded meeting held on 24th January 1933, indicates this section was of 1,000 yards of carriageway with an estimated cost of £10,000. Consequent meetings disclosed the cost of each section of carriageway, which included ancillary work, drainage, kerbing, footpaths and fencing. Following the need to replace or realignment of property boundaries that fronted the Lower Dicker (A22) road, new fences were manufactured and supplied by the local Victoria Fencing Works. By 1936, the road reconstruction had been extended to just east of Hackhurst Lane and was completed as far as the new Boship Roundabout by about 1938.

Throughout, the construction had been fraught by traffic problems, with sections open in only one direction, complicated at weekends with coach day-trippers *en route* to and from Eastbourne, the one-way system caused both minor and serious accidents.

As reported in the *Sussex Express* newspaper:

"Dicker Road Fatality.

"Employees of the East Sussex County Council engaged on the reconstruction of the main London road at the Dicker, were involved in an alarming accident.

"On Thursday, 28th November 1935, an accident occurred on a section of the concrete road not yet open to traffic between the junction of Camberlot Road and Nash Street, (near the bakehouse). A car travelling on a section where one-way traffic was in operation and controlled by 'stop and go' signs, when it ran onto a section not yet completed and collided with workmen taking their dinner break. Three workmen were seriously injured, 31 year old Mr Eli Brinkhurst, a bachelor from Ringmer, later died of his injuries in hospital."

Despite the use of barriers, 'stop and go' signals to control one way traffic and warning boards 'Go slowly for ½ mile – single way traffic', accidents continued to occur.

Extract from the *Sussex Express*, 15th May 1936.

"At 11.05pm on April 7th, a bus coming through a one-way section on the main road at the Dicker, a car approaching at a fast speed from Golden Cross, when it endeavoured to get round the bus as it was coming out of the section, crashed into a barrier consisting of drums of beach and an arrow direction board was damaged.

"Defendant was fined £2, with costs of £3 5s. 4d, and his driving licence ordered to be endorsed."

Again on 21st August 1936, the newspaper reported:

"Sequel to Dicker Accident.

William Warren of London, denied that he drove a car without due care and attention on the Lower Dicker road. PC Von Der Hyde stated, he was on traffic duty near single-way traffic that was waiting owing to road works . The traffic signal was at 'stop' and traffic was waiting to go through. He saw a car driven by the defendant, approach the line of traffic and swerve to the off-side of the road, which then struck and damaged the last stationary car. Defendant was fined £1, and costs of 15s. 6d."

Despite all the traffic trauma and upheaval to the local residents (the Medhurst family were unable to move into their new bungalow 'Agra', in August 1936), the new Dicker section of the A22 road was completed. Over the five years (1932 – 37), documentary evidence from the ESCC meetings gave an estimated cost of £51,384 for the Golden Cross – Lower Dicker section (it is conjecture whether this included a Government grant). By 1937, the Ministry of Transport had already approved the plans and expenditure for the construction of dual carriageways which would become the Hailsham by-pass from Arlington road joining the Dicker on the Hailsham side of Boship Farm, and including a new concrete bridge over the Cuckmere River. Plans were also approved in respect of carriageways past Nightingale Villas at Woodside to Polegate, and a new section of link road running north east to join the Tunbridge Wells road near Lobdens Farm. The total cost of all these road works was estimated at £217,000.

FOOTNOTE: Due to the war years (1939 – 45), some of the dual carriageway and link roads would remain unfinished until the hostilities were over.

Transport

For centuries, the rural populace had little need to travel any distance. For most, if the need arose, journeys would have been by shank's pony (on foot) using the network of footpaths that criss-crossed the rural landscape. By the mid 1800s, journeys of any distance for those less affluent, would have been with the local carrier, whose prime function would have been to convey goods to local villages and market towns: those of Hailsham, Heathfield and Lewes. The carrier's vehicle was generally a horse-drawn tilt-covered waggon; a fitted bench would have provided seating for one or two passengers.

A Carrier in the village of Upper Dicker.
The old village bakehouse is in the centre of the picture

Kelly's Directories confirms that two members of the Westgate family were carriers between 1866 and 1882; also from Chiddingly were Silas Jenner, Gavis Guy and Arthur White, who operated between Golden Cross and Lewes. Henry Wooller and James Parsons combined the occupations of carrier and farmer, operating from the Dicker between 1895 and 1903. Probably the last carrier to operate from Lower Dicker, was Charles Hamper, listed in 1906 as coal, coke and wood merchant, between 1915 and 1938 and was listed as 'carman' (carrier). Carriers operated on given routes, on appointed days, the early irregular passenger service for the ordinary man, and the forerunner of the country bus service.

The advent of the twentieth century brought cheaper and more accessible modes of transport, that of the bicycle and the country bus.

The late 1800s saw the arrival of the safety bicycle but not until 1909 with improved manufacturing methods, was the price (£4) brought within the reach of more people. At that time the bicycle was seen as the rural revolution of the age; it became the conveyance of the worker and was noted that with "courtship mobility",marriages occurred between couples as far as 12 miles apart!. Its popularity in the 1920s-30s was such that James Crossingham at Golden Cross and Martin & Son at Lower Dicker were "Cycle Agents"; also Samuel Miles and George 'Shoppey' Akehurst were cycle engineers. 'Shoppey' Akehurst resided at 8 Elm Cottages, Upper Dicker; and in his younger days was a keen amateur cyclist, but latterly ran his repair business from a large shed behind his house. In wartime Britain, the petrol shortage curtailed public transport and the bicycle was the obvious alternative in rural areas. By 1952, it was recorded that 23 million cycles were owned in Great Britain, with the younger generation cycling to the cinema, not to mention the Saturday night dance in Hailsham. Eventually the motor car dominated both town and village life.

By 1916, the south east of England saw the country bus as a new mode of travel, and many rural carriers motorised their services. Never before had the 'country mile' with its all-too-frequent corners been so shortened by a new passenger service. Like the carrier before, the omnibus became the conveyor of parcels and packages. Pick-up points were The Potters Arms and the Dicker Stores.

Within a short time, the whole of Sussex was covered by a network of rural bus routes, and this brought Ernest Piper into prominence as a bus proprietor. Although no date is at hand to confirm when the Red Saloon Bus Company started, by the mid 1920s his fleet of buses provided a regular service from Golden Cross, via Hailsham to Pevensey Bay and Eastbourne – for a return fare of a shilling and four pence. The company offered, "comfort, reliability, safety, civility and a frequent service" to all destinations. The Red

Saloon buses were garaged at Lower Dicker in a building believed to have been erected by Ernest Piper, and which had previously been in use at the old Airship Station at Polegate. In a short time, the Southdown, a company formed in 1915, plied for passengers on the same routes as the Red Saloon, whereupon each endeavoured to eclipse their rival on these commercially viable routes. With guile and skulduggery the Red Saloon Company strived to fight off the larger operator who threatened their existence! Hearsay has it that Mr Piper induced the local kids with a penny to ride on the Southdown, thus allowing his Red Saloon buses to pick up the more lucrative longer distance passengers to Eastbourne! During the struggle, the local residents were very supportive of the Red Saloon. Probably due to an offer he could not refuse, Ernest Piper sold his company in 1928 to the Southdown and moved to Devizes in Wiltshire, where he started up again as a bus proprietor.

Red Saloon Bus Company
From left to right: Arthur Hoad, Fred Page, Jim Wallace, Don Wallace, Frank Parsons, Don Martin, George Walker, Joe Cornford, Ern Milham and Ernest Piper

ADDITIONAL SERVICE to Time Table published April 15th, 1927.

FROM								W.S.O.
GOLDEN CROSS	7 0	9 40	1 40	3 40	5 40	7 40	9 40	
Hailsham (via Leap Cross)	7 20	10 0	2 0	4 0	6 0	8 0	10 0	
Stone Cross	7 35	10 15	2 15	4 15	6 15	8 15	10 15	
EASTBOURNE (arr.)	7 45	10 30	2 30	4 30	6 30	8 30	10 30	

FROM								W.S.O.
EASTBOURNE	8 0	10 30	2 30	4 30	6 30	8 30	11 0	
Stone Cross	8 15	10 45	2 45	4 45	6 45	8 45	11 15	
Hailsham	8 35	11 5	3 5	5 5	7 5	9 5	11 30	
GOLDEN CROSS (arr.)	8 55	11 25	3 25	5 25	7 25	9 25	11 45	

W.S.O.—WEDNESDAYS AND SUNDAYS ONLY.

SPECIAL DAY RETURN TICKETS.

Golden Cross and Eastbourne both ways (all Buses) .. 1/4.
Dicker Stores and Potters Arms ,, .. 1/2
Golden Cross to Hailsham .. .. 6d.

NEW ROUTE—Hailsham, Polegate, Pevensey.

							S.O.
HAILSHAM (Crown)	9 15	10 45	2 15	3 45	5 15	6 45	8 15
Polegate (Rlwy. Hotel)	9 30	11 0	2 30	4 0	5 30	7 0	8 30
Dittons	9 35	11 5	2 35	4 5	5 35	7 5	8 35
Stone Cross (Red Lion)	9 40	11 10	2 40	4 10	5 40	7 10	8 40
PEVENSEY BAY	9 55	11 25	2 55	4 25	5 55	7 25	8 55

							S.O.
PEVENSEY BAY	10 0	11 30	3 0	4 30	6 0	7 30	9 0
Stone Cross	10 15	11 45	3 15	4 45	6 15	7 45	9 15
Dittons	10 20	11 50	3 20	4 50	6 20	7 50	9 20
Polegate	10 25	11 55	3 25	4 55	6 25	7 55	9 25
HAILSHAM	10 40	12 10	3 40	5 10	6 40	8 10	9 40

	Single.	*Return.*	FARES.		*Single.*	*Return.*
Hailsham to Polegate	5d.	8d.	Polegate to Pevensey	5d.	9d.
Hailsham to Pevensey	9d.	1/-	Stone Cross to Pevensey	4d.	6d.

Red Saloon timetable, April 1927

With people's desire to travel to events and venues not previously feasible, the early charabanc proprietors started day trips much further afield. Unlike the train, the coach picked the tripper up in the village and brought them home. From the early 1920s, coach outings became popular among members of Dicker's Mother's Union and Women's Institute, and others on private excursions. One such trip was to the British Empire Exhibition in 1924, while another was to see the Silver Jubilee decorations in 1935, which for many, was probably their first visit to London. Superseding the early canvas-top charabanc, coach travel had become more passenger orientated, with emphasis on comfort and a greater choice of excursions. The established firm of Wise Tours based in Upper Dicker for the past fifty years, has operated coaches for both day excursions and holiday breaks.

In post-war years, mammoth changes have occurred to both road development, such as. motorways, and to the vehicles that serve the traveller and carry freight, as it was transferred from rail to road. There was none so herculean as Robert Wynn's transporter which brought Upper Dicker to a standstill in 1985, conveying a massive transformer through the village with a police escort from Shoreham to Ninfield.

The motor car is now owned by almost every household, placing man and car in conflict with the environment and lack of parking space!

Wise Tours coaches

1998

Wynn's transporter brings problems to the village

1985

Chapter 5

THE VILLAGE SCHOOL

Concern for a rudimentary education for children of the labouring classes was accentuated in the early 1800s but was slow in it's introduction. Dicker's earliest school building was not purpose-constructed, and was held in the abandoned Wesleyan Chapel building.

Sussex Advertiser, 20th July 1844:

"The desire to educate the children of the agricultural labourers in the district of the Dicker has been manifested during the present year in the establishment of a school for the purpose, supported by voluntary subscriptions. There are at present upwards of 90 children under tuition, and their progress is strongly shown by their improved conduct in daily life. This school is in evidence of what may be accomplished by the inhabitants of any neighbourhood in which a similar feeling prevails."

An entry in *Kelly's Directory* of 1855 confirmed there was an established school in the village and by 1866 indicated the school had been made over to the incumbent of the church by Baroness Buckhurst, the then Lady of the Manor. As the school was situated on glebe land opposite the pleasure ground, this suggests it was a National (Church) School.

The early system of education was on a voluntary basis and the school-room was of diminutive size, it is difficult to imagine 90 children fitting into the small schoolroom.

The Forster Education Act, passed in 1870, was to ensure that every child received a basic education, with School Boards set up with the powers to raise the necessary funds to build and maintain their own schools. At a meeting of Arlington Parish Ratepayers held on 31st October 1870, "it was resolved that Mr Barber should inform Lord Buckhurst that a committee had been formed to initiate plans for an Elementary School at Upper Dicker, and if he so desire to assist in the scheme". At that meeting it was agreed the financing would be obtained by a property rating, provided that such a school could be operated free of government management and left in the control of the ratepayers. At a subsequent meeting held in December of that year, it was resolved a voluntary rate of 3d in the pound would be made, also that the committee had the capacity to spend £40 towards starting the school.

While plans continued and a site for the new school was being sought, the 1875 O.S. map shows a school still functioning opposite the pleasure ground.

1910

Park Mead School

1920

By 1879, transitional changes came when the old Church School was designated the Board School, with Miss Elizabeth Clarke as Mistress.

School Log entry:

"Open this school on 3rd February 1879. There were 27 children present. Number on the attendance book 33. Applied to the Clerk of the Board for Registers and Log Book.

'Admitted Albion Dobson on 3rd February, aged 8 years."

School Log 7th March 1879:

"Received the following new articles of school furniture, viz: Desk, Cupboard, Table, Mounted Slate, Dial, Ball-frame, also books, pencils, slates etc.

"Several of the older children have been out to work during the past week."

Urgency for a new purpose-built school was shown in the school's 1880 Annual Report when Mr Barber (Clerk) emphatically declared, "The Mistress is working well but there is need for improvement in the premises and apparatus. The room is damp, and the one small fire-place is not sufficient to warm it. Many cap and bonnet pegs are broken. The offices [toilets] should be partitioned and a urinal put up on the Boys side."

Such a run-down, inadequate schoolroom, must at that time have galvanised the School Board into action regarding the building of the new school. The location was a parcel of land which formed part of Park Mead field, (which later bestowed its name to the new Board School).

On the 13th October 1881, the Rev. Farebrother gave permission for the children to take half a day holiday, in order that furniture, books etc., could be transferred from the present school to the newly built school. The following day Park Mead School was officially opened; although designed to accommodate 120 children, only 28 were present on this auspicious day! However, by 1882, it was reported that the school still had an unfinished look about the playgrounds and fences, also that some of the work had been badly done by the contractor.

During the school's first four years, attendance figures fluctuated greatly. In addition to the 1876 Education Act for compulsory attendance, the 1880 Act again, strengthened overtures for regular attendance. Entries in the school log indicate attendance ebbed and flowed regularly, i.e. 71 children on the register – only 49 present; with many absent helping with haymaking and at harvest time; some were absent a month or more whilst hop-picking with their parents. In 1885 the new headmaster, Mr Roach, reported, "The excuse that 'mother wants him or her' is often given as a cause of absence, this not being a reasonable excuse for a child losing 3 or 4 attendances per week." In an effort to alleviate this problem, the headmaster and the School Board adopted an award scheme to encourage more regular attendance.

Prize Scheme

Blue tickets value ½d to each child who attended a whole week.
6 blue tickets to be exchanged for 1 pink ticket.

2 pink tickets earn 6d prize		
3	earns a 9d prize.	
4		a 1 shilling prize
5		1 shilling and 3d prize
6		1 shilling and 6d prize
7		2 shilling prize

(9th October 1885 – 45 children earned a full attendance prize!)

FOOTNOTE – the new attendance scheme brought immediate success, the log book entry for 2nd October 1885 records "88 children present – 94 on registers"!

Throughout the early years, the new Board School saw problems, changes and improvements; in 1886 alterations to the classrooms had taken place, and new desks had arrived for the infants. The newfangled 'gallery desks' drew the interest of Mr Hide, clerk of Chiddingly School Board, who was to visit the school two years later. The 1895 Annual Report, stated that the closets were better illuminated but were still not properly divided; it was suggested it could be resolved by a wall that would divide the playground, and build a urinal for the boys. The school was wholly dependent on a well for its water supply; from this (it is believed) water was pumped into a tank situated in the school roof, bringing unforeseen problems. As pupil numbers increased (in 1898 they peaked at 113), coupled by summer drought, immediate steps were called for in 1893, when D Hide, a pupil, was sent to the village on a quest for water. Dependency on the well was again apparent when Mr Pitcher was summoned to repair the well.

Extract from the *Sussex Express*, dated 3rd June 1893:

"THE WATER AT THE SCHOOL

Doctor Andrew Wilson FRSE (editor of Health) writes, 'It may interest your readers to know that an analysis of the water from the tank at the Park Mead School, Upper Dicker, is a dirty yellow colour and full of suspended matter. I am of the opinion, in its present condition is totally unfit for domestic use. Suffice it to say, the water is not what I would give my dog to drink.'"

The early days of compulsory education were not only a learning curve for pupils but the teachers as well. A teachers' handbook of the time (1880s) stated, "Every child should understand that there was a time for work and a time for play", a directive which became apparent to four boys when Mr Roach made an entry in the school log on 31st Dec 1888: "Have been obliged to administer corporal punishment to Alfred Smith, Reg Pettitt, Henry Funnell, and F Coleman for stone throwing etc., after due warning and the confiscation of slings and catapults." The log also noted confrontations between the headmaster and the School Board, alleging neglect of duty and deception, also matters concerning school discipline. The Board's differences with the headmaster seemed to have over-ridden the note-worthy aspects of Mr and Mrs Roach's administration, for example, the introduction of the Attendance Prize Scheme, the Clothing Club (1885) which helped parents afford footwear and clothes for their children, and the introduction of a harmonium (1888) to aid with the singing. Having threatened the Board with his resignation, it was five years later (in 1893) that the School Board gave Mr and Mrs Roach (assistant mistress) notice to quit. From this date Mr Alfred Charles Lay and his wife were to take charge of Arlington (Park Mead) Board School.

Apart from the rigours of learning their 3 R's, the children of Park Mead had their lighter moments; school holidays included Benefit (Fete) Days, the Jubilee Days of 1887 and 1897, and the School Treats held on Friday 12th July 1889 and Saturday 11th January 1890.

Extract from *Sussex Advertiser*, 17th July 1889:

"On Friday last, a treat was given to the children of the Board School. They assembled at the school at 2pm, and marched in procession with banner, flags and bouquets of flowers through the village to the Pleasure Ground, where, after singing one of their school songs, they were dismissed for games. Swings were a great attraction. Mr Page entertained the boys at cricket and other games, and the Messrs Dunk, Vinall and Haffenden rendered valuable assistance at many other amusements provided. Many ladies also came forward as willing helpers to entertain and amuse the children. At 4pm, the children, 122 in number, assembled around the master at the harmonium, and after singing, an excellent tea was partaken of. The children were then arranged in a group and photographed by Mr Baker. By the generosity of Mrs Bottomley, (who already subscribed handsomely), many useful presents were given as a tangible memento of their treat. The whole affair was much enjoyed by the children and friends."

This 'treat' was probably to celebrate Park Mead School's 10th Anniversary.

Extract from *Sussex Advertiser*, 15th January 1890:

"School Treat – On Saturday last the children attending the Board Schools were invited to a tea in the School-room by Mrs Horatio Bottomley of London and Upper Dicker. At four o'clock a sumptuous tea was provided to which ample justice was done, and which was thoroughly enjoyed, as the bright eyes and smiling faces of the children fully testified. After games the crowning point arrived in the presentation of a beautiful or useful article given to every child. It was a treat to be remembered, and seemed all the more generous on the part of Mr and Mrs Bottomley, as only a few days before they had given a dinner to 1,000 poor children in London."

Lessons in Board Schools ranged from the basic subjects to poetry, object lessons, occupation (needlework), drawing and music, with physical exercise included in 1902; later in 1910, hygiene and nature study were encompassed.

Periodically the school log minutes the whole school being tested on 'foolscap.' The week 17th – 21st July 1905 was taken up by examinations. The 1910 Annual Report indicated that the use of 'slates' had now been abolished and the staff had been temporarily increased until the contemplated classroom extension had been effected. School was closed from the 11th September for a week on account of the building work. As numbers gradually increased more children had to fit into the same amount of classroom space. From the outset, children were admitted whenever they 'came of age', and would leave once a certificate of exemption had been granted by the authorities, leaving age being 12 years in 1916 and 13 years by 1918. Possible confusion over school age limits became apparent when Mrs Caroline Smith brought her son Thomas to be admitted, but since the boy was only three years old, the headmaster was compelled to cancel his marks.

Attendance continued to be fragmented by spates of illness and epidemics: in 1899 pupil numbers were decimated by whooping cough and mumps. Ensuing epidemics saw the school closed due to measles in 1900 and 1909, influenza and chicken pox (1902) from March until May, and scarlet fever (1910/11). At times this had tragic overtones. On 4th October 1901, the headmaster received the news that Bertie Bennett had died of typhoid fever. Later, in 1921 more deaths occurred, when Maudie Smith, Cicely Kingman and Phoebe Clapson, succumbed to a diphtheria epidemic. Their graves were marked by identical small stone crosses in the village churchyard.

Bad weather affected attendances with flooding at Michelham and Wick Street. Heavy snow was also a factor on 13th January 1903 when only 9 were

1913

present of the 128 registered. Many at that time, were without adequate footwear for such adverse weather.

Always known affectionately as 'Boss' Lay by the pupils, 1913 saw the retirement of Mr Alfred Lay as headmaster of Park Mead School; subsequently Miss Joiner commenced duties as principal teacher. The following year confirmed Mrs Farrant as teacher in charge of the infant classes.

On Friday 2nd February 1915, the prompt action of the teachers saved the school from near disaster when the new stove in the south classroom set light to the floor beneath it. Previous fire drills had enabled a swift evacuation of pupils, while Miss Joiner prevented the escalation of the fire by dowsing the immediate area with water while awaiting Hailsham Fire Brigade. With disaster averted, the school re-opened the next day, the classes condensed into the remaining rooms while repairs were carried out.

Extract from the *Sussex Express*, dated 15th February 1915:

"SCHOOL ON FIRE

Considerable excitement was aroused in Hailsham on Tuesday when the fire rocket went off and news spread that the Upper Dicker school was on fire. The call was received between 10.30 and 11am and the Hailsham Volunteer Fire Brigade were very quickly on their way, followed by a trap containing extra lengths of hose and other appliances. On arrival it was discovered that the floor of the back schoolroom had become ignited through the heat from a square stove. Prompt efforts to prevent the fire spreading were taken by Miss Joiner, the headmistress, and her staff. The firemen ripped up the floor and poured water on the smouldering timbers, and eventually succeeded in putting out the fire.

The damage done was not very extensive.

The orderly manner in which the children at the outbreak of the fire assembled and were marched out, speaks volumes for Miss Joiner as a discplinarian. The children had a holiday for the rest of the day."

The years of the Great War (1914-18), again brought fluctuations in attendance, due to boys who had prematurely left to replace men called up into the armed forces. Many helped on farms or, as in the csae of Percy Guy, left school to help deliver bread and groceries due to the enlistment of Mr Dunk's son; and John Mercer helped on his father's butcher's round. On the other hand, on Friday 13th July 1917, the cause of absence was a circus at Hailsham which many children decided was far better than time spent in school! To aid the war effort, in March 1918, the older boys cultivated an area of the playground to grow potatoes, and pupils pledged time to blackberrying trips. During the summer of 1918, 12 cwt. (approx. 609 kg) of blackberries were gathered and dispatched by carrier to Newberry's jam factory at Battle. At this time, the school received new desks for the infants and juniors, and cookery classes were introduced at Hailsham, when groups of senior girls were conveyed each week by horse-drawn wagonette or walked accompanied by a teacher.

In accordance with the school manager's instruction, on 11th November (1918) time was taken in singing patriotic songs in honour of the "Glorious news of Peace". A year later, the older children attended a short service in the Church for the 'Great Silence'. Towards the end of November, the school attendance was greatly affected by the influenza epidemic which was prevalent throughout Britain, with only 14 children present on November 22nd, the school closed until 9th December.

1915

Standing from left to right: *Ethel Baker, Kate Ovenden, Ada Brett, Alice Oliver, Dorothy Guy, Primrose Vitler, Grace Haffenden;*
Seated: *Winnie Kingman, Tilly Chilton, Hilda Kirby, Dora Goddard, Dolly Austin.*
The girls were dressed in national costume to celebrate the sinking on 9th November 1914, of the German cruiser Emden by the guns of HMAS Sydney of the coast of the Cocos Islands; in 3 months the Emden had sunk 16 British ships.

Once physical exercise had been introduced into the curriculum, progress was made in the introduction of team games. In 1914 a cricket team comprising John Wheatley, Bert Kingman, Harry Cleeve, Jim Kirby, Percy Guy, Ernest Smith, Reginald Pettitt and John Batho, was selected to play against Hellingly on the recreation ground; later in 1921 another team played Chiddingly on a ground opposite Carpenter's Yard. In 1919, a football was purchased from the proceeds of a jumble sale and in 1924, new stoolball and cricket equipment was bought at a cost of £3 6s. By 1927, the Sports Fund stood at £1 4s. 4d, one shilling having been used on a telegram to inform Hellingly boys that the pitch was flooded!

1917

Standing from left to right: Sidney Smith, Ben Wheatley, Will Kirby, Basil Shepherd, Fred Mitchell, Charles Vitler, Albert Mitchell, Edward Butcher;
Sitting: George Oliver, Gordon Pettitt, Algie Sutton, Jack Kirby, Bert Guy, Eric Akehurst, Bill Gower.

The school log disclosed that on the 7th March 1928, "the older girls were taken to Chiddingly School by bus in order to see a game of netball played". The equipment for this game had been purchased out of the Sports Fund. The acquisition of a maypole in 1919, purchased for £3 2s from proceeds of a Concert, was probably seen as creative exercise for the girls. Although physical exercise was encouraged, in 1922, Miss Joiner (headmistress) forbade the use of pogo sticks in the playground!

Staff changes occurred with some frequency during the 1920s; Miss Joiner ceased duties as headmistress on the 28th June 1923 after 10 years as principal teacher at Park Mead School, with Miss James taking temporary charge until the new headmistress arrived in July. The school log 1913-23 gives a graphic account of children raising funds during that time. 1914: Prince of Wales Fund £5, Dicker War Equipment Fund £2 18s. 6d; 1915: Jack Cornwall Memorial £1 2s. 6d, Nurse Cavell Memorial 3s. 0d; 1916: RSPCA Sick and Wounded Horses £1

0s. 6d; 1920: Lifeboat 5s 0d. In July 1923, Miss A.M. Cowell commenced as headteacher until 1926 when Miss Prentice (supply teacher) took charge on a temporary basis, when Miss M Coster became headmistress. A year later in 1927, Mrs E.F. Newson was appointed principal teacher.

1919

Left to right: *unknown, Sue Davis, unknown, unknown, Florence White, Marjorie Catt, unknown, unknown, Daisy Vitler, Gladys Dadswell,* **(pole)** *Bessie Kingman, Maudie Smith, Alice Shoosmith, unknown, Pearman, unknown*

During the 1920s, the school log records events and innovations which took place. On 8th April 1920 children were taken into the playground to observe an eclipse of the sun and in December of that year, the heating ceased to function due to a depleted coal stock – two boys were sent on an errand to purchase coal from Mr Dann! In 1924 and again in 1925, groups of older pupils were taken to the Empire Exhibition at Wembley. Following an enquiry by the school managers into the plight of Arlington children who were obliged to walk to school, at times negotiating the flooded road at Michelham, Mr Kelly's charabanc commenced conveying them in 1925. A new central heating system was installed and was first used in October 1927 and reported to be working satisfactorily. In September 1928 a 'swing' water barrel had been supplied to convey water to the school during a drought – at such times no drinking water was available on the premises! Following the removal of some of the older desks on 4th June 1929, new dual desks were delivered for the senior room.

FOOTNOTE – Although little has been recorded about privately run schools in the Dicker area, Hellingly School records indicate a 'dame school' was situated on the Dicker in 1887, where pupils paid 9 pence a week. During the 1920s, Mrs Bassett-Smith administered private education to children at the Vicarage, Upper Dicker; also sometime earlier, a small school was run by Miss Ade at Ades Farm Cottages at Lower Dicker.

Park Mead started the 1930s with 79 children on the school roll but numbers were dramatically reduced by the government's 1935 re-organisation scheme which specified that senior pupils (11 year old) were to conclude their education at Hailsham Secondary School. At that time, the school was left with only 44 pupils. Throughout, frequent visits were made by the resident incumbent, Rev Bassett-Smith, while the school correspondent, Mr Terry and managers ensured the school provided an excellent standard of education; the school doctor, dentist and nurse attended to the welfare of the children. During 1935 a milk scheme was introduced, whereupon each child would receive free milk each morning.

On the 5th January 1932, Miss E M Rogers replaced Mrs Newson as headmistress. It was Miss Rogers who put on record that the timetable for the 11th November (1932), "was not fully worked during the morning as the service at the Cenotaph was heard on a wireless [radio] set." This is the first time a radio was mentioned being used in the classroom. Education extended beyond the classroom when gardening was included into the curriculum. In 1933 the school garden was entered in a competition in conjunction with Hailsham Flower Show. The school won second place and was complimented on the excellency of the garden. On another occasion in 1937, Miss Rogers accompanied older pupils on an educational visit to Dicker Pottery.

The 1933 log's first entry is of a scholarship exam for acceptance to the County School at Lewes, when Beryl Parsons attended the second (oral) part. In 1937 Theresa Fletcher, Betty Wooller and Daphne Marshall were awarded places at the County School, and during that year, Joyce Everatt, Rita Parsons, Ronald Fowlie and Leslie Page, "could attend as fee paying pupils if they so wish". This was probably the most successful year for Park Mead.

Relief from the classroom syllabus came on 15th September 1931 when pupils performed 'A Pageant and Flowers' at Michelham Priory in aid of the Village Hall Building Fund; and on Friday 21st July 1933, when Park Mead School held its first Sports meeting, thereafter to be held annually.

Extract from *Sussex Express*, 28th July 1933:

"Park Mead School, Upper Dicker, held its first sports meeting last Friday in the school playground, and the event was favoured with glorious weather. Many friends and parents were present. The children showed marked enthusiasm and had gone in

for intensive training beforehand. There were some exciting tussles and in contrast , plenty of fun occasioned by the dressing-up race and bun-eating competition. Money for purchasing prizes was raised by a jumble sale in June.

Miss Rogers, Miss Coster and Mrs Farrant (teachers) acted as starters and judges for the races'.

The results were as follows.

Running	(babies)	1. Alfred Phillips	2. Rosemary Vinall
	(infants)	1. Gerald Taylor	2. Herbert French
	Std 1.	1. Alec Bishop	2. Daphne Marshall
	Std 2.	1. Ronald Wood	2. John Peckham
	Std 3.	1. Rita Collingham	2. Hedley Phillips
	Senior girls	1. Violet Phillips	2. Lily Crichmere
	Senior boys	1. Ted Stephens	2. J Harrison
Egg and Spoon	(infants)	1. Elsie Skilton	2. Fred Parsons
	Std 1.	1. Daphne Marshall	2. Ella Parsons
	Std 2.	1. Ronald Wood	2. Roy Blackwall
	Std 3.	1. Rose Haffenden	2. Joan Parsons
	Senior girls	1. Lily Crichmere	2. Violet Phillips
	Senior boys	1. Cecil Young	2. Frank Harris
Sack Race	Senior girls	1. Edna Blackwall	2. Violet Phillips
	Senior boys	1. Ted Stephens	2. Frank Harris
Wheelbarrow Race	Std 1.	1. Alec Bishop and Leslie Page	
		2. Margaret Phillips and Theresa Fletcher	
	Seniors	1. Lily Crichmere and Dorothy Smith	
		2. Cecil Young and Frank Harris	
	Juniors	1. Doris and Joan Parsons	
		2. Hedley Phillips and Donald Butters	
Hopping	Std 1.	1. Margaret Phillips	2. Joyce Roberts
	Std 2.	1. Mary Clark	2. John Peckham
	Std 3.	1. Rose Haffenden	2. Donald Butters
	Senior girls	1. Violet Phillips	2. Edna Blackwall
	Senior boys	1. Ted Stephens	2. Tom French
Jumping	Senior girls	1. Violet Phillips	2. Mary Taylor
	Senior boys	1. Frank Harris	2. Ted Stephens
	Std 1.	1. Dorothy Skilton	2. Violet Haffenden
	Std 2.	1. Joan Parsons	2. Donald Butters
Bun eating	Seniors	1. Cecil Young	2. Jesse Bishop
	Juniors	1. John Peckham	2. Alec Bishop
Three legged race	Std 1.	1. Theresa Fletcher and Rose Haffenden	
		2. Joan and Marjorie Arnold	
Three legged race	Seniors	1. Edwin Stephens and Tom French	
		2. Frank Harris and David Fletcher	
	Juniors	1. Rita Collingham and Rose Haffenden	
		2. Donald Butters and Hedley Phillips	

"After the races each child was given lemonade and buns, those who did not win a prize, were given a penny."

As with many other schools, disruption from wartime activity and events, was troublesome and unsettling; in 1939 the school commenced the term on the 18th September, (two weeks later than scheduled) due to the arrival of the evacuees from the New Road School in Rotherhithe. Classroom space at a premium, it became necessary to use the village hall twice weekly to alleviate the overcrowding. As the war intensified, in June 1940, most of the London evacuees were relocated in Wales. Apart from other wartime activity the school maintained a degree of normality. The constant air activity, compelled Arlington parents to complain, regarding the absence of an air raid shelter at the school. Subsequently the cloakrooms were designated refuge (shelter) rooms, and a ballast wall was built to protect the main entrance. As on previous occasions, "on the 25th October 1940, the children were to take refuge for over two hours due to continuous aircraft activity".

In October 1940, Miss E M Rogers relinquished her duties as

1937

Front row from left to right: *Douglas Cox, unknown, Raymond Fowlie, Reginald Haffenden, Bert Skilton, unknown, Alan Page, Robin Gray, Dennis Gray, Maurice Pelling, Roy Pettitt, unknown;*
Second row: *Ronald Medhurst, Rosemary Vinall, unknown, Margaret Levett, unknown, Margaret Wooller, Patricia Farley, Christine Farley, Sheila Butters, James Cox;*
Third row: *Leslie Medhurst, Gladys Skilton, Reginald Evenden(?), Fred Parsons, Nelson Pelling, Dorothy Moore, Theresa Fletcher, Ann Levett(?), Arthur Evenden, Lionel Cox, Phillip Wooller, Elsie Skilton, unknown;*
Fourth row: *Jean Page, Rita Parsons(?), Joyce Everett, Mary Bishop, Betty Wooller, unknown, Joyce Blackwall, June Gray, Barbara Levett, Desmond Fowlie, unknown;*
Back row: *Len Medhurst, Ivor Feakes, Leslie Page, Alec Bishop, unknown, Herbert French, Fred Pearce, Ronald Fowlie*

headmistress, when Miss Margaret Thornton (latterly Mrs Robinson) took charge.

The children's welfare being paramount, cod liver oil and malt extract was made available, and in 1940, the milk quota was accessible to all on a daily basis. Canteen dinners were made available on the 24th November 1943, having been conveyed from Hailsham Senior School and served by members of staff. Although the children still succumbed to chicken pox, whooping cough etc., it was no longer necessary to close the school. On the 1st April 1941, Dr Douglas gave the first inoculations for protection against diphtheria.

The war continued to disrupt, and gas mask drills were carried out with regularity. A warning was received, that on 29th July 1941 a tear gas exercise would be implemented in the district, coupled with a gas mask drill. Visiting ARP personnel helped to improve the children's awareness of the dangers from unexploded ordnance they might find. The glass partition dividing the infant and dinner rooms was removed, for safety reasons. Classroom disruption again peaked during 1944, when the home counties faced the onslaught of the Doodlebug (flying bomb) campaign.

Extracts from the School Log (1944):

"5th July – Very heavy machine-gun fire experienced during the dinner-time. The children knelt under the tables.

6th July – There was enemy activity between 1 o'clock and 1.30. Two robot planes brought down near Berwick but there were none near the school.

10th July – It has been decided to keep the school open. The children have been under the desks only once during the day.

11th July – A fairly quiet day. The children have been under the desks 5 times because of flying bombs, but none of the bombs have passed directly over the school.

14th July – Notices concerning evacuation received this morning.

20th July – Doctor Gillett visited the school for medical inspection of mothers and (8) children who were to be evacuated.

21st July – The children sheltered under desks 16 times during the day.

24th July – News has been received this morning that 3 Morrison shelters are to be delivered to the school.

FOOTNOTE – The threat of the flying bomb caused Miss Thornton (headmistress) to introduce an early warning system of a pupil positioned outside, who would scan the sky and blow a whistle if a robot plane was observed. (Basil Funnell had been selected for Park Mead's front line defence!)

Unlike the previous war (1914-18), the children had found themselves in 'front line' danger. The only recorded instance when the school was damaged, was on Saturday 24th June 1944, when blast damage occurred to windows, doors and ceiling. Throughout, Park Mead children continued with their 3 Rs, with more gaining entrance passes to the County Schools at Lewes. Outdoor activities consisted of blackberrying coupled with Nature Study; a Young Farmers Club was formed in 1942, involving pupils in the school garden, also chicken and rabbit husbandry, and there were annual visits to the Rural Activity Rally held at Mayfield.

May 1945, brought on end to the war in Europe; the school closed on the 8th-9th May for Victory celebrations. The year also brought the retirement of Mrs Farrant after 31 years dedicated service to the school, Mrs Piper, a supply teacher, becoming the replacement.

The immediate post-war years brought several staff changes: Mrs M Robinson's departure as headmistress brought Mrs Kilkenny as principal teacher in December 1946. After only a few months Miss Weedon left in early 1947 and Miss Bonnick was appointed head of the infants' classroom. Other changes came about when Mrs Tatnall and Mrs Vitler took up their roles as domestic (canteen) helpers, thus relieving the teaching staff. Also on 15th April 1947, Mrs Lilian Creasey became the new clerical assistant, (which was to last for 20 years.) The school log noted that the classrooms and dining room were decorated in August 1948, also, in the December, stated, "It is exactly 12 months since the house and school were wired for electricity, but we are still not connected to the Mains". The School was eventually connected on the 6th April 1949.

A climbing frame was installed in July 1947 and the annual School Sports Day was held on the recreation ground. The following year (1948) the school took part in the Hailsham/Heathfield School Athletic meeting. Children were still encouraged to participate in team games of stoolball, cricket and football. On 18th February 1948, the school football team (B Wright, J Green, P Peach, B Cornford, E Staplehurst, N Page, J Hollobon, D Pelling, M Westley, A Shier and B Cull) played Hailsham CP School, and lost 8-0. But scholastically the school fared well in the 1949 and 1950 entrance exams when nine pupils (Brian Cornford, Doris Dudley, John Green, Cynthia Guy, Glenys Levett, Julian Jourceaux, Mavis and Brenda Peach and Maurice Tester.) gained places at the Lewes Grammar Schools.

Post-war years brought changes to the school. Mr Kelly's old charabanc, which for many years had conveyed children from the village and outlying areas to both Dicker and Hailsham schools, was superceeded by transport operated by Mr Ben Wise. No longer would the boys chant

"Old Mr Kelly with the bamboo belly
and his tits tied up with string.
With a trumpet stuck up his bum
playing God Save the King".

In August 1956, work commenced on a new staff and store rooms; also the exterior of the school was repainted. The following year further work was undertaken when the school and adjacent house were re-tiled, a new tarmac drive was laid, and fencing and gates installed. Following closure for the 1961 summer holiday, Mrs Kilkenny reported in the school log that classrooms were to be redecorated but the firm failed to comply with the stipulated colour scheme: "the junior classroom colours were put in the infant room, the infant room colours which should have corresponded with the dinner room colours, were put in the junior room". For many years, the north classroom roof had always caused problems during periods of adverse weather. Reports of flooding in 1919, 1924, 1940 and 1945, necessitated repairs being made in October 1964, following serious leaks, and again in 1975. Visits by county officials during 1963 and 1964 brought a proposal for a new toilet block; also recommendation for the purchase of adjacent land for an extended playground and sports field. Park Mead's first Sports Day on the new field in 1966 was marred by inclement weather; after a postponement of two days, it was finally held on the 22nd July when The Vikings (Yellow) team were winners with 155 points. Refurbishment brought about the delivery of new chairs and tables for the infants room (1965), together with desks, cupboards and bookcases in 1966. Following consultations with Thomas Rich and Son (builders), alterations to the kitchen were concluded. Subsequently the entrance hall and kitchen were redecorated and a new oil-fired boiler installed in 1970, replacing the time-worn coke boiler.

The school year included educational outings to the Festival of Britain (1951), Portsmouth (1952) when 45 children, 22 parents and teachers visited the *Victory* and the Isle of Wight (cost – parents 14s. 6d, children 8s.); Boulogne (1960), the Houses of Parliament (1966); and on the 3rd July 1970 when two coaches conveyed 52 children and 26 adults to London, which included visits to the Tower of London, and a river cruise to Greenwich to see the *Cutty Sark* and the Maritime Museum. Local visits covered history and local studies: Bodiam Castle, Battle Abbey, Hailsham Market, Bates Green Farm, Bluebell Walk and Abbott's Wood and Pevensey Castle etc., hoping this approach to the curriculum would broaden the young mind.

There were also changes in the staff. Following Mrs Kilkenny's departure as principal teacher, Mr J D Rees took charge of Park Mead on the 8th January 1962. Those who were worked at the school during 1959-1979, were: Mrs Mobbs, Mrs Harris, Miss Pearson, Mrs Denham, Mrs Perks, Mrs Duff, Mrs Rees and Mrs Cottingham. On 20th December 1968, Mr J Rees and Mrs E M Rees relinquished their duties as headmaster and infant teacher, when Mr Steadman assumed the post as the school's headteacher.

Other changes also occurred: following a parents' meeting in 1951 school uniforms were discussed, (no other reference can be found in the school log regarding their introduction). In 1964 when Mr Rees (headmaster) placed a requisition for a typewriter, and the following year a television set was installed. On the 28th February 1967, the school received 265 children's books from the County Library, but due to lack of shelf space, 65 of the books were returned on 9th March. The school's own sports field was host to the inter-school team sports. Groundsmen arrived on 21st January 1969 to mark out a small football pitch. On 16th January 1970, Mrs Brooks (teacher) was present at a meeting concerned with sex education in primary schools.

The 1935 Government scheme of re-organisation requiring older pupils to attend Secondary Modern Schools reduced the number of Park Mead pupils to a new low. This re-organisation, in time would culminate in the closure of many village schools; with only 54 pupils on the register in 1964, Mr Rees (headmaster) records his concern in the school log dated 22nd July 1966: "Ten children leave for Secondary schools, 3 others leaving the district – one new entrant" This was a serious situation, bringing the numbers dangerously low – 58 children on the roll. By 1971, pupil numbers had advanced to 92, and Mr Steadman (now the headteacher) pressed for additional classroom accommodation. During August 1971, "a new classroom (building) was erected, enabling the lower juniors to move out of the North classroom", and a second infant class came into being, with Mrs J Hellier in charge. By the following year, pupil numbers had increased to 102, in 1977 numbers increased further to 113 and three years later were an unequalled 128.

Parent commitment to Park Mead had been strengthened following the inaugural meeting held on the 23rd September 1970, when the Parent-Teacher Association (PTA) was established; its function was to assist in the school's activities. At a meeting in October, the headmaster (Mr Steadman) and the PTA assessed the idea of a swimming pool. Until then swimming had been held at Devonshire Baths, Eastbourne. At a PTA meeting held in 1971, the committee made final arrangements with regard to its construction, involving an intense three years of planning and fund-raising before work commenced in April 1974. Throughout, a group of parents consigned both their spare time and considerable effort to the pool's construction, changing rooms and adjacent paved area. The pool project was finalized and declared in working order and swimming commenced at Park Mead on 12th June 1975. The swimming pool was the PTA's first major project and is typical of the parents' dedication to the School. In 1981 ten parents volunteered to become members of a 'reading support group'. Following the 1982 A.G.M., the title of Parent-Teacher Association was changed to the 'Friends of Park Mead' and Mrs Olive Maggs was nominated and elected as the next chairman.

For many years, School House had been the residence of the principal teachers, however the log minutes that by the kind permission of Mrs Shields (tenant), on the 20th April 1972, the house was used for interviews for the post of infant teacher, 'Members present were Mrs Appleton (chairman of the managers), Mr Fisher, Mrs Love and Mrs Gottlieb (managers), Miss Johnson (school adviser). The candidates were: Mrs Dennis, Mrs Viccars, Mrs Vince and Miss Salvage. The successful candidate was Mrs Vince. During 1972, work commenced on alterations to the staffroom, kitchen, cloakrooms and exits; two years later, the school was connected to the main drainage system, and with great emphasis, Mr Steadman recorded in the 1976 log – "Decorating of all classrooms completed", the first time in 12 years!

Since the 1960s, the introduction of safety awareness was brought to the children by police liaison officers, their visits focused on many diverse safety topics: Road Safety, Talking to Strangers, Cycle Maintenance, Water Safety, etc. On 1st May 1979, PC Prout visited to instruct the children on the dangers of skate-boarding.

Changes to aid the curriculum took place at Park Mead, in 1983: electronic calculators were introduced to assist with maths and on 18th January 1985 the school took delivery of a new computer work-station. Following the start of the 'Farmer adopt a School' project in 1984, visits to local farms were videoed and later included in the schoolroom curriculum.

Changes also occurred as space within the school became critical. In 1977 a caravan was purchased from funds raised by the PTA, which would accommodate group-work and staff meetings. Again in 1984, saw the official opening of a new infant extension and sports building, which temporarily answered the dire lack of space. Only four years later, following consultation with the authorities, plans were submitted for a single mobile classroom.

Since the introduction of a library service, Park Mead pupils had enjoyed the variety of books provided, but for whatever reason the county library van ceased in 1984. However, 1988 saw the re-launch of a new mobile library service which again would supply all rural schools.

Staff changes came about on the 15th September 1980, when Mr S H Woodhouse replaced Mr Steadman as headmaster. Following interviews, Mr Clive Hale joined Park Mead in January 1981 as deputy head. The county education authority's analysis of expenditure and manning levels meant staff cut-backs were essential and Park Mead School was no exception. Those who suffered from the staff cuts were: Mrs Morgan (10 years service to the school), Mrs Stevens (8 years) and Mrs Harmer (Kitchen/Dinner staff – 11 years). In the meantime the following teaching staff were to commence the 1981 Autumn term –

Mrs Vince	Infant Reception.
Mrs Duff	Infant/Junior transition.
Mr Hale	Lower Juniors.
Mr Woodhouse, assisted by Mrs Bartlett	Top Juniors.

Over the years many people have contributed appreciable effort and time to the school; whether teacher, caretaker or parent, all are important in the effectiveness of a primary school. Ancillary staff who gave their time, were Mrs Dowling, Mrs Doreen Goodchild, Mrs Valerie Graham, Mrs Pamela Harmer, Mrs Christine Leeves, Mrs Audrey Page, Mrs Sylvia McCarthy/O'Shea, Mrs Helen Nicholls, Mrs Elaine Rushbridge, Mrs May Shier, Mrs Iris 'Ginny' Spiers, Mrs Wise, David and Elsie Mozely(caretakers), and many others. The PTA (later Friends of Park Mead) has been instrumental in the school's well-being and all are praiseworthy for their efforts. Only the names of Mr and Mrs Peter Everest (whose son Christopher was tragically killed in a road accident) are recorded in the school log, and who gave their time and efforts, both before and after that tragic event.

1991

The longest serving dinner lady in East Sussex, Audrey Page retires after 34 years at Park Mead School.

Well in advance of Park Mead's centenary in 1981, teachers and parents had embarked on plans for a programme of celebratory events that would charter the school's 100 years of history. Plans were formulated in January for a new Centenary Garden, the main feature being walled flower beds in the shape of a '100', installing a greenhouse and seats provided by the PTA. The combined efforts of the teachers and eight parents, and weekend gardening sessions brought about the completion of the garden. The garden was officially opened on the 14th July 1981 by Mr D Major (Warden of the East Sussex Rural Studies Centre). In addition, the infants presented 'Boys and Girls Come Out to Play' and class 4 presented a puppet show, followed by an evening of celebration designated 'family fun', when over 200 people enjoyed games, swimming and disco dancing. Following the start of the Autumn term, the staff and pupil's diligent hard work brought 'Park Mead's Centennial Day' to a memorable conclusion with an ambitious programme held on the 14th October (date of the school's inaugural opening in 1881) in the Village Hall. The pupils and staff gave a performance showing aspects and events against during the school's rich history. Guests invited on this auspicious evening of entertainment were, Mr and Mrs T Woodward (Mayor and Mayoress of Hailsham), Mr A Razzell, Mr P Burton, Mr D Pinn and Dr L Bolwell. The 20th January 1982 saw the publication of the Park Mead booklet, 'The First Hundred', produced as a graphic record of the 'Upper Dicker Board School' and then on 3rd April a commemorative oak was planted by Mr C M McCutchan, chairman of the governors.

The 1980s would see further staff changes: Mrs Vange resigned her duties as secretary after 10 years' service, being replaced by Mrs Clement; Mrs Murrell took charge of Class 2 in 1982; two years later saw Mr Hale commence duties as acting headmaster with Mr Woodhouse being seconded to Brighton Polytechnic for a year.

In 1987, Mr Hale became the school's principal teacher; a role that lasted until 1998. During this period, following preliminary discussions, a mutual help link was established between the school and St Bedes (Upper Dicker), and meetings between Mr Hale and Mr Berryman (St Bedes), resulted in an excellent working relationship by St Bedes' visiting pupils. In 1985, Mrs Hale and Mrs Armitage (both parents) formed the school's drama club, prompting the production of the 'Wizard of Oz' staged on the 4th July 1985. The school's log minutes, "This was a unique event for the school, a most creditable effort". Park Mead's curriculum extended to an educational trip to the Isle of Wight, when 40 pupils (25 from class 3 and 15 pupils from Hurst Green) were accompanied by Mr Hale, Mrs Bartlett (teachers), Mr Wood and two parents.

Itinerary

Monday 13th May	*Depart from school.*
	Visit : Weald and Downland Open Air Museum, Singleton.
	Ferry crossing, settle into Hotel, explore locality.
Tuesday 14th May	*Visit a.m.: Museum of Smuggling Ventnor.*
	Visits p.m.: Blackgang Chine and St Catherine's Quay and Sawmill.
Wednesday 15th May	*Visits a.m.: Alum Bay Glass, Needles Battery and Alum Bay.*
	Visits p.m.: Old Smithy Godshill, Godshill Model Village and
	Gardens, Natural History Centre and Tropical Marine Aquarium.
Thursday 16th May-	*Visit a.m.: Robin Hill Adventure Park.*
	Visit p.m.: Carisbrooke Castle.
	Last night Disco/Bar-B-Que.
Friday 17th May	*Visits a.m.: Lilliput Doll Museum, Osborn-Smiths Wax Museum*
	and Animal World.
	p.m.: Ferry crossing and return to school.

Front row from left to right: Louisa Godfraddi, Lisa Hobden, Rosalyn (surname unknown), Anna Farrell, Penny Stevens, Sarah Wye, Jeremy Samson, Thomas Briggs, Myra Berryman, Sam Franklin, Amanda Hurston, Katherine Ansell, Tristan Pengilly;
Middle row: Pippa Spencer, Danielle Borrer, Matthew Pope, Steven Ellis, Marianne Wise, Mark Gribble, Ian Burton, Susan Holland, Steven Graham, Simon Hobden, Stuart Lester, Tina Hobden, Victoria Ansell, Jessica Griffin;
Back row: Liz Cottingham (teacher), Philip Apps, Stephen Godfraddi, Melanie Spencer, Shirley Errey, Kerry Pottinger, Louise Nightingale, Carl Joy, Martin McDermott, Simon Neville, Emma Cull, Paul McDermott, Alison Olive, Elizabeth Fradd, Clive Hale (teacher)

At its conclusion the 1985 log entry records, "An excellent week, enjoyed by all. All staff are exhausted".

FOOTNOTE – The school logs which had been painstakingly kept since 1879, and which were a concise record ceased to be used after 1987 for reasons at this time unknown.

During 1988, the county education authorities deemed that the now vacant schoolhouse should be adapted and used as staffroom, offices, small group teaching and meeting rooms. In 1992, plans were also approved for the improvement of the school's surroundings, which included the transformation of the old swimming pool changing rooms into a science and environment room, and the replanting and maintenance of the school garden.

When Mr Hale secured the post as headteacher at Polegate, Mrs R Ross became principal teacher of Park Mead Primary School, ensuring the school would move successfully into another era of educational excellence.

In March 1999, both the headteacher and parents showed extreme concern that without an injection of finance by the education authorities for repairs and modernisation, Park Mead was on the back foot of a downward spiral. At a meeting in October, governors, staff and parents rallied in a bid for £250,000 to revamp the school, which would ensure new classrooms and a hall would be built for physical education and assembly, also new toilets. An Ofsted report, followed a visit by inspectors who reported, 'the quality of teaching to be consistently good' and Mrs Ross was praised for giving a very clear educational direction.

The approach of the new millennium with possible modernisation together with the continued support of Friends of Park Mead, would ensure a favourable future for the school.

By the new century, Park Mead School had 109 children on the roll, the school was staffed by the headteacher Mrs Rebecca Ross, supported by, assistant headteachers Mrs L Holyoake and Mrs E Walton, and teachers Mr J Entwhistle and Miss V Clarke, classroom assistants Mrs Iris Spiers, Mrs C Blakiston and Mrs S Hale. Others who helped keep the daily functioning on course were, Mrs I Sampson, Mrs A Robb, Mrs S Talmadge, Mrs G Brooke and Mrs P Beaver.

Chapter 6

WELFARE IN THE PARISH

The 1601 Act formed the basis of welfare relief within the bounds of a parish, installing overseers to provide for the needs of the old and infirm, and support those who were unemployed and had families. Arlington, as with other parishes, was a local government entity and provided for the impoverished of Upper Dicker. The Knatchbull's Act of 1722 enabled parishes to combine poorhouse finance with an imposed residency as a condition of relief payment. In theory, each person had a 'place of settlement' where he or she belonged, i.e. they were born in the parish, were working or apprenticed within the parish or residing with a settled employer of the parish. Whenever it was possible to divert the responsibility for funding to a third party, overseers were prompt to seize the opportunity to do so.

Extract from Arlington Overseers Accounts, 8th Oct 1766:
"Letter from Samuel Boys to Gerard Masson (Overseer) at Wick Street, Arlington; agreeing to take Edward Geer as an apprentice ox-boy until Michelmas 1767, and desiring Masson to grant Geer, − 3 shirts, 1 waistcoat, a round frock, a pair of breeches, two pairs of stocking, a pair of shoes and a new hat."

The overseer's obligation to provide 'cradle-to-grave' poor relief to an aged inhabitant was evident from the Accounts book when it recorded, that on June 1st 1795, Dame Fox of the Dicker received eight shillings poor relief over one calendar month, and on September 7th, two shillings was paid for firing (wood). Poor relief continued until December 1803, when Dame Fox was recorded as 'dead'. In an entry for 2nd January 1804, Mr Dobson's bill for Widow Fox' goods (chattels) was eight shillings and ten pence, indicating the overseers were bent on recouping whatever expenditure they were able against the deceased.

Further Account entries record poor relief expenditure –

"2nd May 1796 –	*Jos. Lambert, wife and two children*	*£1 2s. 6d*
	Thomas Gosden, keeping Ann Prodger	*4s. 0d*
	Elizabeth Blaber, nursing Dame Fears	*13s. 6d*
5th June 1797	*making Henry Lambert breeches*	*8d*
1st Sept 1800	*Dame Lee – doing for her, mend her clothes, milk and shoes.*	*11s. 6d*
	cleaning the room, airing the beds.	*2s. 0d*
6th Dec 1802 –	*laying out Dame Hickner*	
	doing for her and nursing.	*8s. 0d"*

These entries give an insight into how poor relief functioned; those in need, whether sick, old or unemployed, were cared for within their own homes. The sick were nursed for by a woman with aptitude rather than skill, the aged were given rent and nursing, and if necessary, were buried at the expense of the parish. A pauper, if providence prevailed, would be given a decent coffin, borne and followed by mourners, all encouraged by a dole of bread and beer from the overseer.

Accommodation for the impotent poor and a parish's need to provide a 'convenient house' within the parish, a poorhouse was established at Cane Heath, Arlington, in 1800.

Extract from Vestry Accounts, 30th March 1800:

"Agreement by the Vestry, that the £200 lent to the Parish by John Tourle of Landport, Lewes; for the erection of a poorhouse at Cane Heath, should be secured by the surrender of copyhold tenements held by the Manor of Michelham Park Gate, by William Hide of Arlington, [yeoman], in trust for the parish, to Tourle and the churchwardens and overseers should enter into a bond."

Arlington's Workhouse was situated adjacent to the old Beerhouse (now the Old Oak). Now with a functional poorhouse which would serve both Arlington and Upper Dicker, the overseers were probably content that it solved some problems of an outdated system. A continual weekly payment of five shillings recorded in the Account Books to Lucy Page (widow) of Chiddingly probably indicates she was in charge at the Workhouse. She was followed in 1817 by William and Sarah Hermer.

The parish expenditure for not only the poor relief, but for the maintenance of roads, bridges and water-courses etc, was assessed at a rate of 3 shillings in the pound. Arlington's account books give a graphic account of the magnitude of the cost of maintaining the poor relief within the parish. Astute overseers were prompt to employ out-of-work men and boys in flint digging on the Downs to mend the parish roads. In April 1828 ten men and boys were employed digging flints at a cost £2 19s. 1d, and in November 1829 fifteen men and boys worked on the roads, costing £5 14s. 5d. Soaring poor relief expenditure threatened to bankrupt the worst hit parishes. Fears over spiralling numbers of unemployed due to the agricultural depression (1815-30), put a strain on the overseer's definition of the deserving and the undeserving poor. A condition of paying relief to the unemployed; was that no relief would be given without work atonement.

"Samuel Prior, for 6 days thatching Workhouse Lodge – 8 shillings.
William Colbran, for digging 24 rods of ground – 4 shillings.
John Huggett, for 6 days faggot carrying – 10 shillings & 6 pence.
Edward Parris, for 5 days on road repairs – 8 shillings & 4 pence.
Henry Pollard, for 4 days flint breaking – 2 shillings."

The depression in agriculture continued to force many into

unemployment and many over-stretched parishes faced an unavoidable financial dilemma, the already inadequate system had brought desperation to Arlington's overseers William Hide, Thomas Shoesmith and Thomas Ogden. The demands on the poor relief coffers by the rural parish were numerous:

> "September 1834 – paid bills for cheese and flour   £9 14s. 1d
> paid for 500 faggots   £3 0s. 0d
> paid for 200 cabbage plants   1s. 0d
> 19th January 1835
> Gave 7 old men in the Poorhouse to buy tobacco –   3 shillings & 6 pence
> Gave John Fox for relief of his family and to pay for coffin for his daughter –   £1 10s. 0d"

Until now, the parish had been realtively self-sufficient but faced by escalating costs, poorhouses had become overcrowded; Sussex parishes had the reputation of having the highest poor-relief expenditure. Consequent to the 1834 Poor Law Amendment Act, the existing poorhouse system became defunct and was replaced by a central Union (Workhouse) administered by a Board of Guardians, which would serve the needs of rural parishes. By 1843, a Tithe map and schedule indicates that the then redundant poorhouse at Arlington became dwellings which were occupied by Rueben Colman and others.

    The new Hailsham Union came into being in 1836, whereupon the vestiges of elementary help and care were found within it's grim façade and harsh interior, it being the intention that those unfortunate enough to fall on hard times would have instilled an immediate desire of self-help rather than prolong their stay.

    Arlington Parish, along with those of Chiddingly, Hellingly, Heathfield, Herstmonceux, Hooe, Laughton, Ninfield, Warbleton and Wartling now came within the jurisdiction of Hailsham Union, eradicating much of the financial burden on parish resources.

    Overseers were still resolute to minimise or divert parish expenditure,

    Extract from Parish Minutes, 29th April 1850:

> "This meeting consents to the Board of Guardians expending the sum of four pounds towards assisting George Lambert, wife and two children to emigrate to Australia."

    Seven years earlier, the churchwardens and overseers spent £100 to defray the expenses of the emigration of poor persons having settlements in the parish, such was their endeavour to minimise prolonged expenditure against the Parish.

    Extract from the *Sussex Express*, 1st June 1850"

"*ARLINGTON*

A meeting of the ratepayers of this Parish, (the Rev Beleney in the chair.) recently passed a vote of thanks to Earl Amherst for having generously employed for several months past, a considerable number of labouring men, who otherwise must have gone into the Union, in straightening and widening the course of the Cuckmere, which runs through his lordship's property here."

Far reaching government legislation had brought an era of welfare change and reform, the new central Unions had relieved parishes of the financial burden of not only the aged and sick, unemployed and destitute, but also the insane. Reform in the latter part of the 1800s led to the building of hospitals in Eastbourne and the Victoria Isolation Hospital in Hailsham. In 1903, the County Lunatic (Mental) Asylum was opened at Hellingly.

Parishes were now discharged of welfare responsibilities, and an era of self-reliance was evident in rural communities; whereupon Benefit Societies came into being, which would provide a safeguard against financial hardship caused by loss of earnings due to sickness or a bereavement. Upper Dicker's Friendly Society (later known as the 'Hand in Hand') was formed in 1871, with a Club or Feast Day held annually on the last Friday in May and was deemed a holiday for everyone.

Extract from Park Mead School log, Thursday 29th May 1879:
"Tomorrow being Club Fete, the school will not be opened, as no children would attend."

By 1889, the local newspaper reported that the village's Friendly Society was flourishing, with new members and a good financial balance sheet. Festivities were held at the Plough Inn and were presided over by Doctor

Upper Dicker Hand in Hand Benefit Society   *1907*

Billings, whereupon, Mr Gutsell provided a capital dinner, and the gathering were entertained by Alfriston Brass Band.

The Upper Dicker Hand in Hand Society continued to extend financial help to a growing membership; in 1907 they held their first march headed by an illustrious banner, and the whole village was thrown into a festive holiday mood.

Extract from *Sussex Express*, 8th June 1907:

"VILLAGE CLUB ANNIVERSARY. – Fine weather on Friday last enabled the members of the Upper Dicker Benefit Association (called the Hand-in-Hand) to participate in a pleasant holiday in connection with their anniversary, which was their thirty-sixth. The village was enlivened all day by the strains of the Heathfield Brass Band and other music, and when the members formed up in procession at their headquarters, the Plough Inn, spectators took a keen interest therein. Their first march, headed by their conspicuous banner, was for church, where the Rev J.M. Russell (Vicar) and the Rev Thompson (Vicar of Laughton) conducted the service, the latter gentleman being the preacher for the occasion. A perambulation of the village was made when this was over, and at the Vicarage the members were hospitably entertained by Mr and Mrs Russell, for whose pleasure the band played one or two selections in capital style. The all important function of the day was the annual dinner, when Mr and Mrs David Gutsell catered in their usual bountiful and excellent manner in a tent in a field opposite the hostelry. The Vicar (the Rev J.M. Russell) occupied the chair, and was supported by the Rev Thompsn, Mr Crowhurst (Hailsham), Mr Vine, Mr Huntley, Mr Austin, Mr S. Haffenden, Mr Foster, Messrs James Parsons, A. Gutsell, J. West, E.E. Rudd, Perry, F. Lovell, C. Griffin, A.A. Wheatley, J. Coleman, D. Smith, W. White, A. Gander, F. Smith, T. Wheatley, W. Barden, and Mr Luther Page (Sec.). After full justice had been done to the repast, and the toast of 'The King and Queen' had been honoured, the Chairman submitted the toast of the day, and congratulated the members of the club on having made such progress as to have just over £300 in the reserve fund, the membership of the club being 40. It had only been good management, and by all the members pulling together, that such a result had been arrived at. He was exceedingly glad to see how much use the club had been to those members who had been sick. He welcomed one or two of the older members, and spoke of the continued generosity of the Southdown Brewery Company in contributing one guinea half of which was for the club funds, and the other half for lemonade for the members' (hear hear, and laughter). He also remarked that by the work of the Secretary and the energy of the members they wanted sufficient honorary subscriptions contributed to pay for the club day expenses. He congratulated the Members on their balance sheet, and hoped in a few years to see the £300 in reserve increased. Mr Luther Page (the Secretary) thanked the Vicar for the kind remarks he had made about the Hand-in-Hand Benefit Club. He himself was proud to say that they had over £300 in hand, and he pointed out that if they could increase their members by the addition of young members, they would be one of the finest village clubs in the surrounding neighbourhood. The health of 'The Chairman' was proposed in a few well-chosen words by Mr Crowhurst, and the Vicar, in reply, remarked that he wanted the members and parishioners to 'turn round in

the way he wanted them to,' and further said that it would be a sorry day for every country parish if the Church of England were pulled down as some threatened. – Mr Foster responded for 'The Honorary Members,' and after 'the Host and Hostess' had been toasted, the afternoon and evening was given up to pleasurable pursuits."

An air of despondence prevailed when the Society held their feast day in 1912; even though the balance sheet recorded £399, mixed feelings would have been felt regarding the threat from larger Equitable Societies, for example the Foresters and Tunbridge Wells Equitable. In addition the pending Insurance Act if instituted, would probably sound the death-knell of the smaller societies. Mr Gwynne affirmed that if Benefit Clubs were terminated by events, the members would have to seek other means of security and the village would be denied its festive gathering!

Mrs Amy Wooller (born 1901) recalled many years later that, as a young girl, saving pennies all year, as she looked forward with great excitement to the annual Club Day, and would walk with her parents from her home at Sessingham Farm, at Arlington, and would spend her precious pennies on the side shows and swings.

Upper Dicker's Hand in Hand Benefit Society continued to function until 1914, but due to hostilities across the Channel, remained suspended until 1922 when it was revived. Club Day was again celebrated on the 25th May 1923, and was believed to be one of the few societies still remaining in the district. The day-long celebrations of 1923 were both pleasurable and well received, according to the local press, with a roundabout, swings, shooting and dart galleries much in evidence; a large marquee and beer booth accommodating food and liquor were provided by Mr and Mrs Pugh of the White Hart, Horsebridge.

Following the event, Stanley Pugh (publican) appeared at Hailsham Petty Sessions on Wednesday 27th June, summoned for selling liquor without having taken out an excise licence as required by the 1910 Finance Act. "PC Peters stated, that at 2pm on the 25th May, he was on the Upper Dicker Recreation Ground, where a Club Day was being held, the defendant was selling liquor in a booth and asked to see his licence. When questioned, Mr Pugh said he had applied for magisterial consent but did not realise he required a licence, – he had only gone into business in March and had yet to acquaint himself with all the intricacies of the licensing laws as he ought to have done!" The Bench dismissed the case.

As village benefit societies fell into decline and were replaced by equitable societies and the national insurance scheme, the Dicker Hand in Hand Benefit Society ceased its beneficiary activities. Alternative assistance was given by slate clubs affiliated to local hostelries. Members paid a weekly contribution into the club, and in December received shares which were similar to those of the now defunct benefit society.

The slate club provided a welfare structure for the working classes, and helped alleviate anxiety about financial provision in sickness. This continued until the 1950s.

The slate club was probably responsible for some minor transgressions – Frank Page used to tell his wife he was just going to slip up The Plough to pay the 'Club', when in fact he was going for a pint or two!

Extract from *Sussex Express,* 22nd December 1906:

"SLATE CLUB DINNER.

Mr R. Holden presided at the annual dinner on Friday at the Rose and Crown. The balance sheet showed that sick pay had been paid out to the amount £1 6s. 8d out of a total receipts of £40 5s. 3d. The share out to the members was £1 4s. 8d. Mr J. Rowland presided at the smoking dinner that was held afterwards."

Granny Cottington outside her home at Body's Farm   *1910*

Apart from an unheralded journey in either a St Johns ambulance or the yellow horse-drawn fever van to Hailsham's Isolation Hospital, the village was reassured by the ever-present resident (unqualified) local midwife whose claim to fame would be to 'hatch and despatch'. For many years this role was carried out by Granny Cottington who resided at Body's Farm. After a call to lay out a body, her white aproned figure would have been seen in the village, followed a day or so later, by Mr Dunk's horse-drawn bakers van used as a hearse for conveying the deceased on their ultimate journey!

In 1917, villagers mourned the death of 'Granny Cott', who for so long had administered to their welfare; in the fullness of time she was replaced by a newly appointed District Nurse on her trusted cycle in fine and inclement weather, administering to those in need of her services.

Mrs Calloway (District Nurse)

In 1925 a whist drive was arranged by Mrs Bassett-Smith to raise funds for a parishioner who had been seriously ill. The generosity of Dicker's inhabitants was extended further afield, when a fund was set up to aid the Welsh colliery disaster in 1934, when an explosion killed 265 at Gresford Colliery.

The need for financial support for hospitals brought about the annual Sunday Hospital Parade. The first parade was held in 1921 and secured £30 for Princess Alice Hospital, and in the ensuing four years, Upper Dicker's benevolent endeavours raised a further £102 for local hospitals. Like the previously held Benefit Society Club Days, Sunday Hospital Parades were a grand undertaking, fronted by one or more bands, and a procession which followed a route from the Dicker to Horsebridge and back.

Extract from *Sussex Express,* – 26th August 1921:

"SUNDAY PARADE FOR HOSPITAL

For the first time a parade and service on behalf of the funds of the Princess Alice Hospital, Eastbourne , was held at Upper Dicker on Sunday, and the organisers are to be congratulated upon the success which attended their initial effort.

A procession was formed at the Plough Inn at 2.15pm, comprising the members of the Hand in Hand Benefit Club (with their banner), the Plough Slate Club, the Football Club, Cricket Club and Stoolball Club. Some members of Chiddingly Equitable Friendly Society also attended. The Chiddingly Brass Band, the Hailsham Town Band, Upper Dicker Fife and Drum Band were present, and played en route. The procession marched to Horsebridge via Coldharbour Road, returning along the Lower Dicker and Camberlot Road to the Plough Inn, where the bandsmen sat down to tea. Afterwards, the procession was reformed and proceeded to the Recreation Ground where a special service was conducted and an appropriate address was given by Rev Hubbard of Hartfield, (who was assisting at the church during the holiday of the Vicar.) A house to house collection was made throughout the ecclesiastical parish during the previous week. The expenditure was greatly reduced owing to the generosity of Mr Harry Page, who provided motor conveyance for the Chiddingly and Hailsham Bands, free of charge. The total amount obtained was £33 19s. 4½d.

House-to-house collections were made by Mrs W.G. Wright, Miss L. Page, Miss D. Guy, Mrs Goddard and Miss R. Harmer.

Collecting boxes en route were organised by Mr E. Guy, Mr J. Brett, Mr F. Oliver, Mr C. Pettitt, Mr E. Smith, Miss M. Parsons, Mr F. Sutton, Miss L. Page, Mr W. Pearce, Miss D. Guy, Mr A. Moore, Mr J. Hunnisett."

In 1926, fine weather favoured Dicker's annual parade which was again enthusiastically supported, and £40 7s. 9d was subsequently forwarded to the Princess Alice Hospital fund.

Sunday hospital parades were instrumental in raising funds until the end of 1933, when they were replaced by a 'Hospital Box' scheme, in which every household held a box and was responsible for its own hospital donations. From the outset in January 1934, 104 households were associated with the new scheme, £57 4s. 9d being donated to Princess Alice Hospital in the first year. This amount had eclipsed any previous annual donation made by Upper Dicker residents to the hospital coffers.

Throughout the 1930s, the Upper Dicker Hospital Committee continued to be instrumental in social events held in the village hall in aid of hospital funds. A dance held on Tuesday 2nd January 1930, raised £2 15s, and a more successful dance held on 2nd February 1934 and organised by Mrs E.M. Wright and Mr Percy Parsons, when over a hundred danced to the music of Stanley Warren's Band of Polegate, raised £6 12s which was forwarded to the Princess Alice Hospital. Funds also came as a result of the occasional 'Pound Day' organised by Mr John Dunk of the shop and post office, when groceries were donated by the villagers and were dispatched to the local hospitals. In 1930, 135lbs of assorted groceries were donated to Eastbourne's Ear and Nose Hospital. And in 1939, in connection with the Womens Institute, a whist drive was organised to raise funds for the blind at St Dunstans.

By 1939 and subsequent years, Upper Dicker's benevolent endeavours extended to previously unknown bounds, when organised fund-raising events gave financial aid to the funds for the armed forces, Red Cross Day and the St Johns Ambulance Brigade.

Welfare care had undergone major change, from welfare in the parish to the radical workhouse reforms, the benefit society and the National Insurance Act. The 1942 Beveridge Report recommended the forming of a National Health Service, which came to fruition on the 5th July 1948, and promised free medical and dental treatment to all.

The National Health Service remained in place until the formation of NHS Trusts in 1991, as health care moves into a new era.

Chapter 7

COMMERCE AND EMPLOYMENT

Farming

Since man's progression from hunter-gatherer to farmer, over the centuries there has been a vast change in the landscape as man's ever-growing demands necessitated encroachment into the forested areas of Sussex. Today's landscape can be attributed to farming needs which saw the enclosure of common land and the felling of immense swathes of woodland.

Most who farmed or gained a livelihood from the land were employed or tenanted to a major landowner. The early method of land cultivation was known as 'husbandry', much later referred to as 'agriculture'. It was labour-intensive and gave employment to the greater number of people living in a rural community, which included children until compulsory education removed them from the equation, (although Dicker school log books until the 1920s, reported pupils absent due to the pressure of harvest time). The multitude of landless labourers, who were without rented land to work, were greatly dependent on the changing economical fortunes of their employer. Throughout the 19th century, the agricultural labourer's circumstances had changed little. Not only crop failures but also the change of farming methods were responsible for unemployment.

The improvement by using the horse-driven threshing machine that had denied the workers their winter employment, was cold comfort to the farm labourer who struggled to support his family on nine shillings a week. In the end the labourers were in open revolt in what is now known as the 'Swing' riots. Anarchy first occurred in Kent on Sunday 29th August 1830 and quickly spread to Sussex and other adjoining counties, where demands were made for a living wage. An exasperated 150 labourers met with Lord Gage (a principal landowner) on Ringmer Green to present a letter regarding poor wages and demanding the parish overseers be more sympathetic to their plight. According to a newspaper report, all requests were granted and the gathering dispersed, but in doing so some over-exuberant people on their way home, damaged the village grindstone.

During the discord in Sussex, 145 incidents were reported, seventeen perpetrators were charged with causing unrest and damage, and were sentenced and transported to penal servitude in Australia. The Swing riots quickly collapsed, but were a spontaneous gesture by farm labourers who had felt their livelihood was threatened.

During the 19th century, employment in agriculture continued to be the principal occupation. In 1851 it was recorded that over two million gained employment from the land, but due to changing methods and mechanization, by 1881 the number had fallen dramatically to 1,633,000. Due to the complexity of Dicker's parish boundaries, it is difficult to determine exactly how many were employed on the land, but the 1841 census records 76 residing in and around Upper Dicker, and working on the land, which, ten years later, had risen to 99.

Early documentation indicates the land in and around the Dicker fell mainly within the bounds of the Manors of Alciston and Laughton, and that of Michelham Park Gate.

Kelly's trade directories indicate the principal landowners were the Hon Mortimer Sackville-West, Duke of Devonshire, the Earl of Chichester and Edward Shoosmith in 1874, and by 1895 records that of Sir James Duke Esq and the Viscount Gage. Four years later (1899), Horatio Bottomley Esq had purchased land on the Dicker, and by 1907, so had J A E Gwynne Esq and Mr Charles Morrison, who had acquired Camberlot Hall and the adjacent farm of 157 acres in 1892 from Mrs William Hickman.

Not always were major landowners committed to farming directly themselves. They often installed a bailiff or a tenant farmer who paid rent on a given quarter-day, his tenancy probably held on an annual covenant. The size of Dicker's farms on the whole were of 60 acres or less, many deemed by today's standards would be called a small-holding. The 1851 census records those occupied by Cornelius Fox – 6 acres, Henry Bishop – 6 acres, John Pitcher – 8 acres, David Butters – 3 acres, Henry Bourne – 8 acres and Samuel Dearing – 4 acres. The smaller tenant farmer with a holding of a few acres, would almost certainly have had to hire themselves out as agricultural labourers to others with greater acreage. Many also relied on 'rights of common', which gave free access to grazing, firewood and litter, with bracken as bedding for one or two animals. Others would be involved in a dual occupation, dividing their time between farming and brickmaking, for example. The 1861 census shows Stephen Haffenden as a farmer and beer retailer, Edward Miller as a farmer of 21 acres and potter, and Trayton Parris as a farmer and 'Ag lab', indicating he hired his labour out to others. In 1871, James Goldsmith's dual occupation was that of farmer and brickmaker and Richard Manser, who resided in Mount Lane, was both farmer and engineer, being in partnership with Thomas Boys, running an engineering business with steam threshing machines. Although few in number, one of the larger farms encompassing the Dicker in 1861, was that of the Boreship: the 400 acres farmed by Algernon Pitcher, who at the time employed 13 men and 3 boys. Earlier documented evidence records on 31st Aug 1818, a lease signed by William Stone (gent) of Framfield, granting land to John Bourne of Hellingly (farmer of Boreship). The 1861 census shows a farm of 400 acres at Michelham being farmed by Elizabeth Child. Of the larger farms at that time, others were Hackhurst (140 acres), Camberlot (152 acres), Coldharbour (100 acres), Clifton (80 acres) and Park Wood with 240 acres, overseen by William Lambert, bailiff for Mr George Woodhams.

Whether by changing fortunes in agriculture or other reasons, land holdings of some farms differed as one tenant farmer succeeded another. One instance was in 1861, when Boreship Farm had assets of 400 acres but twenty years later Charles Cane farmed only 104 acres. In a sale document dated 26th July 1922 when Coldharbour Farm was sold, the acreage had plummeted from a holding of 92 acres to just 14 acres.

In Sussex agricultural practices varied greatly due to the diversity of soil structure throughout the county. The well-drained region of the South Downs, where sheep and cereal farming were predominant, were quite different to the Low Weald where cattle rearing and dairy farming were favoured. The clay which had effectively contributed to the brickmaking and pottery industry, impeded the ploughing of the Low Wealden fields around Dicker, clinging as it does to everything – hence the Sussex lament of "luvin' mud". Despite that, the soil structure was not suitable for cereals; hop production was taken up by some farmers. Muggeridge's map dated 1844, records that 114½ acres were under cultivation in the parish of Hellingly. Although hop growing was more predominant nearer Kent, *Kelly's* 1870 and 1874 directories record that hops were grown on the Dicker by Algernon Pitcher at Boship Farm and William Russell at Hackhurst Farm.

Intense grazing of common land resulted in it being exhausted as ideal pasture. Many commons had been enclosed before 1700, and early 19th century legislation was deemed necessary to accelerate agricultural change and improvement. Following a general Enclosure Act in 1801 and subsequent acts, commissioners were appointed to survey the land deemed as 'Waste Ground', and to administer and set out allotments (awards), that would enable millions of acres to be used more productively.

Previous to the 1813 Enclosure Act when the enclosure of the Dicker Common took place, grants and licences to dig clay for brickmaking had been granted. The size of the common had been previously documented as being of 1,000 acres, its extremities encompassing common land in the parishes of Arlington, Chiddingly and Hellingly. The waste ground known as Milton Hyde has never been enclosed and until the 1940s, 'Arch' Haffenden was the last to claim 'rights of common'. Some land grants or apportionments remain

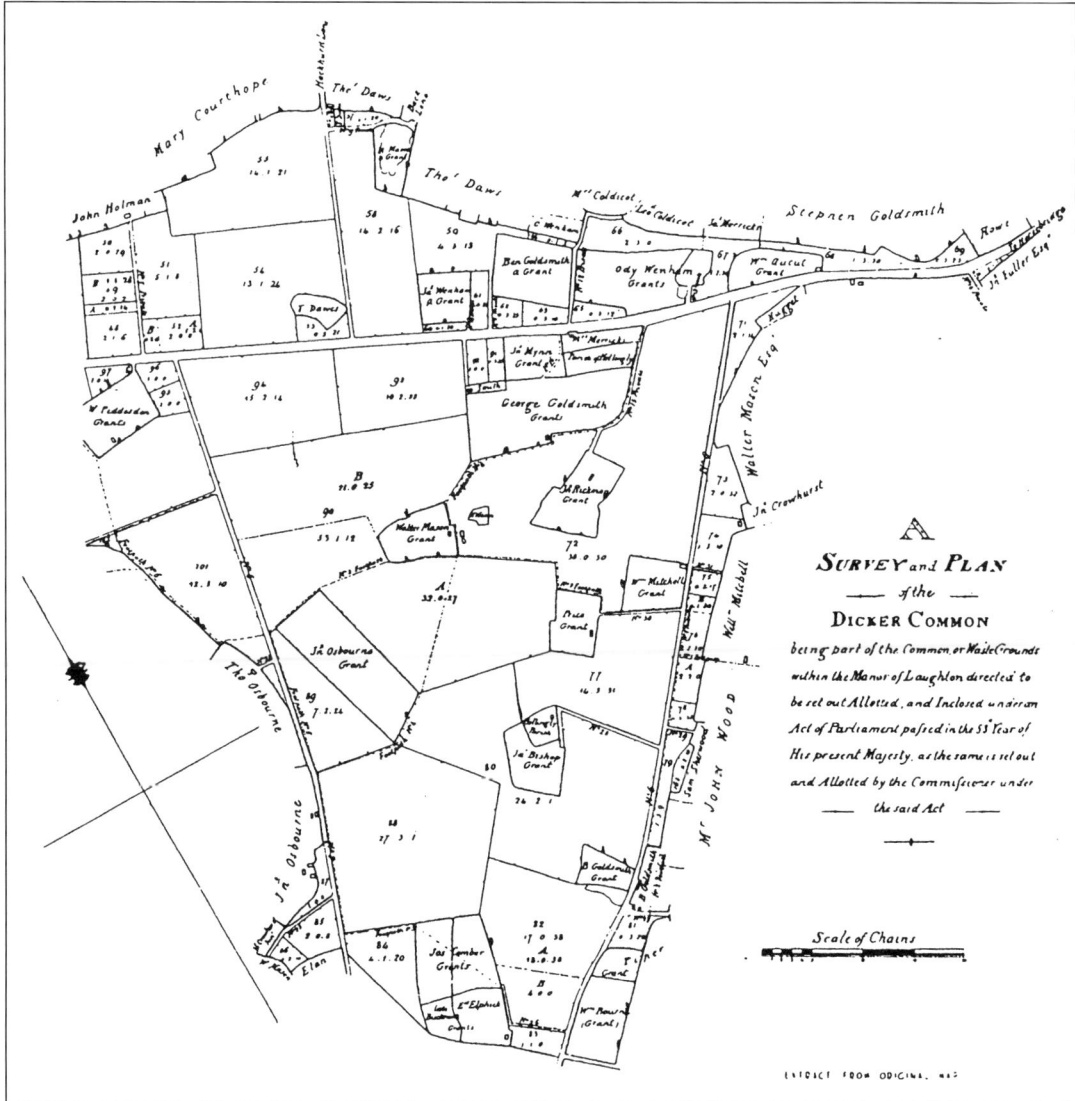

1813 Enclosure map of the Dicker Common

an enigma; for whatever reason, land was granted or sold to both the parishes of Chiddingly and Hellingly, land was also acquired by auction for the benefit of the Radcliffe Asylum in Oxford.

The end of enclosure of the Dicker Common occurred in 1855, when vestiges of land bordering the village of Upper Dicker, previously copyhold of the Manor of Michelham Park Gate were attributed to the following:

> *Parcels of land and cottage known as Shermans (nos. 187, 190, 190a, 194 and 201) – to Dennett Huggett of Lewes (pork butcher).*

**1855 Enclosure map of the Dicker Common
(identified by numerals in designated land apportionments bordering Upper Dicker)**

Land (184, 193 and 193a) to William Body of Arlington (yeoman).

Two parcels of land (182 and 192) to Thomas Austin of Hellingly

Land (185 and 196) to William Burton of Hellingly (bricklayer) – purchased from
John Gosden

Strip of land (181) in front of Providence House – to William Cowper of Arlington (dissenting minister).

Land (189, 191 and 197) to Leonard Cruttenden of East Hoathly (farmer).

Land (183, 186 and 198) granted to Robert Reeves of Chiddingly (farmer).

As already mentioned, the complexity of the Dicker boundaries initially due to encroachment into neighbouring parishes of Arlington, Chiddingly and Hellingly, prevents a determination of an exact acreage of farmland. The 1874 *Kelly's* trade directory assesses the parish as having 1,852 acres being farmed. The enclosures in 1813 and later of 1855 of the Dicker Common, where before gorse and poor grazing had previously existed, would have increased the acreage of viable pasture and advanced the progression of 19th century farming.

Farms in the area varied greatly in size, the larger being that of Boship and Michelham, both of around 400 acres, Park Wood Farm with 200 acres, and Starnash where Samuel Deadman farmed 242 acres and employed six men and two boys in 1871. The greater number of farms during the 19th century remained diminutive in size.

The origin of the name of some properties is very old. In Richard R Creasey's publication *The History of Hellingly*, he mentions that in 1578 certain lands were named Hackers (now Hackhurst), and a tenement at Bowershippe (Boship); also in 1561 two tenements with 30 acres of land and wood known as Bowles lying near le Dicker were held chiefly by John Woodhams and were valued at 5 shillings. (probably Bowlers, or in more recent years Clover Farm, farmed by the Hicks family.) Place names, so much a part of local history, can change and go undetected losing their association with the past. Whereas the origin of some farm names have been lost, many remain. The 1841 census and earlier documents record tenant farmers whose surnames would eventually endorse the name of a farm, for example that of Bourne, Body, Caldicott, Price, Lambert and Sharrard.

Methods of farming had progressed little for centuries, even with the innovative horse-drawn drilling and hoeing machines invented by Jethro Tull in the 1700s. Farming remained labour intensive, and provided a livelihood for the rural work-force; for farmers labour was cheaper than machinery. But there were those who saw change as fundamental to farming and to their own prosperity.

William Child moved to the Dicker in 1791, his attitude towards progressive animal husbandry brought acclaim throughout the county and prominence to Michelham, which became associated with cattle breeding. Such was his enthusiasm for efficient farming and stock breeding, he along with others, proposed in 1806, a Sheep Fair to be held annually on the Dicker

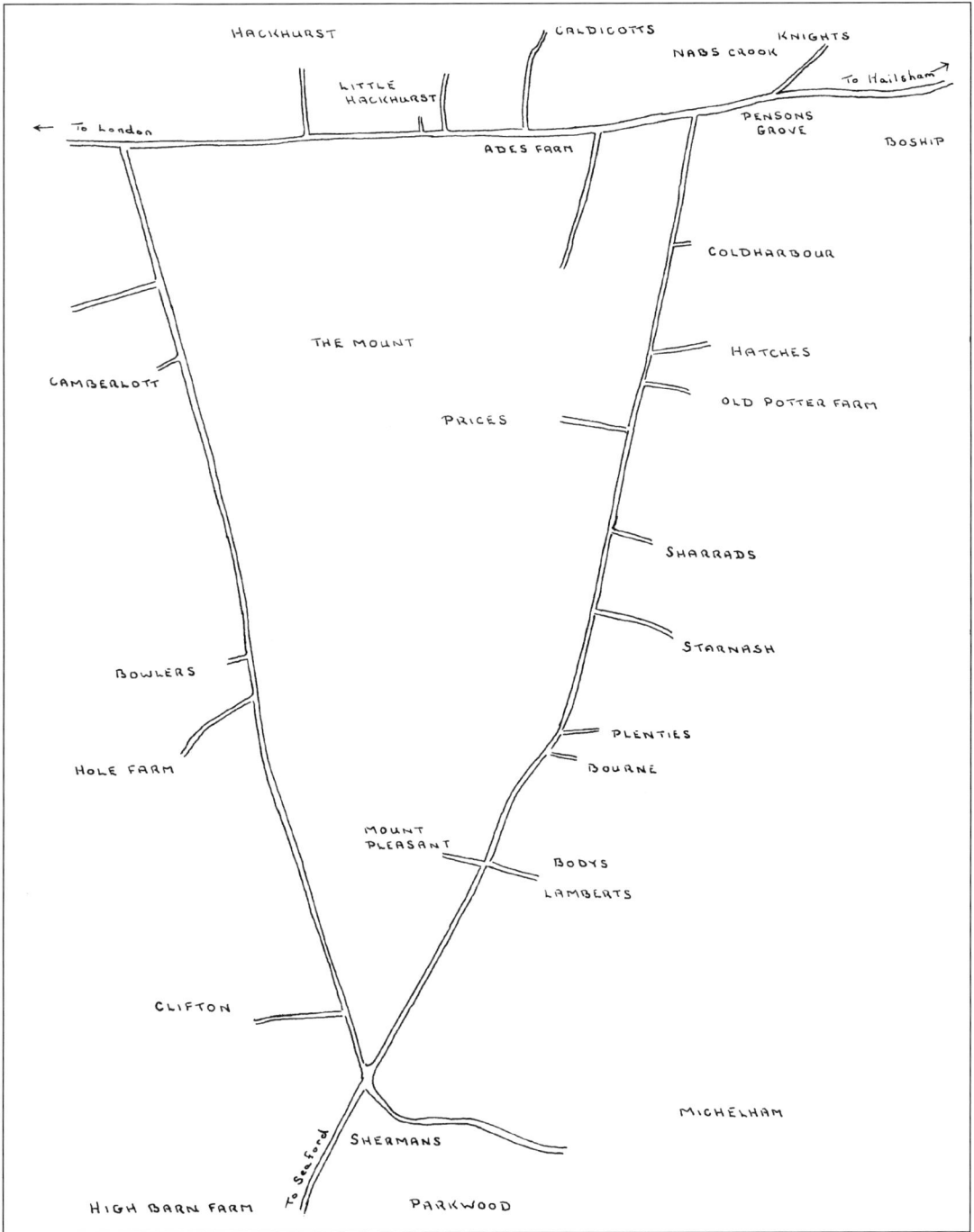

Diagram of approximate location and names of farms situated on the Dicker

(probably the Bat and Ball Fair). The *Sussex Advertiser* reported that in 1807 and again in 1817, he had been instrumental in the improved management of Lewes Sheep Fair and Corn Market, like John Ellman of Glynde, a man of his time. By 1818, Thomas Child had assumed the running of the Michelham Estate which included the leasehold of Wilbees and Colman farms near Arlington. During the Swing Riots of the early 19th century, William Child subscribed one guinea towards a fund to encourage the apprehension of the transgressors who had set alight a hayrick at Friston in 1800. Some methods of cattle breeding were thought by some members of the established church to be incestuous, and this brought about Thomas Child's dissension from the established church. Whereupon he formed an affinity with the chapel at Alfriston, but for this came to an end some years later and he returned to his Anglican roots.

Finally cattle breeders overcame the prejudicial attitudes of the time, and Michelham became synonymous with their breed of Sussex Reds.

Although earlier records had indicated Michelham bred cattle had been entered in shows, it was in 1819 that a two-year-old bull from Michelham stock and owned by Mr Heath, gained a first prize at Bramber Stock Show. Now firmly established as breeders of premier cattle, not until 1834 did the Child family enter their cattle in Stock Shows themselves. The superiority of Michelham stock was evident from the many awards gained, from 1819 to 1859. records show that Michelham cattle had been entered in 44 Stock Shows, with 40 first prizes being awarded. In 1837, Thomas Child was appointed steward of the West Firle Stock Show and ten years later, was made a member of the County Cattle Show committee.

The agricultural depression from 1854 until 1861 saw a decline in the fortunes of cattle breeding at Michelham. Following the death of Thomas Child in August 1854, most of the herd were sold and Francis Child remained as tenant farmer. An era of cattle breeding which had spanned 70 years, came to an end in 1861 when the Child family concluded their association as tenant farmers at Michelham, and moved to Lewes.

Throughout, farming had been reliant on the good fortunes of both the elements and the market place, which had suffered the doldrums of depression and misfortune. Farmers would have been alarmed when it was reported to the Hailsham Division of Cattle Diseases, that an outbreak of foot and mouth disease had occurred on three farms in the area.

Extract from the *Sussex Express,* 24th December 1881:
"SERIOUS OUTBREAK OF FOOT AND MOUTH DISEASE

We regret to state that foot and mouth disease has broken out in this division, three farms having already been affected and there are fears lest the mischief should spread still further. The Fair at East Grinstead on the 12th instant is reported to be the source. After the Bench (at Hailsham) on Wednesday, the Local Authority under the

Cattle Diseases Act, met at the Sessions House to receive reports, and take steps to isolate the disease. Supt. Waghorn (the inspector) presented reports showing that the disease had broken out on Bowlers Farm, Arlington, in the occupation of Mr Brown, where 10 animals out of 17 had failed. Other affected Farms were Lee Bridge at Hellingly and at Manksey Marsh on Pevensey Level, where 17 out of 33 beasts had been affected. It was at once decided to proclaim infected areas, into and from which no animals could be removed without licence. Other farms proclaimed as affected in the Dicker area were – High Barn Farm, Hole Farm, Camberlot Farm, Clifton Farm and land in the occupation of Robert and Samuel Gutsell."

The government's 1889 Farming Act which brought into being the Board of Agriculture compounded the necessity for improved farming; many who farmed on the Dicker probably would have felt that government bureaucracy unnecessary and an intrusion on the way they managed their farms; distant legislation may have been beyond their comprehension. Change is not a thought they would have contemplated! There were many who would have continued with the farming methods of their forebears, – "there's none more stubborn than Sussex folk," – "You may push and you may shove, but I'm hemmed if I'll be drove"! But changes to farming methods were deemed necessary to feed the ever growing urban population, farmers were encouraged to improve productivity to satisfy demand.

By the 1860s the cramming (artificial fattening) of poultry was centred particularly on Heathfield and the immediate area, and many local farmers took advantage of this new effective method of farming which, to some, became a primary source of income. The rearing and fattening had two distinct operations, although sometimes a 'fatter' of chickens also reared them, but generally chickens were reared by one man and fattened by another. So lucrative was this means of farming, almost every farmer in the district reared chickens. They depended on a collection network of higglers (carriers) who drove round two or three times a week, calling on a farmer once a fortnight to collect fattened chicken, conveying them to a railway station for distribution to supply the ever-increasing demand by the greater centres of population. The operation of cramming whereby chicken were force fed twice a day over a period of three to four weeks, gave the farmer a constant means of revenue. Growth in chicken farming was evident in 1894 when a *Sussex Express* report "Poultry Rearing in Heathfield" declared, "In 1884, dead poultry sent by the LBSC railway from Heathfield was estimated at a value of £60,000, whereas ten years later had risen to £140,000 which accounted for 30 to 40 per cent increase. The quantities of dead poultry dispatched from Heathfield and Uckfield stations in 1893 were 1,8400 tons, representative of 1,030,400 chicken." During the ensuing years, many farmers would combine poultry rearing and fattening as a progressive means to their farming.

Harry Smith who farmed sixteen acres at Lamberts Farm, had numerous chicken night arks, and a cramming shed which bore witness to his commitment to poultry farming. The 1911 *Kelly's Directory* also records that Robert Cree was a poultry farmer at Laurelhurst Farm, Lower Dicker, James Keeley was at Little Hackhurst Farm, and Harry Bramley operated a poultry business at Upper Dicker until the 1920s. An extract from the *Sussex Express* refers to a poultry sale held on Tuesday 16th December 1924 at Allander Poultry Farm by the auctioneers, A Burtenshaw of Hailsham, when around 300 head of poultry and appliances were sold. In addition 30 "nearly new" sectional laying houses came under the hammer. It seems that farmers and small-holders found the practice of force feeding poultry was in decline, and more veered towards dairy and mixed farming.

The market place which had always been of integral importance to rural commerce, their locality determined from the Middle Ages by a charter granted by the Crown to a named person for a particular place; or in some cases that of a borough status. In 1252, the rights to a Market in Hailsham were granted to Peter of Savoy by Henry III, with an agreement that a toll would be collected in the market place every Wednesday. Thus through the centuries, the market, as with many others in Sussex, was of great importance to local farmers, (long before motorised transport, goaded their cattle along the rural

1916

Chicken cramming at Lamberts Farm.
Harry 'Snapper' and Ruth Smith with Maudie youngest of their thirteen children.

byway to market.) Travelling to market wasn't without misfortune or adversity, for in 1844 two accidents were recorded in the newspaper, whereupon injuries were sustained.

Extract from the *Sussex Express*, dated 18th May 1844:
"ACCIDENT

On Wednesday last, as Mr David Oxley of Lime Kiln Farm, Chiddingly, was returning from Hailsham Market, he was thrown from a colt which was but recently broken in, in consequence of the animal taking fright and becoming unmanageable by the sudden attack of a dog from the roadside. The horse endeavouring to go through a gateway unfortunately came in contact with the post which caused the rider to be thrown. Mr Oxley was taken home, which was but a short distance, in a state of insensibility, but after being put to bed he revived, and we trust the care of his medical attendant he will soon recover. We hope this accident will be a sufficient warning to those in our neighbourhood who keep dogs, not to allow them to range at liberty in the public thoroughfares."

Extract from the *Sussex Advertiser*, dated 20th July 1844:
"SERIOUS ACCIDENT

On Wednesday last, as Mr Thomas Jenner of Bentley Farm, was passing across the Dicker, on his way to Hailsham Market in a gig, his horse suddenly slipped and fell, pitching Mr Jenner out with great violence upon his head. Assistance was soon at hand, when he was taken into the house of Mr Wenham (grocer), and the medical assistance of Dr Cunningham of Hailsham procured, when it was ascertained that his collar bone was broken, and he had sustained some serious injuries in the head. In the latter part of the day he was removed to his home, but he is not considered to be out of danger."

Until 1868, Hailsham's market had been held in the High Street and other adjacent roads in the town. Following a meeting held in the Crown Hotel on Tuesday 19th July 1870, the purpose of which was the curtailment of the selling of livestock and the dealing of other commodities in the street, all trading was to be concluded within the bounds of the new walled-in market. Whereupon the pedestrian should no longer accidentally procure repugnant footwear due to the misdemeanour of a four legged beast.

Although sited in the Parish of Chiddingly, the Bat and Ball Sheep Fair was referred to as being on the Dicker, and was important to the farmer who sought revenue from sheep rearing. The *Sussex Weekly Advertiser* reported in July 1806 that the determination and resolve of John Ellman of Glynde, (regarded as the county's leading farmer) with Thomas Child and others, brought about the founding of the Sheep Fair to be held annually in fields adjacent to the Bat and Ball Inn. In 1840, it was recorded that 4,000 sheep and lambs had been penned at the fair, but six years later, rumours were prevalent that due to poor location, and in order that railway facilities might be secured, it would be possibly held on Berwick Common. Even in the following year some said that if the fair was not moved to Berwick, then it should be relocated in Hailsham! Eventually all discord was laid aside, and by 1850, the Bat and Ball Fair had attracted greater entries, when in excess of 18,000 sheep had been penned. Although the 1862 Fair had only attracted 6,000 entries, it was reported that the display of excellent 'modern' farm implements by Messers Cheale Brothers of Lewes, stimulated the attention of local farmers, (if not being so strapped for cash, they would have undoubtedly subscribed to the age of farm mechanization).

In 1854 the Bat and Ball Farmers and Tradesmen Benefit Association was founded to give financial assistance to its members, with an annual Feast Day being held in a marquee in the field adjacent to the inn. By 1880, the Benefit Association's accounts recorded a reserve fund of £203 7s. 1d, an indication it held a secure future for its members. Many who subscribed to its success, were stalwarts, Messers H Wenham (chairman), G Turner, M Ford, E Wickens, O Sifflet, A Hall, S Follington and W Whitborn. But with the passage of time, the Association became stricken by a decline in membership and funding. Once again, members had received their tickets for the Benefit Association's 1906 feast day but during the proceedings it became apparent all was not satisfactory with the club's financial state. "From the annual statement of accounts, [read by Mr G W Deadman, secretary] it appears that the receipts amounted to £115 13s. 6d. The expenditure for sickness (including £16 16s. due to the honorary treasurer); with £22 paid out for three funerals, the management expenses were put down at £7 2s. 5d, dinner expenses were £12 5s. and £5 for the band, made a total of £222 16s. 11d. The reserve funds showed a total of £283 5s. 2d." With such a financial statement, Mr H Richardson of Hilders Court (presiding) expressed concern as to how the Club was to survive, and further criticised expenditure; he suggested that the committee should draw up new rules and induce better support than they now had! No doubt, once the furore had abated, the gathering of about a hundred enjoyed the repast and Sussex ale in good measure.

By 1909 and the near demise of the Benefit Association three years earlier, even heavier demand on the society's income had depleted the previous years funds of £205 9s. 11d, to a reserve of £170. The committee resolved that the contributions of the members should be raised to 7s. 3d (37p) a quarter, and that in future the expenses of the annual feast should be met by members and not from general funds. Festivities being favoured by fine June weather, were carried out again with amalgamation being made with the Chiddingly branch of the Equitable Society. With the closure of the old Bat and Ball, the 1910 festivities were held on Thursday 16th June within a large marquee in a field adjacent to the Golden Cross Inn. Although the usual toast was proposed, "Success to the Bat and Ball Club", the increased demand on their financial resources by members, compelled a resolution to be passed that burial remuneration should be reduced to £4. (The reserve funds were now only £137 10s. 3d.) Eventually it would be the equitable societies and the government's pending national insurance scheme that would sound the death knell to the Bat and Ball Benefit Association, and many local societies.

The old-established Bat and Ball Fair which over the years, had seen thousands of sheep penned saw a further decline. Apart from five years in the 1880s when over 60,000 sheep had been exhibited, the subsequent years saw numbers plummet, in 1899 only 3,000 were penned. A serious accident befell Mr Faulkner, (a blacksmith from Lewes) in 1840, when he was thrown from a horse he was endeavouring to purchase, and in 1872 when Mr Ralph Verrall of Falmer was robbed of £85. The good years seem to have vanished, gone were the times when one exhibitor alone would have penned 400 sheep, as did Mr J Carey Pitcher in 1881. Selling transactions changed dramatically in 1910 when the Fair was conducted by auction for the first time, contrasting with previously when deals were executed by the striking of hands.

"One instance of the manner in which business was transacted, we may mention that one party sold lambs at 30 shilling each and appeared to be well satisfied with the money, but on hearing that the lucky purchaser had soon afterwards disposed of them for 35s, it would be natural that he should bite his fingers with vexation! It was even heard that a second buyer in his turn, sold the lambs for even a greater profit!"

Whether due to its location or something else, the fair that had been important to the sheep breeders' calendar, attracted only 1,800 entries in 1914 and seemed doomed as a sheep fair. At some time, it was relocated near the Chalvington road junction at Golden Cross, by 1922 was being conducted by Messers A Burtenshaw and Sons of Hailsham. Although no sheep were entered due to a restriction order that year, over 300 head of store and dairy cattle were sold, the principal lots obtaining good prices. Eventually this small market ceased to operate, when Burtenshaws concentrated their auctioneer's business within the confines of Hailsham market.

During the 19th century farms on and around the Dicker, had been tenanted, but when the gentry disposed of major land holdings, the occasional sale occurred making it possible for the tenant farmer to be in possession of the land he farmed.

A sale document refers to property being auctioned known as Potkilns, a substantial brick and tile house containing six rooms, with a lean-to building; also a cottage of two dwellings then let on a quarterly tenancy of £1 1s. 3d to James Medhurst and John Payne, and various other buildings, productive gardens and orchard, a well with a good supply of water, at the Crown Inn, Hailsham, on the 8th August 1877. The document advocates the property (containing 6½ acres – 4 acres are freehold, the remainder being copyhold of the Manor of Laughton) would be well adapted for dairy farming or the fattening of chicken.

The name of Potkilns derives from the bricks and pottery previously made there. William Cuckney established a kiln in 1765, which continued in production until the 1840s, when the land reverted back to farming. Consequent to the purchase of the two dwellings now known as Old Pottery Cottages by Mr E Shoosmith, around 1955 were sold to Mr Laurie Parker for £500 (deemed a munificent amount from wages earned at MacDougall's Mill at Horsebridge.) Following conversion of the property by Richard Parker in the 1970s, Old Pottery Cottage was sold in 1986 for £92,000 to a Mr Charles Smith. This was an era when people had the desire to own what was once a modest rural property, and it became a 'Des Res' (desirable residence).

Not dissimilar were other small farms that changed ownership in 1881 and 1909 and were reported in the *Sussex Express* newspaper.

Extract from the *Sussex Express*, 15th October 1881:
"SALE OF PROPERTY

Mr David Guy (auctioneer), submitted to public competition on Wednesday, several lots of valuable property, belonging to the late Mr W Medhurst. LOT 1., was a compact property situated on the main Dicker to Ripe road, comprising a dwelling house, barn, piggeries, garden and orchard, and three small enclosures of grass land (2a. 0r. 19p.) with frontage of 330 feet to the main road; also a piece of grass land, having a cattle shed and a pond of water." [The property was purchased by Captain Taylor of Glenleigh for £370.]

In 1909, the small farm known as Pensons Grove on the Dicker, which comprised a cottage, garden, buildings and about 4 acres of pasture land, had been included in an auction of property by Messers Burtenshaw and Son. It was withdrawn at £360 but was later sold by private treaty.

Farming suffered a succession of bad winters and wet summers. This was followed by the worst depression to hit farming since the 1870s. In 1896 the Agricultural Rates Act helped farmers by providing a concession on their rates. At the turn of the century the smaller farms on the Dicker were family owned. The 1901 census shows that in a national population of 41.5 million the average number of children per family was six. Such an increase in population prompted the government's call for an increased yield from farmers.

The introduction of steam powered ploughing and threshing in the 1850s, later forming the basis of the Boys and Manser business at Lower Dicker, brought with it an advanced dimension to agriculture. With horses, an acre ploughed in a day had been regarded as a good stint and would have involved walking ten to twelve miles behind the plough. Whereas with steam ploughing, twelve to fourteen acres could be achieved without any untoward effect on the farm labourer's legs! But many farmers would probably have preferred the old tested method of horses.

Although steam traction engines had been important to farming, they were slow replacing the horse. The numbers on farms peaked at the start of the 20th century. Even after the introduction of the tractor, the horse still remained the only motive power for those who farmed on the Dicker. In consequence of which, the local blacksmiths Thomas and Herbert French were jubilant that the newfangled contrivances hadn't made them redundant – all was rosy down at the old Dicker forge!

The horse that had for so long been man's best friend, could also have an off-day like their master, when injury could occur because of the animal's change of mood, all to the cost of young Donald Atkin.

Extract from the *Sussex Express*, dated 17th July 1914:

"KICKED BY A HORSE
ACCIDENT TO A DICKER FARM HAND

At half past eleven on Saturday, while harnessing a horse to a rake, Donald Atkin, aged 17 of Pottery Cottage, Dicker, an employee of Mr Charles Hamper, Caldicott's Farm, Dicker; let part of the harness fall against the animal's hocks. The horse kicked, and the hoof caught the unlucky youth on the head, injuring his left eye and also hurting his right leg. He was taken in a motor to Dr Walker, Hailsham, who dressed his wounds and then on to the Princess Alice Hospital, Eastbourne."

Even after the introduction in Britain of the Albone tractor during the early 1900s, many farmers saw no advantage of the tractor over the horse. By 1918, it was estimated only 7,000 tractors were in use. (At the time of writing, it is unknown by whom and at what date, the first tractor was used on a Dicker farm.) An advertisement in a 1921 *Sussex Express* newspaper states that a Fordson tractor could be purchased for £225, nearly half the amount paid by Henry Smith for Lamberts Farm in 1925.

Within the advertisement, Henry Ford, manufacturer of the tractor, extols the benefits from machine-powered farming.

"In the tractor the farmer now has a machine in which is harnessed one of the most adaptable, efficient, economical sources of power in the world – the internal combustion engine.

The tractor will multiply the productive capacity of each individual farm worker from three to four times.

It will put the farmer on par with the city manufacturer. It will put his produce-producing factory – for that is what a farm is – on an efficient production basis.

It will enable each worker to earn so much more that he can be paid more and still leave a greater profit for the man who employs him. It will enable the farmer to work fewer hours in the day, giving him more time to enjoy life."

"I believe the tractor will make farming what it ought to be – the most pleasant, the most healthful and the most profitable business on earth."

Although farmers relied on the horse well into the Second World War, the

Harrowing at Starnash Farm
Charles Vitler with Goad

1920s

Mowing (possibly Hole Farm)
Edmund Smith on the mower

1920s

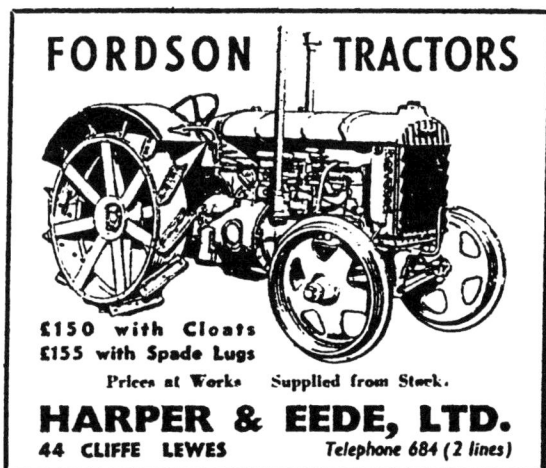

dire need for increased home-grown food production, led to a rapid introduction of the tractor. By 1944 it was estimated that 173,000 were in use and by 1950, this had risen to 332,000. In the immediate post-war years, the Ferguson TE20 produced at Coventry, with its hydraulic system and range of implements, revolutionized mechanisation in farming. Many other manufacturers' names became synonymous with tractor development, such as Fordson Major, John Deere, Case, Field Marshall and many others. Over the last ninety years, the tractor has evolved from a slow cumbersome machine into the high-tech computerised tractor now sold by the Lower Dicker based firm of Palmer Agricultural.

The enclosure of the Dicker Common and the necessity for increased hedged field boundaries, would probably have been the only significant visual change to the farming landscape, but those who farmed the land were part of Dicker's farming history. So below is a list of farmers from the years 1841-1924 compiled from *Kelly's* directories and census returns.

1841 Census

Susannah Bishop (Hatches)
William Bourne
Thomas Child (Michelham)
Arthur Fox
James Harmer
William Huggett (Pensons Grove)
James Hide
James Lambert (High Hids)

John Noakes (Coldharbour)
Eli Page (Clifton)
Susannah Price
William Russell (Hackhurst)
Richard Smith (Bowlers)
Thomas Thatcher (Starnash)
Frances Wheeler (Boship)

1851 Census

Henry Bishop
David Butters
Thomas Child (Michelham)
Arthur Fox
Cornelius Fox
David Funnell (Coldharbour)
James Harmer

William Huggett (Pensons Grove)
Algernon Pitcher (Boship)
John Pitcher (Plenties)
Robert Pitcher (Camberlot)
William Russell (Hackhurst)
Thomas Thatcher (Starnash)

1861 Census

Walter Bourne
Henry Bourne
Elizabeth Child (Michelham)
John Dodson (Clifton)
Samuel Dearing
Samuel French
Cornelius Fox (High Barn)
David Funnell (Coldharbour)
Richard Gander

William Gutsell
Stephen Haffenden
Mary Huggett (wid)
William Lambert (Park Wood)
Edward Miller
Trayton Parris
Algernon Pitcher (Boship)
William Russell (Hackhurst)
Robert Wright (Camberlot)

1871 Census

Thomas Boys (Knights)
Arthur Butler (Coldharbour)
Thomas Brown (Michelham)
Henry Cousins (Crossways)
Samuel Deadman (Starnash)
Emily Dearing (Sharrards)
Samuel French (The Mount)
David Funnell (Hatches)

James Goldsmith
Robert Gutsell (Shermans)
Charles Goldsmith (Bourne)
James Lower (Valley of Achor)
Richard Manser
Richard Mitchell (Mount Pleasant)
Algernon Pitcher (Boship)

1881 Census

Henry Aucock (Park Wood) (bailiff)
James Brotherhood (Clifton)
Thomas Brown (Michelham)
Thomas Boys (Knights)
Arthur Butler (Coldharbour)
Henry Cousins (Crossways)
Charles Cane (Boship)
Emily Dearing (Sharrards)
John Deverall (Camberlot)

Samuel French (The Mount)
David Funnell (Hatches)
Robert Gutsell (Shermans)
Charles Goldsmith (Bourne)
James Goldsmith
James Lower (Valley of Achor)
Richard Mitchell (Mount Pleasant)

(Starnash shown uninhabited.)

1891 Census

Charles Barrett (Upper Mount)
Alfred Brett (Starnash) (bailiff)
William Brauch
Henry Brown (Michelham)
Charles Cane (Boship)
Henry Ford (Clifton)
Samuel French (Hatches)
Robert Gutsell (Shermans)

Frank Goddard (Park Wood)
Orpah Guy (Little Hackhurst)
Edwin Jenner (Manor House)
William Medhurst (Caldicott)
William S Piper (Knights)
John Tillywhite (Sharrards)
Henry Wooler (Osborne)
John Wheatley (Camberlot)

1911 *Kelly's Directory*

George Brett (Starnash) (bailiff)
Thomas Clark
Robert Stanley Cree (Laurelhurst)
Henry Ford (Boship)
George Gardiner (Bowlers)
Joseph Johnson (Michelham) (bailiff)

William S Piper (Knights)
Noakes Brothers
John Stone (Park Wood)
John Wheatley (Clifton)
Henry Wooler

1924 *Kelly's Directory*

Allander Poultry Farm Ltd
James Benjamin Chilton (Prices)
Robert Stanley Cree
Mrs A Dadswell (Old Pottery Farm)
Sidney Dinnis (Park Wood)
George Dann (Coldharbour)
Albert Gander (Mount Pleasant)
Albert Harmer (Bowlers)

John Harvey (Camberlot)
George Hoddinott (Clifton)
James Keeley (Little Hackhurst)
Richard Pratt (Boship)
Henry Smith (Lamberts)
Frederick Vitler (Starnash) (bailiff)
Sidney White (Plenties)
Henry Wooler (Hatches)

Throughout farming's chequered past, the running of individual farms changed with regularity, whether instigated by change of fortune or pastures new. John Wheatley was at Camberlot Farm in 1895, had moved to Bowlers Farm by 1899, and by 1909 was farming at Clifton Farm. In 1922, the running of Clifton Farm altered course yet again when James Elliott quit the farm and retired. On Friday 30th November, good prices were to prevail at the sale conducted by Messers A Burtenshaw and Son, as indicated in the *Sussex Express* the following week. Lots ranged from two Jersey cows to "Tom" a sixteen-hand brown cart gelding which sold for 25 guineas, an eight year old van mare sold for 29 guineas and a sow with ten piglets for £10 10s. A cross section of poultry, turkeys, geese and 40 guinea fowl gives an indication of mixed farming in the 1920s. The last lot which came under the auctioneer's hammer was a covered motor van with new body by Davis of Hailsham, which sold for £55.

Further changes occurred when the 15-acre farm known as Little

Hackhurst was submitted for public auction on 29th August 1894 at the East Sussex Auction Mart, in Hailsham. The property comprised a newly erected dwelling, with gardens and orchard, which had replaced an older dwelling as shown on the 1875 OS map. An account of the auction testifies that bidding had commenced at £150 and quickly rose to £690, but with no further advances being made, the property was withdrawn. The 1891 census affirms that Isaac and Orpah Guy occupied Little Hackhurst at that time, so it may have been Isaac Guy who had been instrumental in the construction of the new dwelling. Another six or seven decades would pass before there was further change, when Little Hackhurst farm buildings were converted into a dwelling (now Pear Tree Cottage).

A farm that also saw change was that of Black Barn Farm which had been farmed by Isaac Clark for a number of years. His retirement from farming culminated in an auction held on Saturday 29th September 1894; it was reported "a large number had been present and bidding had been brisk."

A report in the *Sussex Express*, records that sales of dairy stock and Southdown sheep were held in October 1894, emphasizing the end of an era of farming at Michelham Farm by Thomas Brown and his sons Thomas and Henry. Thomas Brown who had commenced farming at Michelham in 1861, became renowned throughout for his approach to progressive farming, and was acclaimed for well-bred shorthorns and a cross-bred dairy herd, and a flock of Southdown sheep. On his visit to Michelham for the 1881 census, the enumerator set down that Thomas Brown (aged 55) farmed 400 acres and was a miller, employing 9 men, 2 boys and 2 millers; also that his son Thomas farmed 140 acres. Changes occurred in 1887 when *Kelly's* directory listed Thomas and Henry Brown as farmers at Michelham Farm, (it is not possible to tell whether this was father and son, or his sons Thomas and Henry who were running the farm). The 1891 census states that Henry Halcombe Brown was in sole charge of Michelham, with Frederick Colman as farm bailiff; so why did Henry Brown retire from farming, aged only 32? The interest generated by the importance of Michelham's stock sale would have been paramount, farmers would have travelled many miles in their endeavour to be at such an outstanding sale. The sale commenced on Wednesday 3rd October, consisting mainly of dairy cows all of which were purchased for their good milking qualities, with an average price of £16 10s. per animal being realised. Among the purchasers were Mr F Alderton of the London County Lunatic Asylum, Claybury, Essex (credited as the largest buyer), Messers A Wadman, J Tompsett (Piddinghoe), W Medhurst (Lewes), A D Mannington (Hellingly), C S Simmonds (Eastbourne), and A Barden (Laughton). No doubt Mr A Burtenshaw, with his auctioneer's commission in mind, concluded what was considered a most successful sale on the following Monday; it comprised 405

Southdown ewes and lambs, and 12 draught horses and realized upwards of 35 guineas. Also sold, was Mr Brown's seven year old hunter Michelham, purchased by Mr De Costabadie for 22½ guineas.

The sale catalogue indicated the great affinity a farmer had with his dairy herd, given names like Primrose, Blossom, Frosty, Damsel, Kitty etc; and his working horses, Boxer, Mover and Turpin.

Large landowners who had purchased land according to their aspirations, with a desire to own and administer vast acreages of farmland, began to change their minds. Farmers who had previously been a tenant, during the 1920s and 1930s, found that farms became available as large estates were fragmented and sold, and ownership became a possibility. The 800 acre Folkington and Michelham Estates owned by Colonel Roland Gwynne were auctioned at Hailsham's Corn Exchange on Wednesday 24th June 1925, and Lamberts Farm (in the 1840s known as High Hids) in Upper Dicker, a farm of 16 acres, six-roomed house, garden and pasture, was sold to tenant Henry Smith for £550. Also Fair Place, with two enclosures of land and cattle lodge adjacent to the church, was purchased by Mr R Fletcher for £100. Other land holdings were, Park Wood Farm with 287 acres, farmhouse, buildings and pair of cottages £6,000 and Pit Field, 13½ acres of pasture opposite Park Mead School (with vacant possession). Both were withdrawn but were later sold by private treaty.

The interest in farm ownership was still apparent in 1932 when, in accordance with orders from the executors of Mr B T Tillerstone-Rogers' estate, farms, cottages and land which fronted Coldharbour Road came under the auctioneer's hammer on the 4th May in Hailsham: Plenties Farm with 7 acres of pasture, was sold for £450 to S H White (tenant), and Bourne Farm was purchased by Mr F T Hastings for £400. The auction also saw the sale of Old Pottery Farm to Mr John Wooller for £475 and Old Pottery Cottages to Mr E Shoosmith for £210. Farmers were probably galvanised by increased prices of seven years previously, and the 181 acre Starnash Farm and Prices Farm with 52 acres of pasture, were both withdrawn as both failed to meet the reserve.

After the First World War, farmers experienced a situation in which grain was plentiful but prices had fallen sharply to the guaranteed minimum price which had been introduced when state support was established. The Agriculture Act that had supported farmers, was hastily repealed by the government, which left farmers to fend for themselves. Following the Great Depression in 1929, farmers faced a bleak future, in many areas farm prices had fallen by a third, and farm labourers were forced to vacate the land as farmers were compelled to change to less intensive agriculture. Boship Farm of 112 acres, which had previously been farmed by the Cane and Ford families from the 1880s was purchased by Richard Montague Pratt for £14,000 in 1919. It seems that due to agriculture's impoverished predicament Boship Farm was both farm and tearooms, according to the 1927 *Kelly's Directory*, and remained popular throughout the 1930s. It is likely that the tea rooms were frequented by day-trippers who had earlier enjoyed an excursion to the Dicker Pottery just up the road, – postcards of the day affirmed their popularity.

The farmer had always hoped he would profit from his endeavours, knowing from the past that farming had suffered from pestilence, bad harvests and had been victim to Britain's ever increasing commitment to overseas free trade policy, but the farmer was forever optimistic that next year would be a better one! Probably with this in mind, farmer Gomer Emlyn Jones abandoned hope of successful farming in Wales and searched Kent and Sussex for the ideal farm. In 1933, unaware of the prejudicial views of those who would not entertain a stranger in their midst, became tenant farmer at Knights Farm at Lower Dicker, with a herd of 24 dairy cows. The demand for more milk brought about an increased herd. Previous to the 68-acre farm being purchased in 1968 for £20,000 from the Hancock-Nunn estate, pig farming had been introduced on a large scale with 150 breeding sows, now farmed by John and Mary Jones.

Throughout the 1930s, tenancy and ownership of farms on the Dicker changed, one of the causes of which may have been the depressed agricultural climate during that time; the 1934 and 1938 *Kelly Directories* point to change at Clifton Farm where Alfred Helyer had replaced Thomas Vine; Hatches Farm which had previously been farmed by Henry Wooller and then his son John had now been purchased by Frank Barrows. Ownership of Starnash Farm changed in the mid 1930s when Thomas 'Arch' Piper purchased the 181-acre farm from Charles Botting. Very few farmhouses can ascribe parts of their structure to 1697: 'Starnash' comes from the Saxon 'Stearne-erse', transcribed as 'sea swallows (terns) on the stubble'. At Lamberts Farm, the old farmhouse can attribute origins to close to the Elizabethan period of timber framed, wattle and daub construction, with evidence of stonework probably taken from Michelham Priory following the dissolution of the monasteries by Henry VIII. Unlike so many other farms where old farm buildings were replaced by today's modern wide-span industrial structures, some of Starnash farm buildings retain evidence of a past era and can lay claim to fame as overnight billets for soldiers *en route* to Newhaven and France in the First World War.

With unemployment in 1932 at an unprecedented high of three million, the government hoped to curb overseas imports by the introduction of a tariff that year, and in addition to the 1931 and 1933 Agricultural Acts that had pioneered the Marketing Boards, they re-introduced price control. Boship Farm was ranked a prominent farm throughout the 19th century, and it may

1920

Boship Farm
Jabez and Ruth Ford

Farm Workers at Boship Farm.
'K' Piper, Will Orton, Fred Medhurst, George Young, unknown, Fred Page

be plausible to believe that its farm status had diminished by 1938 when *Kelly's Directory* identifies a change from farming interests, to that of 'Boship Farm Guest House', when farming probably became secondary to the owner's aspirations.

By the 1930s Britain's agriculture had been allowed to fall into decline as government policy was toward imported wheat and meat from the Empire, supplemented by trade agreements. As in 1916 when a poor harvest and Germany's increased threat against Britain's imported foodstuff, by 1935, the Ministry of Agriculture had deemed it necessary to set up a committee to look at the way farming should be organised in wartime. It was to take the possible isolation by Hitler's warmongering in 1939, that would result in maximum agricultural production. Dicker's farmers had eked out a living during the 1930s, and the ensuing war that urged greater productivity, threw farming a lifeline. The Ministry of Agriculture had complete authority to control and direct food production, which included the right to take possession of any farm where the land was deemed to be neglected or poorly cultivated; such a fate befell Boship, Pekes and Black Barn farms, which were run for the duration of the war by the County Agricultural Committee, generally known as War Ags". Following two decades of agricultural depopulation when many had sought employment elsewhere, and by intensive recruitment into the armed forces, members of the Women's Land Army were drafted in to work on some of Dicker's farms. One old farmer who has long since gone to the great pastures above, was heard to say scornfully in his broad Sussex dialect, "Am baint 'aving 'er pull my cows teats about." But such changes were necessary to meet the shortage in both labour and home grown produce.

The wartime approach to farming had seen many changes; those who farmed Dicker farms remained almost unchanged from the late 1930s. They had struggled to meet the M.o.A. wartime demands and had provided food for the nation, and they should be proud of their essential part in achieving victory!

Farmers and farms

Frank Barrows	Hatches
John Cox and Charles Vitler	Bowlers
Wilfred Peerless	High Barn
John Conway	Caldicotts
Alfred Dadswell	Old Pottery Farm
George Dann	Coldharbour
J H Duncan	Michelham
Stanley Dinnis	Parkwood
Gomer Jones	Knights

Don Martin	Hackhurst and Perrylands
Thomas A Piper	Starnash
Sidney Smith	Lamberts
Thomas Vine	Clifton
John Benjamin Wheatley	Prices
? Saunders	Camberlot

The 1939-45 war years had generated maximum productive returns from agriculture, and the 1947 Agricultural Act was designed to save the farmer from the insecurities of post-war farming. By the end of the war there were over half a million full-time workers still working on the land. But in a few years, changes were to occur that would alter the old and tested farming methods forever. One was the introduction of pedigree tuberculin tested cows, another the use of piped water, leading to many ponds being filled in. Bigger and improved cow-stalls and dairies were advised, and the installation of bulk milk tanks would see the demise of the milk churn collection by firms like Matthews of Hailsham. Government legislation would sound the death knell to many small dairy farmers, like Trevor Smith, who gave up a 36 head milking herd.

Probably the farming ideology of 1950s and '60s was that the larger farm would be more profitable and more viable to run. George Dann (the younger) who had inherited a milling business and Coldharbour Farm from his father in 1935, engaged upon greater dairy production, and around 1955 expanded the farm's acreage with the purchase of land from Prices and Mount Pleasant farms, and land adjacent to Camberlot Road. The trend towards larger farms also brought about the removal of many hedgerows across the area known as The Mount. Not since the enclosure of the old Dicker Common, had the landscape seen such change. Coldharbour Farm continued to be farmed by the Dann family until it was sold in 1978 to a Mr Tyoonk. Barns that had once been an integral part of a farm, became impractical were often converted into homes of great character. Retaining the name of the farm, Coldharbour Barn was converted by Aubrey Dann around 1993 and continues to maintain a link with farming history.

Very few farms had remained in one family's farming ownership since the earlier part of the 1900s: Coldharbour Farm which had been purchased by George Dann in 1922, Lamberts Farm purchased by Henry Smith in 1925, and Starnash Farm had continued in one family's ownership for a period of time. Starnash Farm purchased by Thomas 'Arch' Piper in the 1930s, continued in the true tradition of dairy, beef and arable farming, extending into Laughton with the purchase of Michelham Farm, where much of the acreage was taken up by growing cereal crops, necessitating the removal of hedgerows to accommodate modern farm machinery. Two men who had experienced many changing seasons at both Starnash and Michelham were farm manager and stockman Reg Ellery and tractor driver George Harmer. Following the death of his father in 1976, Michael Piper took over the running of the farms until the year 2000 when Michelham Farm was sold.

Two farms which had seen change in either tenancy or ownership were those of Camberlot and Clifton, both fronting the Camberlot Road. Camberlot was a farm of around 170 acres and was owned by Mr Askew of Wellingham, Ringmer. Moving from Winchester in Hampshire, in September 1962, John and Elizabeth Major continued their farming interests at Camberlot Farm, and have now extended their farming commitment to a herd of 80 Friesian milking cows, 160 beef cattle and 500 breeding ewes on 375 acres (15.1 hectres) of pasture that includes Stud and Marnhull Farms at Chalvington.

A document dated 20th February 1764 held at the East Sussex County Record Office, states that land called Cliftons tenement containing 70 acres, a newly erected messuage, barn and garden in the Manor of Berwick, had been bequeathed to Nicholas Gilbert gent, bonding Clifton Farm to its historical roots. It was Benjamin and Mary Ann Balcombe who, in September 1853, severed their ties with the village by emigrating with a party of missionaries to Natal, South Africa, where in 1856 they were granted government farms. It was probably thoughts of Clifton and the village of Upper Dicker, that urged Benjamin Balcombe and his son to name their sugar-producing farms, Clifton and Michelham, and so perpetuate the memory of the Dicker. History has a strange way of linking events through time; an association can be drawn with the Balcombe family's growing sugar cane in South Africa, to nearly a hundred years later when Mr Phillip Lyle (company director of Tate and Lyle Sugar) purchased Clifton Farm in 1947 for £8,000. From 1947, over the ensuing thirty years, Clifton Farm saw seven owners, one being the celebrated Jack Hilton of dance band fame. In 1977 the farm consisted of 85 acres and a farm shop which had been licensed to sell meat and was purchased by Don and Barbara Hutchison. The farm would become notable for the breeding of beef cattle and sheep, much of which was sold to other wholesalers as well as being sold in Clifton's own farm shop. It had been said that people would give their right arm for a taste of Hutchison's sausages!

His whole working life committed to farming and cattle dealing, it was on the 30th September 1987 that Don Hutchison died from injuries caused by a Charolais bull that had unexpectedly turned on him at Clifton Farm. Over the years Clifton Farm had witnessed tragic accidents: in 1929 William Piper died from injuries caused whilst felling a tree; in 1930 Alfred Clapp was killed in a gun accident; in 1940 a shot-gun caused injuries to Jessie Ridley while rabbiting and in 1970 Derek Smith died in tragic circumstances in the farmhouse. At present under the partnership of Barbara and Michael

Hutchison, Clifton Farm (now of 138 acres), plus over 350 rented acres of pasture, can only pledge to the future of farming on the Dicker.

Unlike the ploughed furrow that was always determined by the man who worked the land, farming remains influenced by events far beyond the farmer's control. Depressed prices, government and European Union directives have brought despair to farmers, and the BSE crisis of recent years has seen a downward spiral in farmers' fortunes. Change of ownership which had also brought boundary and diverse land management changes, had seen resolute farming only to a few farms, that of Bowlers, Clifton, Camberlot, Knights and Parkwood Farms, whereas many farms remain in name only, being let for grazing or utilised by other means.

FOOTNOTE – Sources of information about farms and farming are so diverse that only a fragmented account has been rendered, but the hope is that the reader has gained an insight into some of farming's chequered past.

The farm which had been occupied by Richard Price some time prior to 1838 was known as Warren House in 1693. By the beginning of the 20th century it was known as was Price's Farm, and in recent years was renamed Field House. Plenties Farm was purchased by John Fradd, a builder by trade, in 1984 and the old farmhouse was pulled down due to structural faults and a larger house built in its place. It was while the demolition of the derelict Sussex

Razing of Plenties old farmhouse   1985

Old Barn at Plenties Farm

barn was taking place that an old brick culvert was uncovered that may have carried the old road which skirted many of the farmhouses to Upper Dicker village. Time would also see the demise of Hole Farm that had been part of Wick Street Farm in the 1950s, part of which now has five acres of greenhouses.

Although soft fruit had previously been grown at Clifton Farm and on The Mount, the poorly drained land that had lent itself to grazing pasture and the extraction of clay for brickmaking, was never particularly suited to fruit-growing. The drift away from farming came when Simon and Tess Gray purchased the bungalow Millstones in 1992, with 89 acres of land which had been part of Coldharbour Farm. Renamed Meadow Farm, where fields had once been used for grazing, now they saw the return of strawberries and soft fruits being grown on the Dicker.

The trend toward today's commercial horticulture in the area, had been begun ninety years earlier by Ernest William Shoosmith using greenhouses near the Coldharbour Road and listed in the 1911 and 1938 *Kelly's* directories as a nurseryman. It is not certain when the nursery closed but around 1980, Robin Page-Wood purchased the property and started the very successful business now known as Robin's Nursery. The English passion for gardening goes far beyond television's celebrity horticultural programmes as gardeners strive for their "own kaleidoscopic patch of flowers". About 1988 Peter Dann established Coldharbour Nursery. Moving from Wilmington in November 1993, Richard and Julie Owen purchased the nursery and has since provided a range of bedding plants and specialises in hanging baskets.

A ten-acre field that fronts the main A22 road at Lower Dicker is recorded in the 1843 Tithe schedule as owned by Elizabeth Sarah Smith, but the 1875 OS map shows that the field had subsequently been divided into six smaller fields. As early as 1930, what was once farm land was occupied by Victoria Fencing Co Ltd, who advertised their 'chessboard' panel fencing as being, "Cheap, Hard to beat, Easy to erect and British made, for further details – telephone Hellingly 24". Probably sometime before 1938, Victoria Fencing Co Ltd, moved to Staplehurst. Having previously being a haulage contractor during the 1930s, William Colman set up and operated the Victoria Market Garden, sending tomatoes and mushrooms to Covent Garden, London, until it closed in 1956. At some later date, it became the Kennedy Garden Centre, which on the 12th April 1992 was visited by the late Geoff Hamilton (TV's *Gardener's World*), when he planted a tree to commemorate his visit. Change of ownership occurred in 1999 when the Garden Centre was purchased by Wyevale.

Commerce and employment from time immemorial had forever changed direction, probably none more than agriculture and the use of land. In more

Rainbow Farm boot fair at Lower Dicker

recent times of the car boot fair, has given new uses to fields. The purchase of a 15-acre field in 1990 by farm contractor James Vinall, established the venue for Rainbow Farm's Boot Fairs.

Blacksmith and Wheelwright

The arrival of the tractor and departure of outmoded practices eventually brought about an end to the traditional skills of both the blacksmith and the wheelwright, where their presence had been based upon the horse as a means of power and transport, and had been essential to the farmer and rural community. Every village had echoed to the familiar ring of the blacksmith's hammer striking the anvil and the parked farm wagon outside the wheelwright's shop, even the adjacent chestnut tree, symbolic to the old-time forge, had now been consigned to the past!

Upper Dicker's forge stood opposite the church, and had been recorded on the 1843 Tithe schedule as being owned by Edward Parris; Benjamin Balcombe was blacksmith and resided in Forge Cottage. Subsequent to the 1852 Enclosure Act, common land fronted the old forge, which would have given open grazing before present boundaries were established. The enumerator, when recording the 1851 census for the village, listed Stephen Fox, aged 20, employed as a blacksmith's apprentice and stated that he lodged with Benjamin Balcombe and his wife. Two years later when Benjamin

1909

The Old Forge at Upper Dicker
From left to right: Reg Graves, Percy Guy (on the shoulders of) Thomas French, Herb French, Jabez Finch, Ger French and George Haffenden.

Balcombe and his family emigrated to South Africa in 1853, Stephen Fox became resident blacksmith for the next twenty one years until his death in June 1874. *Kelly's* directory for 1878 lists Aaron Firrell as blacksmith; three years later the 1881 census records Stephen Dodson as the village 'smithy' with Alfred Kemp and Arthur Smith employed as "apprentice jobbing blacksmiths". In 1882, the trade directory records Frederick Kemp as the Upper Dicker blacksmith and five years later Thomas French who, in later years, passed his smithing skills on to his sons, Thomas, Herbert and Gerald. Thomas French (snr) retired from the forge around 1911 and passed the running of the blacksmith's business over to his sons Thomas and Gerald, known in the village as Ger. At this point, his son Herbert was the blacksmith at the forge at Lower Dicker.

The blacksmith's day was long and arduous: repair of tools and farm equipment, and household chattels, but the rural economy had a pattern of its own – payment was not always in currency but sometimes by way of barter. The Upper Dicker forge was not just a location for the blacksmith's means of income but on certain evenings became a haven for members of the Dicker Drum and Fife Band (known locally as 'Dicker Spit and Dribble' or the 'Rat Frighteners') to practise and hone their musical prowess. The venue was probably chosen because Tom French owned the forge and was a member of the band, but the warmth generated from the forge's glowing coals would have been quite inviting during the winter months, rather than the cold interior of the Parish Room! The siting of the old-time forge, quite often near the village's beerhouse, must have been contrived by the blacksmith himself; it wasn't unknown for Tom and Ger French to stroll to the nearby Plough Inn for a liquid lunch! The demise of the village forge was brought about by industrial changes and was probably hastened by the impending war in 1939; Thomas French (the younger) was recorded as the last blacksmith to work the Upper Dicker forge, the Church gates are a lasting testimony to his trade.

With the closure of the blacksmith's shop, Forge Cottage became untenanted; in 1943 Benjamin Wise rented the property and immediately after the war purchased the property and adjacent Sideways Cottage (so named because of its position to the road), the old forge and adjoining land. Many blacksmith workshops were to adopt occupations such as motor and agricultural engineering, and this one in the fullness of time became Wise's Garage. Ben Wise's adeptness for things that were petrol-driven started as a 16-year-old grass track and hill climb enthusiast riding Rudge, Cotton and AJS conversion motorcycles. By 1928 he gained an ACU licence for the early form of speedway (dirt track racing), and rode in 1928-9 season for Bristol until injured by a horrendous accident. Recovered from his injuries, he started his first business venture, Boship Farm Garage, buying and selling motor-cycles and sports cars. The fascination for wheeled vehicles and speed was Ben Wise's downfall in 1937 when stopped by the constabulary for speeding!

Extract from the *Sussex Express,* 12th March 1937:

"MAKE IT SNAPPY

HELLINGLY MOTORIST FINED FOR SPEEDING

When Benjamin John Wise of Boship Garage, Hellingly was stopped by a police patrol car at the foot of Chalk-pit Hill, Eastbourne on his way home at 7.55pm on February 13th and was told that he would be reported for exceeding the speed limit, he asked P S Willmer to 'Make it snappy'.

The case went before the Eastbourne Bench on Monday when the Chairman (Lt. Col. R V Gwynne) asked what the phrase meant!

The sergeant replied that it meant the defendant was in a hurry. Further evidence of the defendant's haste was shown when the officer asked to look at the defendant's certificate of insurance, Wise then saying, 'Take it with you, I have a gentleman to pick it up at Hellingly'.

Defendant told the Court that he was rather rushed for time and after overtaking a slow moving motorcycle he forgot to slow down.

The fine was 10 shillings. Defendant was also fined 5 shillings for failing to have a hackney carriage plate fixed to the vehicle. His explanation was that he had forgotten to transfer the plate from a car that had been in an accident two days previously."

The war years curtailed his business aspirations when he was directed to wartime engineering work; at the conclusion of hostilities he started a commercial venture buying and selling surplus army vehicles. A span of nearly 50 years brought Ben Wise into varied business enterprises: involvement in the engineering firm Light Craft, a partnership in Polegate Motors and a renewed interest in racehorses. All vestiges of the old Upper Dicker forge building were eradicated when a new vehicle repair workshop was built in the 1960s, and the installation of petrol pumps – Wise's Garage purveyed for a now car-minded community! The field at the rear of the old forge, which had been referred to as 'House plot' in the 1843 Tithe schedule, later became the graveyard for worn-out vehicles and a source for spare-parts, and in 1988 was transformed into a new housing development.

Granted a trainer's licence in 1966, Ben Wise became renowned as a racehorse trainer with over 200 winners, his first winner being 'Birth of the Blues' at Plumpton in 1968, and the most successful 'Moison' who won over twenty races. Following his father's death in 1991, Richard Wise took over management of the garage and the family firm of Wise Tours, which owes its origins to a 29-seater coach purchased in 1947. A fleet of luxury coaches now operate on selective day excursions and holiday tours, overseen by James Wise.

Only in name, can what was for so long the blacksmith's workshop at Upper Dicker, Forge Garage continues to service and rectify faults for the local motorist; in recent years the garage was sublet to a succession of mechanics, –

The Forge Garage scrap yard.

Brighton Races. (Lester Piggott) Ben Wise (Race Horse Trainer) extreme right

Bill Gravett, John Smart, Richard Lee and Nick Woods; in the six years since 1995, Shaun Barnard has adhered to the motorist's needs.

The forge at Upper Dicker had been built to serve the needs of an agricultural and rural community; the forge at Lower Dicker was quite separate. Recorded in 1843, the forge, stable and adjacent cottage were owned by George Goldsmith, with Stephen Stone listed as blacksmith. The brickyard which later became the Dicker Pottery, (also owned by George Goldsmith) and the forge both contributed to his brickmaking operation, so the forge may only have provided a marginal service to others. For 50 years following the brickyard being sold to Uriah Clark the forge continued as part of the Dicker Pottery infrastructure. The construction of a large cart-lodge and adjoining stables to the rear of the forge sometime before 1875 indicated the important role of the blacksmith to the Pottery's needs, particularly its reliance on horse drawn transport.

Extract from the *Sussex Express,* dated 5th September 1874:
"SERIOUS ACCIDENT TO CARTER.

On Wednesday afternoon a serious accident happened to a man named George Fagg, in the employ of Mr Uriah Clark of the Dicker brickyards. From enquiries made, it seems that Fagg was returning from Pevensey with a quantity of timber in a wagon, and that on his arrival at Sandbanks in this parish (Hailsham), he incautiously attempted to get upon the shafts of the waggon whilst the horses were in motion but his foot slipping he fell to the ground, and the fore wheel passed over his right leg, causing a compound fracture. The crisis of the poor fellow attracted the attention of Mrs Hook, wife of Mr Hook farmer of Sandbanks, who, perceiving what was the matter, called her husband and Mr Fagg was rescued from his still perilous position. Dr Billing was immediately summoned to the sufferer's aid, and Mr Hook having kindly placed a horse and cart at his disposal he had his patient conveyed home, and so successfully exerted his skill that hopes are entertained of Fagg's ultimate recovery without the loss of the limb, and in spite of the crushed condition of the bone".

Throughout the latter half of the 19th century the census identifies those who perpetuated their blacksmith skills at the forge. In 1851 Stephen Hunnysett migrated from Worthing, and worked at the forge for over twenty years. The 1881 census refers to William Burgess, aged 29, blacksmith and residing at No 7 Potteries, Lower Dicker, but ten years later, the enumerator fails to record a blacksmith but lists Charles Carey, a carter and living at Smith's Cottage, which may indicate a vacancy or that the blacksmith was at that time, residing elsewhere. It can be postulated that the forge's owner following the death of Uriah Clark in 1904 was Herbert French from *Kelly's* 1911 trade directory. Herbert French was listed as blacksmith at the Lower Dicker forge, and residing in the adjacent cottage. Herbert's wife, although diminutive in stature, was known for her scolding, because on occasions she would vent her displeasure on her spouse! "Now and then, old Ben Parsons would sit and talk to the blacksmith while he worked in the forge but one day sparks flew of a different kind. Rebuked for talking, he doused her with black forge water from the cooling trough." Even a stroll for a pint at the nearby Potters Arms wasn't without strife; late home for his meal, on the warpath, she brought the plate and placed it on the bar table. His only comment was, "where's me afters"!

Although the 1924 trade directory listed Herbert French still as blacksmith at the Lower Dicker forge, no date has yet been established to confirm its closure. Even long after his retirement, Herbert French continued to use his skills at a small forge situated behind his bungalow at Upper Dicker.

The wheelwright, like the blacksmith, had been fundamental to the needs of a rural community; both needed a workshop in the village. The earlier wheelwright's workshop in Upper Dicker, according to the 1843 Tithe map and schedule, had been situated on land now occupied by Orchard House. But the 1875 OS map bears no reference to the building, an indication that the wheelwright's shop had been relocated. The 1881 census listed Stephen Crowhurst as wheelwright residing at Ivy Cottage, so the wheelwright's workshop was probably situated nearby.

Both the 1841 census and the Tithe schedule show that James Body was wheelwright, and that he paid a yearly rent for both the wheelwright's shop and the adjacent dwelling. The census also has John Pitcher residing at Plenties Farm and a wheelwright by trade. This immediately raises the question as to where his workshop was situated. Ten years later, the 1851 census records him as farmer and carpenter, so he had diversified from being just a wheelwright.

By 1851 William Body had taken over the business from his father, and had become established as the village wheelwright. Subsequently the 1861 census records him as wheelwright and builder. Phillip Walder and David Crowhurst were listed as wheelwright and carpenter, and both resided in Upper Dicker, so it may be assumed they were employed by William Body. The affiliated business of wheelwright and builder continued after 1870 when James Walker Body had taken over the business. A year later he is employing seven men, and is listed as a farmer. Perhaps their business interest over the years had become most agreeable! A Richard Body lived at Body's Farm from 1863 till 1901. The wheelwright business came to an abrupt end in 1878 when James Walker Body died aged 32. Stephen Crowhurst had been in their employ and became the next wheelwright. It seems that when the Body family ties with both the wheelwright's shop and adjoining dwelling ceased, they were pulled down. It is possible that Devon Cottages were built around this time.

Stephen Crowhurst continued as village wheelwright until his death in 1890 when his son William took over the business. By 1891 he was employing 14-year-old Willie Piper as an apprentice. No date can be assigned to when the wheelwright's shop ceased to function. *Kelly's* 1895 trade directory records

William Crowhurst as the last known wheelwright in Upper Dicker.

The structure of the wheelwright's workshop at Lower Dicker remains to this day. In 1987 it still bore evidence of the wheelwright's trade: a dust-covered saw-bench, the shaft and pulley wheels hidden in the diffused light of the roof space, led back to where the Ruston-Hornsby 5hp engine had been housed in a lean-to shed (operating instructions still pinned on the wall); still within the confines of the workshop were many chisels and other tools that had been used by Ernest Lade. A heavy, well-thumbed ledger with dated entries from 1915 gave reference to the type of work undertaken for local businesses:

MR J CARPENTER

30 Mar 1915	Painting three wagons.	£4 10s. 0d
14 Mar 1917	Writing name on car	2s. 6d
29 Nov 1924	New barrow body	£2 1s. 6d
30 April 1928	Repairs to van	4s. 3d

MARTIN AND MEDHURST

24 Jan 1916	Repairing Threshing Machine	11s. 0d
24 Nov 1916	Lining Engine Body etc	5s. 0d
5 Jun 1919	Blue and Red paint	5s. 6d

Mr G DANN

1 Sept 1921	Repair wheel of Coal Trolley	£2 0s. 0d
14 July 1923	Repair Miller's Van	12s. 3d

MESSERS G DANN AND SON LTD

17 Dec 1954	Repair and paint Trailer	£10 4s. 2d

MR D HIDE

8 Aug 1919	Repair wheels on Bakers's Cart	12s. 0d
28 July 1922	14 new spokes + re-make wheel	£2 17s. 9d

MR T OVENDEN

9 Aug 1921	Repair wheels on Tilted Van	£4 17s. 0d

MR E WICKENS

3 Jun 1921	Repair Cart smashed in collision	£8 0s. 6d
27 Jan 1930	Repair to Lorry tailboard	£1 19s. 6d

Although the 1875 OS map shows a house and out-building were opposite Black Barn Farm, no evidence has yet been found as to when the wheelwright's shop came into being. Whether coincidental or by design, the 1895 trade directory states William Crowhurst as wheelwright in Upper Dicker, and confirms for the first time that Obadiah Siffleet worked as wheelwright at Lower Dicker. The question maybe asked whether William Crowhurst and Obadiah Siffleet worked in tandem, or that one capitulated to the other. From 1895, trade directories only listed Obadiah Siffleet as wheelwright on the Dicker.

Ernest Lade had been apprenticed to Obadiah Siffleet, and took over the business around 1914, and at some unknown date purchased the detached house and workshop. The house, part of which had been utilised as a private school, was later converted into two dwellings, and became known as Marigold Cottages, one being occupied by Ernest Lade and his sister Alice. Ernest Lade's death in September 1959 brought an end to the workshop at Lower Dicker, the businesses that had relied on the wheelwright's skills, were no more – James Carpenter's Timber Yard, E Wickens millers at Golden Cross, Harry Page brickmaker and miller at Upper Dicker, Charles Hide baker, Uriah Clark and Nephew at Dicker Potteries and essential work during the war for East Sussex War Ag. Committee.

Marigold Cottages and outbuildings were sold in 1960 to David Cottington for £1,700. Three years later John Cottington purchased No 2 Marigold Cottages and the old workshop, and changed the name to Wheelwrights Cottage.

FOOTNOTE. In 2001, an estate agent's sale brochure lists Wheelwright Cottage as, "an interesting semi-detached cottage, believed to have been constructed in the late 1800s, with attractive brick elevations and having retained the original wheelwright's workshop, – and priced at £125,000.

The Engine Shop

The Engine Shop and the Dicker Garage owed their existence to different eras, both linked to engineering, the former was allied to the traction engine whereas, nearly a hundred years later, the same building was being used as a garage for motor vehicle repairs.

The 1843 Tithe map and schedule show the land as 'Front Field' and attributed to the adjacent farm (later known as Little Hackhurst) owned and occupied by James Wenham. A footpath which had skirted the field, probably gave access to four tenements which were sited near Caldicot Lane, (the 1899 OS map shows the cottages had been demolished), and sometime after 1970, the footpath succumbed to expanding business development.

The early agricultural steam engine which was likely to have been of wheeled portable design and hauled by horses and the logical progression to the traction engine, gave rise to the engineer and agricultural contractor.

No evidence has yet come to hand as to when the Engine Shop was built, but the 1861 census records Richard Manser as residing in Coldharbour Road, and his occupation as "steam threshing machine feeder", evidence of his intended interests in establishing the Engine Shop at Lower Dicker. Ten years later, the 1871 census refers to Richard Manser as 'Engineer and Farmer', now residing in Mount Lane. The census also records Thomas Boys as engineer, William Medhurst (engineer's blacksmith), Frederick Boys (feeder to threshing machine) and George Smith (driver to threshing machine), and probably indicates that the Engine Shop's inaugural years had passed.

It is not clear when the partnership between Richard Manser and

MANSER & BOYS,
Agricultural ✝ Machinists
AND IMPLEMENT AGENTS,
HELLINGLY.

Agent for R. Hornsby & Sons, Limited, and the leading Manufacturers

ROYAL FIRST PRIZE STEAM THRASHING MACHINES.

PATENT STEAM ENGINES,
SOLD BY MANSER & BOYS, HELLINGLY.

Pike's 1886 Directory

The Engine Shop. (Edwin Medhurst)

Thomas Boys was formed, but by 1874 the business was established as Manser and Boys – engineers and machinists, steam threshing machine proprietors. *Pikes* 1886 trade directory describes the business as 'Agricultural Machinists and agents to leading manufacturers'. The partnership came to an end when Thomas Boys died at the age of 52 in 1888, after which Richard Manser continued to operate the well-equipped workshop to maximum effect. Rather than obtaining new parts from the original makers, parts were forged by blacksmith William Medhurst at the Lower Dicker workshop, generally regarded cheaper and quicker. By 1891 Richard Manser was employing David Clark, Albert Bennett and George Smith as engine drivers as opposed to just one man twenty years previously. Richard Manser died in 1894 and was interred in the Zoar Chapel, and Harry Martin and William Medhurst probably purchased the Engine Shop business. After his death, Mount Lane in which Richard Manser had lived, became known as Mansers Lane.

A newspaper of 1897 reported the new Bill before Parliament amending the law concerning traction engine traffic, also highlighted the importance the traction engine had to road haulage and agriculture. It stated that "a ton of stones drawn by a horse over a mile cost 8 shillings and 2 pence", whereas by engine over the same distance the cost was only 5½ pence. But the report also emphasised that local authorities were concerned about broken roads and damage to nearby properties caused by engines hauling excessive loads; even with the restricted speed of 4 miles an hour on country roads. It was felt necessary that engines should be limited to three loaded waggons. Even the series of Parliamentary Highway and Locomotive Acts passed during the 1870s had failed to alleviate unforseen problems; these great chuffing giants were known to create mayhem to other horse drawn traffic! Such was the concern of Police Constable Bond at Horsebridge.

Extract from the *Sussex Express*, 4th November 1899:

"HORSEBRIDGE
THE LOCOMOTIVE ACT

At Hailsham Petty Sessions on Wednesday, William Wallis was summoned for an offence under the Locomotive Act, that he being the owner of a locomotive that did not have a person accompanying such locomotive to give assistance if necessary to passing vehicles. PC Bond said at 9.30am on the day in question he was on duty near Horsebridge Mills when he saw a traction engine drawing two trucks. There were two persons on the engine and one on the front truck. Witness stopped the engine, and asked how it was they had not got a man accompanying the engine, to assist any horses that might pass. The driver replied that it was unnecessary, and witness said he would report the case. In reply to the Clerk, witness said the engine was near a corner. If the road was straight it would be possible to see horses that were approaching, but as there was the corner the person on the engine would not be able to see any vehicles approaching. In reply to the defendant, the witness said the engine was going at an ordinary pace. There were no horses in the neighbourhood at the time. By Sergeant Verrion; If there was a horse round the corner, it would not be possible to see it. A man named Longley in the defendant's employ, said he was the one in the truck watching to see if any traps or carts were coming, and he could jump out and get in front of the engine and assist carts very quickly. In reply to Mr Strickland, witness said they were coming towards Hailsham and had a load of bricks. The Clerk: And how long would it take you to get out of the truck. Witness: Not a minute. The Chairman: Is it not rather dangerous getting out of a moving truck? Witness: Not at all sir! George Longley, a youth, son of last witness, said he was driving the engine when the policeman stopped him. He had with him a man to assist him, and his father was in the truck ready to give assistance to passing vehicles if required. The Chairman: I suppose you are learning to drive like a carter boy learns to plough? Witness: That is it sir. The Magistrates retired, and upon their return into Court, the Chairman said the Bench had decided to dismiss the case. They were, however, of the opinion that the person accompanying the engine should be on the ground."

The 1897 Highway and Locomotive Act legislated that it would no longer be required for a man to walk in front of an engine. The case against William Wallis at Hailsham Magistrates Court shows that two years later such an amendment had yet to come to the notice of the local constabulary.

Under the management of Harry Martin and William Medhurst, the Engine Shop continued to contract engines and threshing machinery to local farms, and the workshop carried out repairs for other traction engine operators. Accidents were numerous and one newspaper report stated, "a traction engine

Dicker Garage (Sylvia Griffiths)
Building in the background relocated from Polegate Airship Station

belonging to Mr French of Alfriston, while being taken from the works at Lower Dicker last Friday, (11th Jan 1907), side slipped on the road and fell on its side in a deep ditch." No injuries were incurred and the engine was later retrieved by crane.

Conceivably the Martin and Medhurst partnership had come to an end when wheelwright Ernest Lade presented his statement for payment to Harry Martin and Son, in July 1920. *Kelly's* 1924 trade directory lists Martin and Son, as agricultural and mechanical engineers, also as cycle agents. Although no exact date has been established as to when petrol pumps were introduced, installation had taken place prior to 1928 when Ernest Piper operated the Red Saloon Buses, which had been garaged behind the Engine Shop. It is likely that by the 1930s the business began to cater for the passing motorist, progressing from Engine Shop to garage. Donovan Martin took over the garage from his father until it was sold to Basil Harris in the late 1940s. After that a house was built at the rear of the garage, and the large corrugated iron-clad building that had garaged two Southdown double-decked buses until around 1957 was demolished. In anticipation of increased petrol revenue, a filling station was erected across the road adjacent to Albion Cottages. The site in recent years has been occupied by Lifestyle, a company supplying and installing u-PVC conservatories.

From the days of Richard Manser and Thomas Boys who laid the foundations for the engineering business sometime prior to 1874, the Engine Shop had experienced transition through differing aspects of transport. After a brief period in the early 1980s when it was used for a caravan business, it returned to its engineering roots when Palmers Agricultural Ltd commenced business in October 1984. David Palmer who, since leaving school had worked for the agricultural engineers James Penfold and Son at Arundel, latterly became director and managed their branch based at Golden Cross until its closure. The company's workshops serve the farmer's needs, being a dealership for John Deere and E P Barris, supplying agricultural and ground-care machinery in Sussex, Surrey and Kent. Following David Palmer's retirement in 1995, the family-orientated business continues under new directors Paul and Karen Palmer, and Martin Coles, supported by thirty one members of staff.

Palmers Agricultural Lower Dicker

Mills on The Dicker

The topography of Sussex is conducive to both the watermill and the windmill and both were relatively evenly spread compared to some other counties. Many windmills were sited on higher ground, and the watermill benefited from the north-south flowing rivers, such as the Cuckmere that provided power to the watermills at Michelham and Sessingham. Records indicate that the earliest Sussex windmills date from at least 1180; conceivably the watermill was already in active use in Saxon England, and initially powered the millstones which replaced the hand-operated quern.

There is documentary evidence for a watermill at Michelham in 1434 when the Prior agreed to pay the Abbot of Battle four shillings annually for water. In common with all monasteries situated close to waterways, they operated their own mills and would have gained revenue from neighbouring farmers. The mill at Michelham had been rebuilt several times, the main timber frame dating from the 15th century. The Bishop's Visitation in 1478 described the mill as "ruinous", so the mill had been in need of urgent repair. With the dissolution of the monasteries Michelham Priory and watermill became crown property; John Foote, gentleman of Arlington, had been tenant since 1542, purchased the Priory and remaining lands.

On the Michelham estate in 1841, Thomas Child was listed on the census as a farmer, and he, in turn, employed William Sinnock as miller. Twenty years later the census records Frances Child, farmer and miller, with Henry Page, James Cooley and his son George employed at the Michelham mill. By 1871 George Thorpe was miller and baker, but it is not known where the bakehouse was sited. By 1881, Wallace Thorpe had taken up the family mantle of village baker and it may be assumed that the bakehouse was, in fact, the one located within the bounds of the village, on what was known as Dicker Road. During the 1890s, Ernest Ball was a miller at Michelham; the 1891 census records him as a working foreman, and indicates others were employed and the mill was a viable business.

J E A Gwynne purchased the Michelham estate in 1896, and the watermill may have been let out on a yearly tenancy. George Dann (the elder) was milling here in the early 1900s. Milling had ceased at Michelham by 1924, all the machinery was removed and the building used as a farm store. In 1925, Michelham Priory and 41 acres were sold to Richard Beresford-Wright of Warwickshire; eventually a modern water turbine was installed in the old watermill in 1933 which generated electricity for the Priory. The event was reported in the *Sussex Express*, headlined, "Mill House Adapted, Electricity Station at Michelham Priory".

Not until 1971, were efforts made to return the derelict mill to full working order; the volunteers surmounted many problems bringing the mill

Michelham Mill 1890s
From left to right: ? Pelling, George Dann, George Dann Snr

once again into operation and attracting tourists. The mill continued to operate regularly until 1995 when the machinery ground to a halt through wear and tear. Again through volunteers' sterling efforts and a Heritage Lottery grant, Michelham watermill returned to full production.

Until the windmill's demise in the early part of the 20th century, they had stood like sentinels over the rural landscape from time immemorial. Even though the 1789 OS map shows three windmills sited on what was proclaimed as the Dicker, conceivably other mills had previously occupied these locations.

Only the roundhouse now stands testimony to the last of the two windmills sited at Golden Cross in 1793, both owned by Joseph Willard. A reporter's 18th century account of "Dicker Windmill Blown Down", and being rebuilt and working six weeks later, is either a tribute to the millwright's exceptional skill or the reporter's over-exuberance to impress his editor.

Extract from the *Sussex Weekly Advertiser*, 29th October 1787:
"DICKER WINDMILL BLOWN DOWN

Last Wednesday in the afternoon, a windmill on the Dicker, the property of Mr Joseph Willard of Chiddingly, was blown down by the violence of the wind; it was observed to totter some minutes before it fell, but the men who were in it (two able grinders) were under great apprehension for their safety, which occasioned one of them to make his escape, he was hurled amidst the ruins to the ground, and had the good fortune to escape entirely unhurt. Had he followed his companion down the ladder, 'tis thought he must have been crushed to death, as several heavy pieces of timber fell thereon immediately after the other had quit it. The mill was almost a new one, being erected only in the year 1785.

Another mill, situated near the above, the property of the same person, was also shaken violently by the storm but Mr Willard being there at the time, he exerted himself in the manner that luckily prevented it from falling."

Extract from the *Sussex Weekly Advertiser*, 10th December 1785:
"TRIBUTE TO FRAMFIELD MILLWRIGHT

'Tis mentioned to the credit of Mr James Laker, millwright at Framfield in this county, and his men, that Mr Willard's windmill on the Dicker, which was blown down at the end of October, is now rebuilt and in a state of work."

Probably by 1839 when the Tithe schedule recorded John Russell as occupant of the Golden Cross mill, the second mill had already fallen into decline and been superseded by the mill built in 1785. In the 1845 and 1855 trade directories, Richard Russell was listed as miller, an indication the mill was still owned by the Russell family. In 1856, George Wickens took control of the mill, extending the family's association with milling at Golden Cross over eighty years. By 1878 Ebenezer Wickens had taken over, but four years later the windmill, associated dwellings and pasture had been committed to auction at the Star Hotel, Lewes, on Tuesday 8th August 1882. The sale document describes the property as being very compact, part freehold and part copyhold, and the mill being in a very favourable position and in excellent working condition. The house consisted of, two sitting rooms, kitchen, dairy, pantry and four bedrooms; Lot 13 also comprised a cottage with outside closet, a two stall stable, cow shed and granary, and was let to Mr Ebenezer Wickens under a lease for seven years expiring at Michaelmas 1883, at an annual rent of £63. Handwritten evidence on the document indicates bidding commenced at £850, and moved on until it reached £1000, when the property was purchsed by Ebenezer Wickens.

The local newspaper's report of a serious accident which had befallen Mr E Wickens while out shooting with friends, may well have robbed the miller of his sight.

Extract from the *Sussex Express*, 7th November 1891:
"GUN ACCIDENT

A serious accident occurred on Place Farm on Tuesday last, Mr E Wickens, miller, was out with a couple of friends, when he was accidentally shot in the face. A partridge rose from the hedge, it is supposed one sportsman was too anxious and firing too quickly, part of the contents of the gun lodged in the face of Mr Wickens, who was on

Wickens windmill

the other side of the hedge. The sufferer was taken home and attended by Mr Holman, surgeon: who, having extracted most of the coins [pellets], it is hoped he is going on favourably and will not loose his sight."

By 1913, Ernest Wickens had already taken over his father's business, dismantling Wicken's Mill in about 1919 and had built what became known as Wickens New Mill on land that had formed part of Dunk's Farm opposite the Chalvington road junction. Inevitably the Golden Cross windmill which had endured high winds and storms since 1785, and had become known as 'Willards' and 'Wickens Mill', stood bereft of sweeps until 1919 when it was dismantled by millwrights Luther Pearce and his son Charles.

The windmill which had been reliant on the wind for power became outmoded by the

Dismantling Wickens mill
Luther Pearce, millwright, and Charles
'Willie' Pearce

circa 1915-20

Wicken's New Mill
Charles Goldsmith, Ebenezer Wickens, unknown

new brick-built mill, the millstones driven by a Ruston Hornsby 40hp gas engine ensuring grinding when desired by the miller. The New Mill building had been enlarged during the 1930s to cope with extended business, grain being transported by lorry from Hellingly railway station. Trade directories listed Ernest Wickens as miller and baker, also corn and coal merchant. Following his death in 1940, executors continued to run the business throughout the war years until 1945 when it was purchased by George Dann, miller at Coldharbour Mill. The Wickens bakehouse was sold to Carter and Sons.

As the smaller rural based mill succumbed to cost efficient roller milling, Wickens New Mill building was used by Sussex Trailers, followed by a centre for a motorhome business operated by Marquis Motorhomes.

A windmill sited near the junction of Camberlot Road and the old turnpike road (now the A22), had been in been here since 1793. The mill was referred to as Dicker New Mill to distinguish it from the one know as Willards, later Wickens Mill, at Golden Cross. As with names of farms, mills known by the name of the previous owners or tenants. It is generally accepted that the windmill had been built and financed by a group of local farmers for their own use.

Walkers Quarterly article (1930), 'Windmills in Sussex' attributes the last known mill here to have been built in 1805; it was 45 feet high, the main post that the mill pivots on was 25 feet long, 12 feet in circumference at the base and 7 feet at the top. Unlike most other mills, the mill body was covered in metal sheeting, and the sweeps were recorded as being 33 feet in length. Within the mill's interior, were recorded dates and events – the great snow storm of January 18th 1881, a damaging flood on October 23rd 1882 and an exceptionally high wind in September 1883.

The Dicker New Mill was worked by a Mr Elphick in 1815; William Hide had taken over the mill in 1829 after the coalition of local farmers sold their rights of ownership, after which the mill remained with the Hide family for eighty years.

As recorded in the 1841 census, Richard Hide had inherited the mill. Documentary evidence reveals he felt it necessary in 1848 to insure the mill and running gear against fire for £350, and the adjacent eight-roomed house for a further £100.

A tragic event occurred at the Dicker mill when a man came to make enquiries about grinding his corn. He inadvertently tethered his donkey to the mill's lower stationary sweep; the miller quite unaware set the mill in motion. It was later proclaimed that after the poor donkey had ascended about sixty feet towards heaven, it became very dead indeed!

By 1882, Benjamin Hide took over the working of the mill, and around this time, installed an auxiliary gas engine which would have provided a secondary source to operate the millstones, and a flour dressing machine. It seems that this was not entirely satisfactory.

Following Benjamin Hide's retirement in 1907, George Dann (the elder) ran the mill in

Dicker New Mill   *circa 1910-20*

conjunction with his recently built Coldharbour Mill and the watermill at Michelham. In 1909, Thomas and Ephraine Ovenden took over the milling business, until Thomas Ovenden died in 1919. There is then conflicting evidence as to who owned what had become known as Ovendens Dicker Mills, a 1924 trade directory states that the mill was overseen by executors of Thomas Ovenden, and three years later listed Ovenden Dicker Mills (F Harbert), an indication the windmill and more modern power-mill had been sold. A trade card denotes F Harbert as proprietor, and that the mill had changed towards grinding agricultural feeds, i.e. ground oats and barley meal, and were also purveyors of English middlings and bran, and linseed seed cake.

As with other windmills which had, over the centuries, been damaged or toppled by gale force winds, a gale brought destruction to the last Dicker windmill in 1929.

Extract from *Sussex Express,* dated 3rd January 1930:

"A prominent landmark on the south side of the main Dicker road, between Horsebridge and Golden Cross, disappeared this week. During the gale on Sunday morning (29th Dec.), the windmill known as "Ovenden's Dicker Mill", was blown down. It was a post mill and the gigantic post which ran through the centre, broke off about 12 feet from the ground. The whole of the wooden structure toppled over with a tremendous crash and only just missed falling on the engine shed of the modern mill, which is close by. The windmill was about 120 years old and was in regular use. It belonged to Mr F Harbert."

At some undisclosed date, it is believed Mr Harbert remained as manager after he sold the modern powered mill to Stricklands of Hailsham, and later had been replaced by George Ovenden as manager. It is not clear when the mill ceased to function, as *Kelly's* 1938 directory listed George Ovenden as miller at Upper Dicker, which may indicate Stricklands had ceased milling at the Lower Dicker mill.

Built by George Dann (the elder), Coldharbour Mill was probably the first of the modern steam or gas powered mills to be built on the Dicker. George Dann had worked as a miller for Ebenezer Wickens before starting his own business of selling garden seeds and other sundries, a business he augmented by chicken farming in a rented field near Little Mount cottage. This may have been the same field where his mill was later sited.

He returned to milling as tenant miller at Michelham, and built the steam-powered Coldharbour Mill about 1901. Eight years later, George Dann was listed in a trade directory as "Corn and Marine store dealer, also Miller (wind and steam)", and evidence of further business diversification came with the purchase of Coldharbour Farm in 1922. By 1924, business could be transacted by using the newly installed telephone (Hailsham 73), and deliveries of milled animal feeds were now carried by lorry. Further advancement occurred in 1927, announced in the local newspaper as a new Hellingly company.

Extract form the *Sussex Express,* dated 1st April 1927:

"George Dann and Son Limited (220570) Registered March 23rd 1927. To take over the business of flour millers, dealers in coal, corn and wood, carried on at Coldharbour Mill, Hellingly, as George Dann and Son. Nominal capital £8,000 in £1 shares, (1000 "A" ordinary and 7000 "B" ordinary). Permanent directors, G Dann the Elder, Hope Villa, Hellingly, (Chairman); G Dann the younger, Coldharbour Farm, Hellingly, (Managing director). Qualification of Directors; £100 "A" ordinary or £250 "B" ordinary shares. Renumeration of above directors; £150 each per annum."

Following the death of his father in 1935, George Dann (the younger) took over the family business. During the post-war years increased business necessitated enlarging the mill in 1952; a year later a grain drier had been installed to meet government contracts. George Dann retired in 1960, and sons Aubrey and Maurice took over the business. In about 1964, further development of the mill took place, but what was once a family orientated business came to an end with the merger with the Dutch firm NGJ Schouten. BV. in 1975. Three years later it was sold to the BSM Group.

Probably due to the location and outmoded buildings, Coldharbour Mill was vacated and sold to a developer, but over the years became a depleted

Coldharbour Mill
George Dann snr.

structure until April 2000 when the mill and associated buildings were demolished by a Swindon based firm Conlon, in preparation of new houses being built by Westbury Homes.

An area near Upper Dicker which was referred to as The Brickyard, was not only part of the brick and tile industry, but also a location for a steam-operated mill which became known as Page's Mill, both owned by Harry Page.

Brickmaking had taken place in the neighbourhood of Starnash from the 17th century; the first documentary evidence for the brickyard (Map ref 4, on page 140) had been a grant to Thomas Wood in 1767. After bankruptcy in 1776, Thomas and James Peckham became the new owners. In 1799, Benjamin Goldsmith acquired the brickyard, and was later succeeded by his son Stephen in 1827. A source states that the brickyard was sold to Samuel Gravett in 1840, who was believed to have leased the yard to George Goldsmith; however, this remains unsupported as the 1843 Tithe schedule listed him as owner and occupier. Samuel Gravett died in 1850 and Stephen Goldsmith occupied the yard.

Extract from the *Sussex Express,* dated 18th June 1870:
"UPPER DICKER

FIRE. – On Tuesday night last, about 8 o'clock, a fire broke out in the brickyard here, which in occupation of Mr Cosham, who resides at Shortgate. There were it seems, two cottages on the premises, occupied by Mr Cosham's foreman, Hutchinson and his carter. Within a few rods of these cottages was a large stack of faggots, from 8,000 to 10,000, and it was from this stack from which the flames were first seen issuing. Close to the stack was a cart-house in which were several carts and waggons, with ploughs and other implements.

There were also two kiln sheds very near the spot, also a barn and stables, the latter were, however, fortunately empty, as Mr Cosham's team had just arrived from Eastbourne, where they had been taking bricks. When the alarm was given no engine was to be procured, but there was fortunately a large pond of water of at a distance of not more than ten or dozen yards. There was speedily a large number of persons assembled, not less than 300 or 400, and Superintendent Waghorne who arrived very speedily, got together a large quantity of buckets, and forming the best men present into a double line, from the scene of the fire to the pond, the whole party was vigorously employed in preventing the flames from extending to the cottages, the barn, the sheds in which bricks are dried, the stables etc, and in this, by the most active and strenuous exertions, they partly succeeded. The two kiln-sheds, however, caught fire and were destroyed, and notwithstanding all the efforts used, the flames also spread to the two cottages. The latter are greatly damaged, the windows being burnt out, and a great part of the poor men's furniture was much damaged and broken whilst being removed. In addition to this, the cart lodge was also burnt down. Whilst these efforts were making to save the cottages, the faggot stack continued to blaze away and it was evidently impossible to save any part of it. The fire only went out, indeed, for lack of material as usual. The premises are, we understand, the property of Mr Goldsmith of Eastbourne, and they are partially insured. The greatest credit is due to Supt.

*Waghorne for the skill and exertion displayed in marshalling the people, and making
them useful in stopping the progress of the flames. We must add that all present,
"worked with a will," and did all in their power to save the property, or the whole of
it must have been burnt to the ground. We understand that the stock of bricks on the
premises is such as will allow the business to be carried on as usual."*

Stephen Goldsmith may have remained owner of the brickyard until his
death in 1876, and the 1871 census states that James Goldsmith, aged 41,
brick and tile maker and William Cosham, aged 29, carter, both occupied the
the cottages. This seems to contradict some of the facts reported in the
newspaper a year earlier.

James Goldsmith was listed as brickmaker and farmer in the 1891 census,
and Harry Page had taken over the brickyard in the early 1890s; twenty years
later, trade directories show that the yard continued to produce quality bricks,
with vast quantities of paving bricks being conveyed to Eastbourne. In the
1920s, an order for new 'hat covers' to protect clamps of drying bricks, had
been placed with Hides of Hailsham, confirming protracted brick production.

The brickyard closed around 1929, and adjacent field levels had been
changed by clay extraction. The pond opposite once known as 'Kel Pond' was
where water had been drawn for brickmaking. Only the cottages that had
almost been destroyed by the fire in 1870, still have the name Brickyard
Cottage, identifying with its industrial past.

Harry Page's readiness to embark upon the brickmaking business at
Upper Dicker in the 1890s had also brought an involvement in farming, and
he is believed at one time to have farmed at Church Farm, Chalvington. The
1905 trade directory which listed him as brick and tile maker, four years later
also recorded him as miller (steam), an indication of diverse business interests.
The mill later referred to as Pages Mill, was built by Harry Page in 1906, along
with two adjoining houses that provided accommodation for Jabez Finch and
James Butcher, who were employed at the mill, which was powered by a
stationary steam engine. Whether the mill was committed to flour or animal
feed production has yet to be established. As with the brickyard, early transport
had been with horse and waggon but later came lorries (one a Maxwell) being
driven by Frank Page and James Butcher. At this time, Edmund Smith (a
carter) refused to transfer from horse to lorry, and without hesitation tendered
his notice! Modes of transport came in many forms; it was said that as an
expectant father, a wager was made with Charles Clark of the Potters Arms (no
doubt over several ales), obliging Harry Page to push a newly purchased pram
from a shop in Hailsham to the Dicker!

Harry Page purchased two cottages in 1922, known as Nos 5-6 Lower
Dicker for £320, also two adjacent freehold pasture fields for £225. Although
he had resided at Orlton Cottage opposite the brickyard, and at Body's Farm

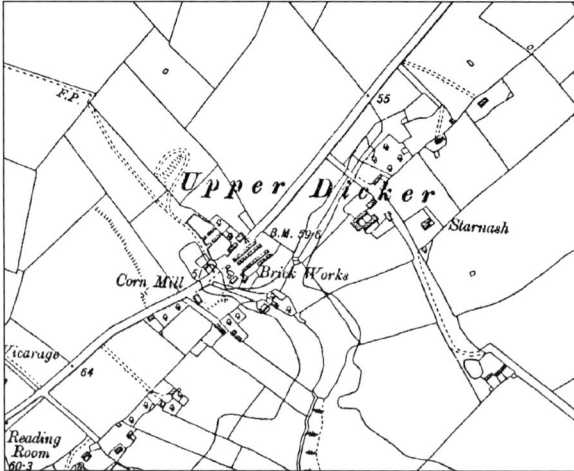
1910 OS map

in 1925, it remains unclear what other property he owned.

Extract from the *Sussex Express*, dated 3rd August 1934:
"CONTRACTOR AND MILLER

Death of Mr Harry Page, who passed away on Wednesday, who was taken ill on the previous Saturday after he had returned from haymaking. Whereupon leaves a son and one daughter. Mr Page was 70 years of age, had spent all of his life at Upper Dicker. Took over the brickyard and subsequently erected the steam mill, and established a haulage contractor's business. The brickyard was closed down four or five years ago. Mr Page also had played cricket for Upper Dicker."

Following Harry Page's death in 1934, George Ovenden purchased the milling business and continued to operate the mill until called for military

Pages Mill
Bill Hannaford second from right

service at the outbreak of World War II. At this point in time, Pages Mill was no longer used for milling and before conversion into a private dwelling, from the 1950s had been utilised by Fred Page in the production of Sussex trugs.

Whilst owned by Mr Michael Norris, the names of Bill Hannaford (who had worked at the mill) and German POWs of the 1914-18 war, were found scribed on one of the mill's timbers. While the Norris family resided at Pages Mill, Upper Dicker's David Norris who had reached the minimum age for speedway racing, made his professional debut for Eastbourne Eagles on Sunday 21st August 1988, and notched a credited two wins and two third places, securing a future as a speedway star!

David Norris awarded the coveted Silver Helmet Challenge Trophy from Eastbourne Eagles boss Gareth Rogers on 3rd June 1989

Brickmaking on The Dicker

The geological strata of brick earth known as Weald clay, started just north of Eastbourne and extended west beyond Horsham. This vast supply of the raw material gave rise to brickmaking in this locality, none more so than the Dicker area.

Brick and tile making was first introduced to Britain by the Romans; examples can be seen by the bonding courses in the walls of Pevensey Castle and traces of tile can be seen at Arlington. After the Roman occupation, the Saxons brought their own timber style construction. Probably the only use of the clay at this time would have been for domestic ware only. Evidence of this was found in Abbott's Wood in the early 1960s, by Forestry Commission workers. Although there had been a medieval kiln sited at Michelham, with timber so readily available, dwellings continued to be timber framed with wattle and daub construction for many centuries. Not until the late 18th century were bricks made on a wider scale, and this brought an increase in permanent brickfields being established.

The immense tract of waste land known as the Dicker Common, was situated on the Weald clay bed, and would, over 200 years, provide a variety of clays – not only for bricks, flower pots and pottery but also a clay which when fired, created a cream coloured brick, seen on many of the Lower Dicker houses, built in the late 1800s.

It is difficult to establish a date when brickmaking was first associated with the Dicker but one of the earliest people was Nicholas Willard, possibly the the same man who rented land near Boship Green in 1703. During the 18th century numerous applications were submitted for clay extraction and siting a kiln on the Dicker Common, followed by copyhold grants being given. Any illegal encroachments on the Common were dealt with by the Manor Court, with the offender being fined.

The Manor Court book relates to those associated with brickmaking on the Common during the second half of the 18th century; William Funnell had been granted land in 1765. By 1773 a new grant was given to his son William, to operate on land called Millbank near the Chalvington road, which was sold to Richard Guy in 1789. (map ref. nos 1-2. page 140)

The demand for bricks and tiles, brought three more grants to brickmakers on land fronting the east side of the Dicker Common (fronting the Coldharbour Road). A grant for a brickyard near Starnash was given to Thomas Wood in 1767 but nine years later Wood went into bankruptcy, when Thomas and James Peckham became the new owners. By 1799 Benjamin Goldsmith procured the brickyard, followed by his son Stephen in 1827, and successive members of the Goldsmith family until the late 1890s, when Harry Page took over. (map ref. no. 4, page 140)

On the east side of Coldharbour Road, was a house referred to as Old Pottery, where Old Pottery Cottage and Old Pottery Farm stand. In 1765 William Cuckney was granted 1½ acres (0.6 hectares) for brickmaking. By 1775, a 'Crockhouse' (kiln) had been erected, an indication pottery supplemented the brick and tile business. In 1787 Cuckney sold the property, and consequently was then run by members of the Mitchell family, followed by Stephen Goldsmith until 1842. Probably soon after this time the site returned to farming. (map ref. no. 5, page 140)

Not all brickmakers were dependent on brickmaking for a livelihood; their main occupation was that of farmer with brickmaking as a secondary

Old Pottery Cottage Coldharbour Road, Upper Dicker

enterprise. One such farmer/brickmaker was Richard Price, who farmed on the west side of Coldhabour Road (a farm later known as Prices Farm, now Field House), until his death in 1838 when it probably returned to agriculture. However records do indicate brickmaking took place at an earlier date, when William Cuckney operated on this site in 1775. (map ref. no. 6, page 140)

The earliest brickmaking operation on the north side of the turnpike (the A22 road), was a site leased to the Wenham family around 1708. Over a period of time, this site had been listed as "Kiln Plot" on the 1813 Hellingly Tithe Award and Nabs Crook in the 1841 census return. It probably ceased as a

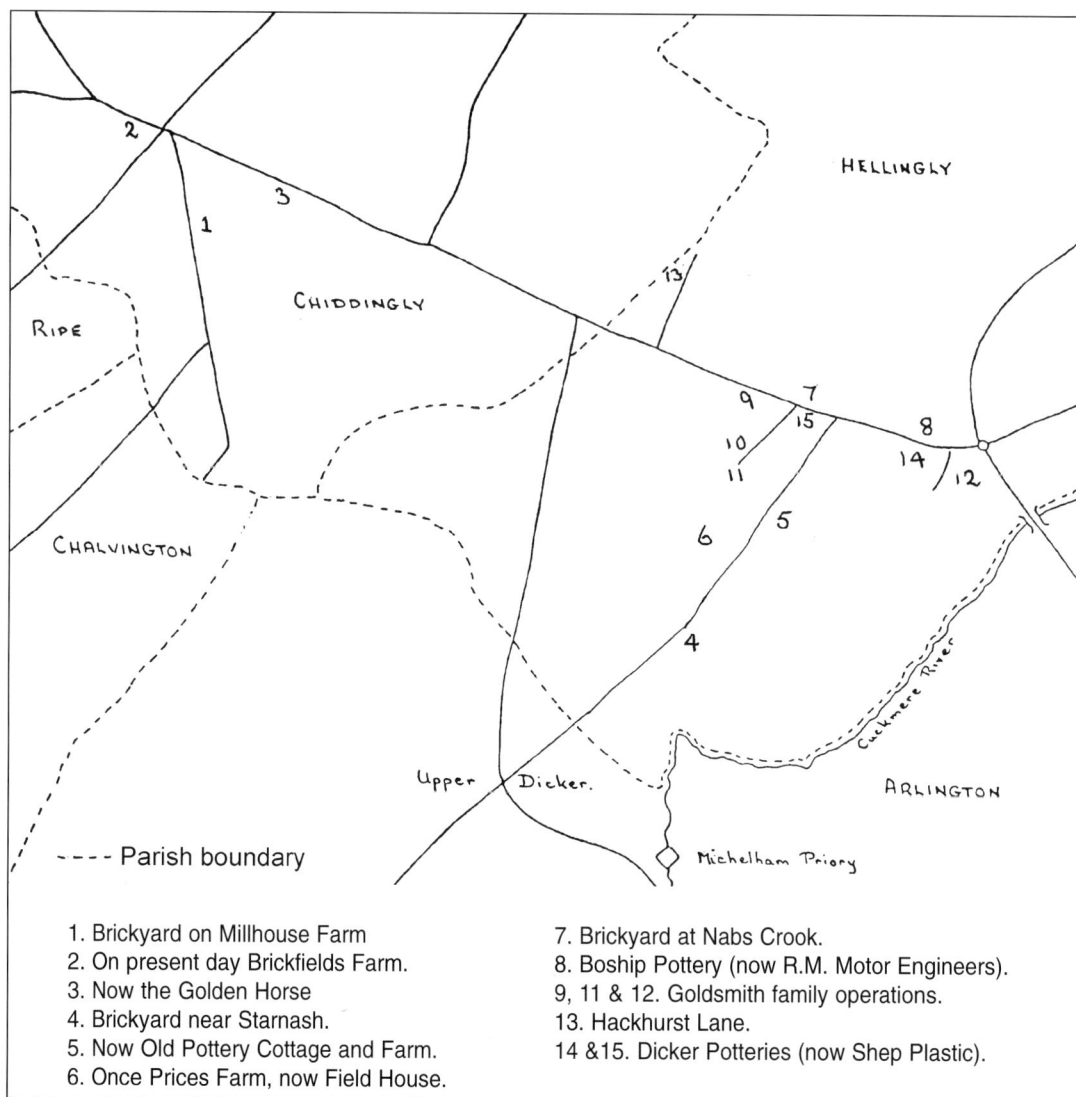

---- Parish boundary

1. Brickyard on Millhouse Farm
2. On present day Brickfields Farm.
3. Now the Golden Horse
4. Brickyard near Starnash.
5. Now Old Pottery Cottage and Farm.
6. Once Prices Farm, now Field House.

7. Brickyard at Nabs Crook.
8. Boship Pottery (now R.M. Motor Engineers).
9, 11 & 12. Goldsmith family operations.
13. Hackhurst Lane.
14 &15. Dicker Potteries (now Shep Plastic).

The location of brick and pottery operations (Courtesy of Molly Beswick) brickyard during the mid 1800s, but throughout its history was run by the Wenhams. (map ref. no. 7, page 140)

As the name of Guy was associated with brickmaking on the west side of the Dicker, the Goldsmiths were predominant on the east side of the Dicker Common. In 1798, James Goldsmith was given a grant of a ½ acre with a cottage (map ref. 11, page 140), with more land granted in 1801 and 1806. About this time, Robert was also given a grant, followed by an additional site in 1806, (map ref. 9, page 140). But due to misplaced investment, both James and Robert saw their brickmaking operations come to a premature end. The longest operation, was the brickyard near Upper Dicker, being run by Benjamin Goldsmith and successive members of his family. Brickyards identified with the Goldsmiths were adjacent to Mansers Lane: the Old Pottery on Coldharbour Road, the Old Brickyard at Boship Green and the Dicker Pottery; (both these would subsequently form part of Uriah Clark's operations. – map ref. 12 and 14, page 140).

In 1821, William Miller of Hellingly, purchased a plot on the north side of the Dicker turnpike road. At some time it was designated as Boship Pottery, and was worked by several generations of the Miller family. Though never a brickyard, in 1842 it was listed as Tile Yard with Edward Miller as owner and occupier. The making of tiles, drainpipes and pottery continued – *Kelly's* 1882 refers to Henry Wenham potter at Boship Pottery, which probably indicates the Miller family were no longer in control, and by the 1890s, William Henry Benjamin Bridges controlled operations. Since his arrival in 1873, William Bridges married Mary Jane Miller, advanced from being just a potter to running the business. Boship Pottery probably ceased around 1898, one can only surmise they could no longer compete with neighbouring Dicker Pottery. (Map ref. 14).

HENRY WENHAM,
BOSHIP POTTERY,
HELLINGLY, SUSSEX.

Pottery and Drain Pipes of every Description, Wholesale & Retail.

Kale Pots, Washing Pans, Bowls, Paint Pots, Milk Pans, Dish Pans, Crocks and Covers Chambers, Pitchers, Bottles, Jars, Chair, Tongue, Foot and Stool Pans, Glazed Basins, Money and Honey Pots, Spittoons, Biscuit Pans, Pipkins, Handled Dishes, Bed Pans, Flower Pans, Seed Pans, Hand Pans, Chimney Pots, Drain Pipes from 2 in. to 12 in., Land Drain Pipes from 1 in. to 4 in., Pan Tiles, Glazed Ridge Tiles for Slate Roofs, Flower Pots of all sizes.

Since its cessation, it is uncertain who owned the Boship Pottery site and buildings around 1900. *Kelly's* 1870 directory referred to Luther David Pearce as a millwright, and in the 1881 census returns as residing at Laurel Cottage, Lower Dicker. By 1907, William 'Willie' Pearce had joined his father in the millwright and engineering business. From 1922 until 1938, *Kelly's* directories still listed him as a millwright but he was also a builder. It is believed William Pearce built a bungalow (known originally as Sutton) adjacent to the Old Boship Pottery buildings. From here he carried out his builder's business. Sutton was later owned by Stanley Woodhams and then Mrs Chinnery, followed by Leslie Earl in 1957 who renamed the bungalow Earl's Court, the buildings again being used for a builders and decorators business. Another change of ownership occurred when Peter New set up a car repair workshop on the premises from around 1968.

More recently in 1993, Richard Millar purchased Earl's Court bungalow and old pottery (kiln) building, and transferred his business from Hackhurst Lane Industrial Estate. From here R.M. Motor Engineers, is a garage which now employs three mechanics.

1997

***Earls Court bungalow and the premises of R.M. Motor Engineers
(the buildings were once part of Boship Pottery).***

From the outset, brickmaking had seen its peaks and troughs. One upsurge in operations was during the latter years of the 18th century, when the Martello Towers were constructed along the Sussex coast, against the threat of invasion by Napoleon (so Dicker bricks may have been used). However, Nelson's victory at Trafalgar in 1805, brought an end to the threat of invasion by France and the demand for bricks was reduced. Prosperous times were at an end: only two brickmakers were still operating on the east side of the Dicker,

George and Benjamin Goldsmith. The enclosure of the Dicker Common in 1813, meant that brickmakers were no longer able to gather brushwood from the common. Wood being in shorter supply, faggots to fuel the kilns would have to be transported from further afield. The depression continued throughout the 1820s, when those still in business had to scale down operations, some returning to farming. Although never restored to the earlier boom years, by the 1850s production had increased due to the expansion of the coastal towns of Eastbourne and Brighton.

The 1851 census return, listed 17 men and 2 boys being employed in brickmaking in the Dicker and Chiddingly area.

Edward Clark	age 35	Herbert Goldsmith	age 17
Thomas Dine	46	Henry Goldsmith	27
Samuel During	30	John Guy	65
John During	32	John Guy	32
Frederick Funnell	19	Thomas Guy	51
Stephen Goldsmith	58	Uriah Clark	26
John Goldsmith	49	Richard Miller	15
John Goldsmith	18	Henry Miller	28
John Goldsmith	32	George Miller	18
Edward Miller	54		

One new brickyard came into being in the 1860s when Benjamin White started brickmaking operations opposite Elm Cottage on the west side of the Dicker. – The first mention is in *Kelly's Directory* for 1867, and the 1871 census records him as "farmer and brickmaker", employing 7 men and 3 boys. The brickyard continued until 1884 after which time the farm's 23 acres returned to agriculture, and by 1899 became known as Willowhurst Farm. (Map ref. 3, page 140)

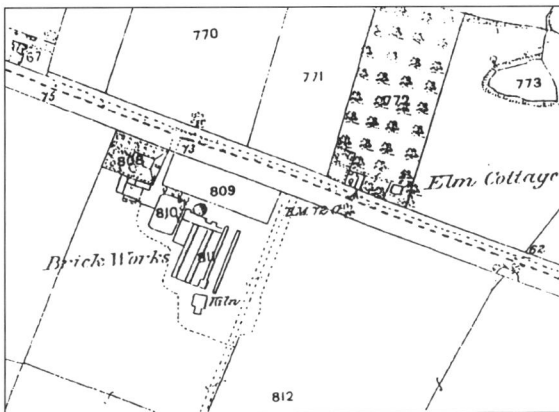

OS map 1875

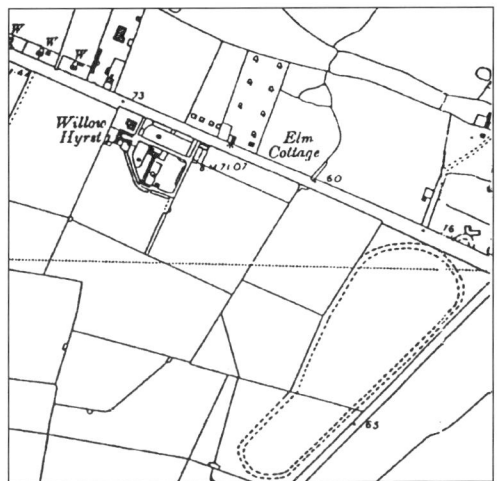

OS map 1930s

A 1930s OS map indicates the farm became an equestrian centre, with a training circuit located opposite the junction of Nash Street with the A22 road. During the war years when farm land was at a premium, it reverted back to its agricultural roots. Sometime later when owned by Peter and Pru Mason, it again became an equestrian centre, and the name was then changed to the Golden Horse Ranch. By the 1980s the house had been converted into a restaurant called the Golden Horse. In 1993, on moving from The Lamb at Wartling, Robert Granville and Carol Coundley purchased the Golden Horse, introducing their own bistro cuisine and catering for individual diners and functions.

Golden Horse Restaurant   *1997*

The brickyard which was sited in Hackhurst Lane, operated for a brief time in the 1920-30s. A wood previously known as Kiln Wood (possibly the wood now known as Dicker Wood) may give an indication of earlier brickmaking operations here (the 1899 and 1910 OS maps give no indication of a brickyard operating at Hackhurst Lane but local knowledge establishes the brickyard as having been started in about 1923-4). William Lancaster owned and ran the brickmaking operation from this date until late 1930. The yard was listed in *Kelly's Directory* in 1938 as the Sussex Stock Brick Company, and probably ceased operations in 1939 due to the war years.

Bricks are still in evidence with the distinctive DICKER impressed in the frog of the brick – it is believed the only bricks bearing a trade mark were made at the Hackhurst Lane brickyard. William Lancaster also owned a parcel of land which fronted the A22 road to the east of Hackhurst Lane. Around 1936-39 he built the properties known as Glen-innes, Glaisdale, Lindyville, Addiscombe, Fairholme and Rosendale. It is probable that his son Edward, a bricklayer by trade, helped his father. *Kelly's Directory* also lists Sussex Sand and Gravel Co. Ltd., owned by Freddie Hastings, operating and extracting gravel from Mill Lane, Hellingly. From around 1936-7 until the 1950s he owned the Hackhurst Lane Brickyard, which again produced bricks during the early post-war years. A change of ownership some time later, saw the old brickyard being converted into an industrial estate (map ref. 13, page 140).

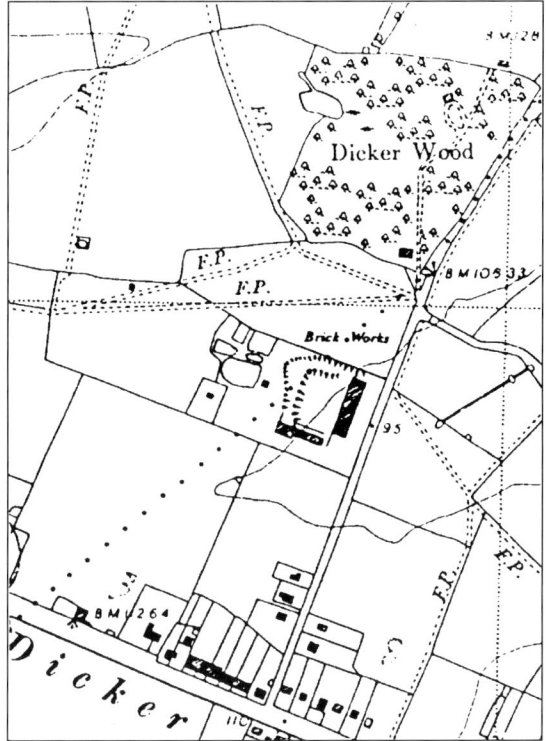

OS Map 1930s

1997

Properties situated on The Croft, Lower Dicker
Glen-innes, Glaisedale, Lindyville, Addiscombe, Fairholme and Rosendale

The Dicker Pottery

By the mid 19th century, a new name would become synonymous with pottery and brickmaking on the Dicker: the brickyard previously occupied by George Goldsmith, was acquired by Uriah Clark in 1843, and this became known as the Dicker Pottery. The 1851 census has Uriah Clark as 26 years of age, a brownware potter and employing 3 men, giving an early indication that pottery was his main concern. The Pottery was adjacent to the Zoar Chapel on one side and the lane to what is now Silver Tree Cottage on the other. Additional buildings and kilns were constructed as his business expanded over the years. An entry in *Kelly's Directory* for 1866 refers to his diversification in business, now as grocer, draper and potter. The 1874 directory entry states, "Uriah Clark – potter, maker of red and white chimney pots, socket pipes and junctions; fancy ridge tiles, plain and paving bricks, all kinds of pottery made to order; coke and coal merchant". The latter suggests that some kilns may have been fired by coal. By now, Uriah Clark was employing 13 men and 2 boys, emphasising the growth in his operation and property holdings. A freehold prospectus dated 1878 indicates Uriah Clark as not only owning the Dicker Pottery and nearby houses but also a considerable parcel of land east of Manser's Lane, land fronting both the main London road and Coldharbour Road, which he had purchased at an auction around that time.

Clay for the pottery's operations was extracted from local clay beds, which gave a variety of grades and textures, which facilitated diversification: from bricks to tiles, bread crocks and flower pots, and the renowned lustred art pottery known as Dicker Ware (the registered trade mark.) For many years, clay had been extracted from a field at the rear of the pottery, which was eventually dug to a depth of up to nearly 2 metres, and also from land adjacent to Manser's Lane. By 1881, such was the growth and productivity of the Dicker Pottery, that Uriah Clark had seen the need to build houses to accommodate his workers, probably these being houses scheduled in the 1881 census as "Nos. 3-17 Potteries".

No 3 "Potteries"	? Wenham	?
4	Charles Carey	labourer
5	Edwin Roberts	postal messenger
7	William Burgess	blacksmith
8	Henry Deadman	labourer
9	Trayton Smith	out of work
10	Elisha Clark	potter
11	Uriah Clark	potter and brickmaker
12	Sarah Lavender	labourer's widow
13	Harry Miller	potter
14	George Miller	retired potter

15	William Wenham	tile maker
16	William Bridges	potter
17	Amos Sanders	tile maker

Dicker Pottery   *1890s*

Uriah Clark was both stalwart and benefactor to the Zoar Chapel, having named his house Zoar Villa, which indicates how important the Chapel was in his life.

The transport of bricks and pottery had changed little through the 19th century. The horse and waggon had been adequate for local deliveries, but with the expansion of the pottery and with orders to more distant customers, Uriah Clark felt the need to use the recently constructed branch line of the LBSC railway. Although extended by 1880 from Hailsham northwards via Hellingly, the station was built only to accommodate passenger traffic. Such was the need for a quicker mode of transport, a meeting was convened on the 27th November 1888 at the Kings Head Inn, at Horsebridge, the purpose of which was to proposition the railway company into providing a goods yard at Hellingly station. Amongst those present were Uriah Clark (chairman of the Parish Council), Messers W.H. Pitcher, J. Clark, Manser, Bridges, Miller, J. Goldsmith, T. and W Gower, Gutsell, Foord, W. Piper, E. Clark and many others. During the meeting Mr J. Goldsmith stated, "that he had recently

URIAH CLARK,
THE DICKER POTTERY WORKS,
HELLINGLY.

Maker of Red and White Chimney Pots.

SOCKET PIPES AND JUNCTIONS,

Slate Crest and Roll, and Fancy Ridge Tiles,

PLAIN AND PAVING BRICKS.

ALL KINDS OF POTTERY MADE TO ORDER.

WHOLESALE DEALER IN

Glass, China and Earthenware.

RED & WHITE TERRA COTTA.

SANITARY WORK, &c.

COAL AND COKE MERCHANT.

THE DICKER POTTERY WORKS,
HELLINGLY.

Pike's Directory 1885

declined an extensive brick order to Mayfield owing to "cost and time involved". Like many others, Uriah Clark, believed a goods yard would also be beneficial to the railway company. A committee was elected which passed the resolution, and in due course their request was granted, in 1890 a goods yard was opened at Hellingly station.

As the Dicker Pottery moved towards the 20th century, great strides were made to extend the range of pottery shapes, and experiments were conducted in new glaze colours, all glazes being held in secret from competitors. The 1899 and 1902 sale catalogues indicate that Uriah Clark's business interest had now extended to being an agent for stoneware sanitary goods, (i.c. closets, sinks, pipes and gullies etc.) having been supplier for some years to corporations, councils and builders. They were also wholesale dealers in porcelain, majolica, china and ironmongery.

Uriah Clark now in his 75th year, was now being assisted by his nephew, evidence of which can be seen by the 1899 catalogue – "URIAH CLARK AND NEPHEW, Dicker Potteries, HELLINGLY". Perhaps it could mean one or even all nephews (Elisha, Abel, Henry and William – who worked at the pottery) in this partnership. Following the death of Uriah Clark on the 23rd February 1904, Elisha and Abel Clark formed a new partnership, renting the kilns and buildings from Mrs Elizabeth Clark.

After only eleven years of Elisha and Abel Clark's direct control of the pottery, 1915 saw the end of the Clark family's 72-year operation. The deaths of Mrs Elizabeth Clark (on 5th Feb), and Elisha Clark just a week later on the 12th February and Abel Clark on the 3rd May 1915 brought about a new era for the Dicker Pottery.

By 1912, the business had been formed into a limited company trading under the name of 'Uriah Clark and Nephew Ltd'. Throughout the 1920-30s,

From left to right standing: Uriah Clark, unknown, unknown, J.Funnell,
unknown, Mark Parsons, unknown, unknown, Elisha Clark, William Clark
Seated: William Hickman , unknown, Charles Carey, the rest unknown

Dicker Pottery employees and their years of service by 4 Dec 1902
From left to right: William Clark (38 years), Elisha Clark (48 years), Jonathan
Wenham (27 years), William Hickman (21 years), Alfred Funnell (25 years),
Edwin Lavender (27 years) with son Owen, Harry Clark (38 years).

it was staffed by many who lived within walking distance, and whose working hours were indicated by a bell mounted on the pottery roof. For the most part, about 15 to 20 were employed, comprising five or six potters (throwers), office staff and packers, potter's journeymen who would have dug and prepared the clay – worked in the glaze room and fired the kilns, and with young boys who worked as handlers. Information is sparse regarding the ownership of the pottery at this time, but Mr Sidney Harte was prominent in the pottery's functioning and direction, and carried out experiments with new slips and glazes. It is believed Mr Harte was married to a member of the Clark family.

Some of those who were employed during the 1920-30s were

Will ('Wink') Bridges	potter	Norman Bridges	
George Price	potter	Owen Lavender	potter
Cecil Parsons	potter	Francis Robb	potter
Ernest Smith	glaze room	Mrs Brett	packer
Harry Bridges	glaze room	Don Lade	
James Harris		Reg Keeley	
Harold Griffin		Don Carey	
Miss Tye	office	Wifred Page	

The Dicker Pottery was renowned for its varied ware of over 200 shapes, many in the distinctive Sussex iron glaze, which gave the pottery a metallic lustre.

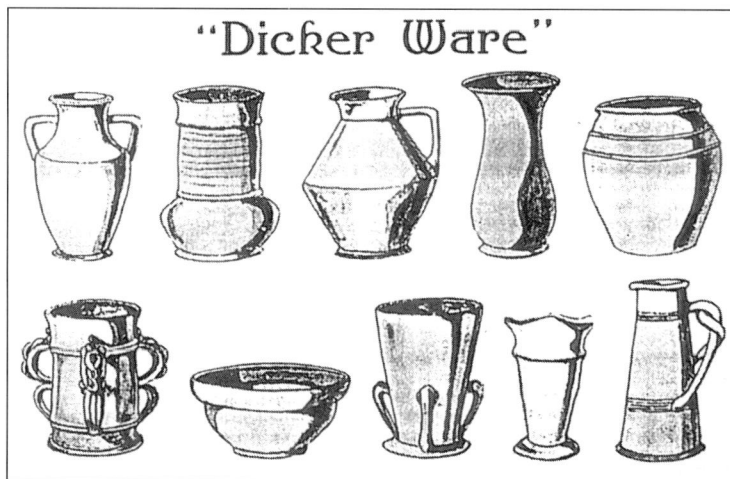

"Dicker Ware"

From 1915 to 1938, it was exhibited at the British Industries Fairs and could be seen at their showroom in Middle Street (opposite the Hippodrome) in Brighton. The acclaim given to Dicker Ware, brought about its being made for both the home market and for export. Such was the interest in this rural pottery on the main London – Eastbourne road, that it became a magnet to

1907

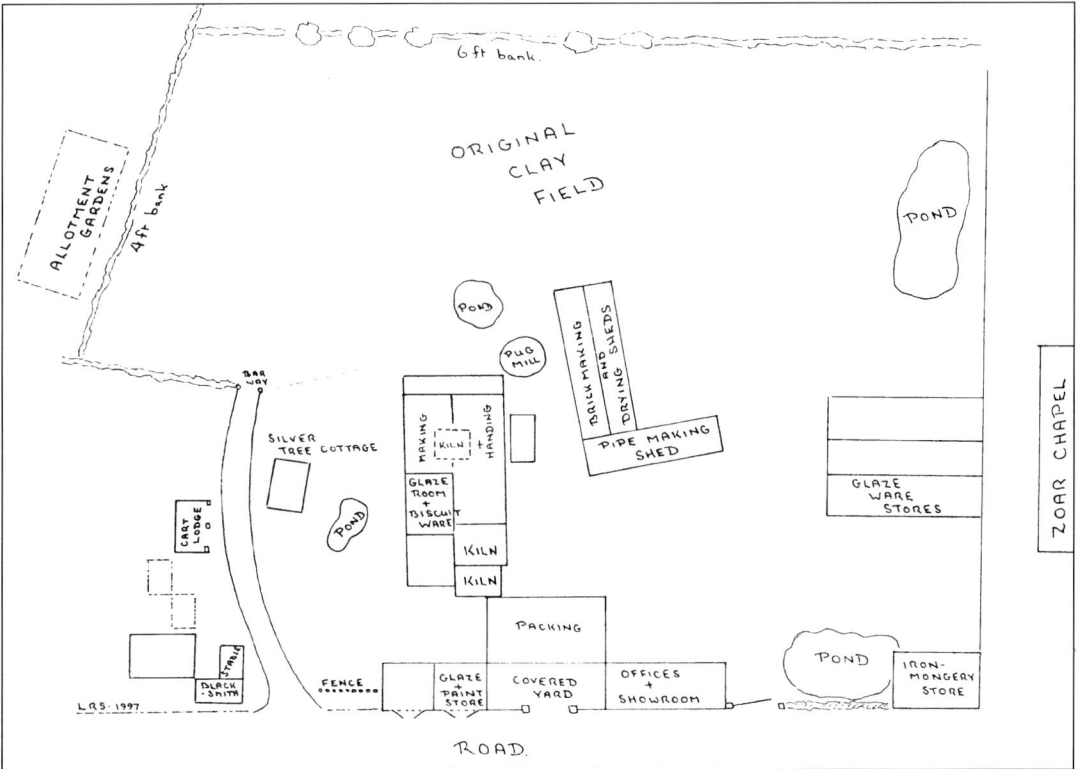

The Dicker Pottery as remembered by Ernest Smith in 1982 who worked there from 1916-1939

British Industries Fair 1915

visitors who arrived by char-a-banc (coach) during the 1920s until the war years. Guided tours of the pottery encompassed the many operations in its production process, culminating in a visit to the Potter's Market, where pottery and souvenir postcards could be purchased.

For well over 75 years, the pottery had celebrated its excellence in iron glaze pottery, but was brushed with fame of a different kind in 1919, when a murder melodrama was filmed there, the workers being used as film extras.

Extract from the magazine *The Bioscope*, 29th July 1920:

"Film Reviews "BURNT IN" featuring – Henry Vibart, Sam Livesay, Oswald Marshall, Bertram Burleigh, Gertrude McCoy, Bert Darley, Jean Miller, Adelaide Grace, Henry Doughty, Hugh Sturge, Stewart Brown.

This excellent English melodrama is notable for it's truthful characterisation and for the consistency and realism of it's atmosphere. The carefully staged pottery scenes add a welcome touch of industrial intest to the picture, whilst the trial is better mounted than any similar episode we can remember in a British film

There can be no doubt that "Burnt In" will prove a popular success. So far as it's acting and production are concerned, it is also a notable artistic success. As a whole, it may fairly be described as the best picture the British Actors Company have yet made."

FOOTNOTE – Amongst those who were film extras in the film *Burnt In*, Ernest Smith, (many years later) reminisced, as a 15 year old, being paid the princely sum of 10 shillings for his minor role and going by chara-a-banc to see the film at a Brighton cinema. Also 'Wink' Bridges shouted with elation when seeing himself on the silver screen. A film archivist informs me there is no known surviving copy of this film, only documentary evidence remains.

During 1925, interest was shown in the strata of clay known as the Wealden beds, at that time, it was considered a more diversified series of clays than any other geological formation used in the industry. A survey took place near the Dicker Pottery; a trial boring in the adjoining fields (12 acres/4.8 hectares), which were freehold property of the company, indicated clay of up to 15 feet (4.6 metres) in depth. If utilized, with modern labour-saving plant installed, it would produce 3 million bricks per annum, providing an overall output of upwards of a 100 million bricks. It was suggested that a new company should be formed, which would pay rental to Uriah Clark and Nephew Ltd. The proposed new company was still viable in 1927, but for whatever reason, survey engineer Mr Arthur Brown's recommendation never came to fruition!

Probably the most extraordinary art pottery ever fired at the Dicker Pottery kiln, was a model of Herstmonceux Castle, crafted by Mr E. C. Hurst JP of Bexhill, from Wealden clay. This exceptional model took twelve years to

Model of Herstmonceux Castle

The Pugmill.
behind are the brickmaking and drying sheds

George Price potter

The drying room

Owen Lavender making handles for 'art ware'

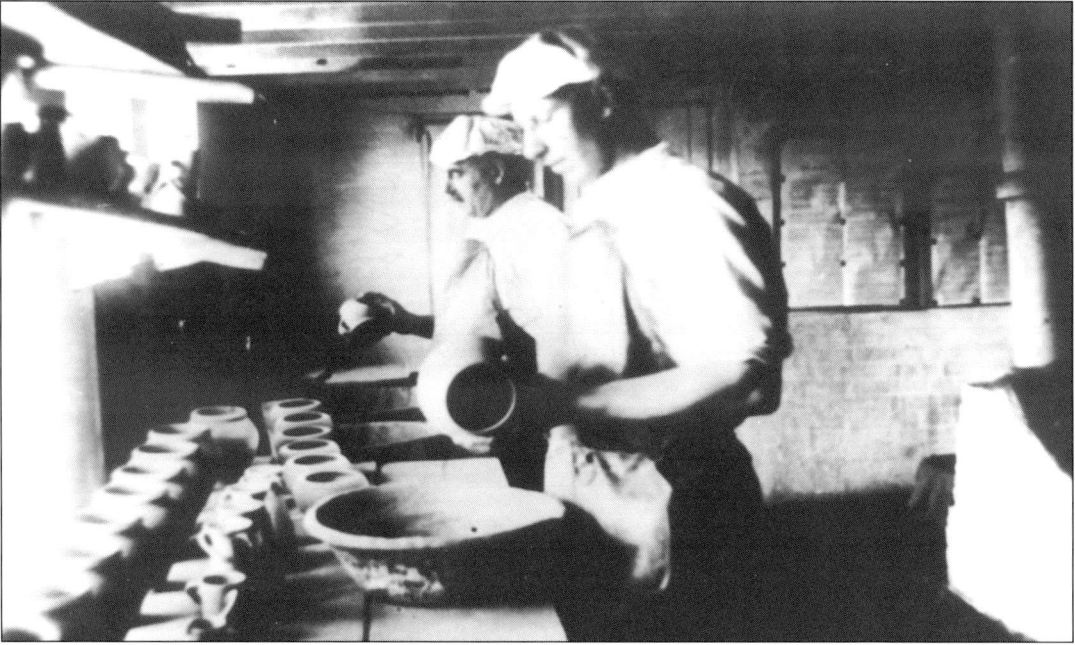

Glaze room
Harry Bridges and Ernest Smith

Display of Dicker Ware

complete, was considered to be the largest example of Sussex Wealden pottery.

The boom era continued, demand not only for the commercially popular Dicker Ware but also for bricks and flower pots, bricks latterly were on a lesser scale. Clay continued to be dug from the land behind the Oak Tree bungalow in Mansers Lane, Which was transported by Charlie Hamper's horse and cart, the short distance to the pottery. Once the clay was dug and weathered for a period of time, the pugmill would purify and help to bring the clay to the correct consistency for the potter's wheel, grading of brick clay being less important. Flower pot and brickmaking were the only operations done by piecework rates. A maker's skill would be gauged on the quantity – a good brickmaker was adept and could produce up to 1000 a day. Once the drying period had passed, firing would take place. With art pottery, greater care was needed to pack the kilns. Firing was 5 days for the up-draught kiln and 3 days for the other down-draught kiln, two men would oversee the firing during the night. An old kiln no longer in use, was used to display Dicker ware for visitors.

Nearly a hundred years after Uriah Clark had acquired the pottery, and a succession of skilled potters with their ancillary workers, the pottery had proved the most successful on the Dicker.

With the onset of war, the loss of men to the armed forces and the war effort, made it difficult to continue production, and by April 1941, with

circa 1930-1935

buildings already requisitioned by the army, the pottery finally closed for the duration of the war and from there on was used as a War Department surplus depot.

Under New Ownership

With conclusion of the war, the pottery could now again look to peace-time trading. In June 1945, licences were granted to certain potteries to produce decorated goods, the old Dicker Pottery could have been one such pottery! Sometime in 1946, Mr Sidney Harte negotiated the sale of the pottery with Mr H. E. Parrish (of Wightman and Parrish – builder's merchants in Lewes), on behalf of a group of partners, Mr Parrish being the predominant shareholder.

During the army's wartime occupation of the pottery, damage had occurred to the buildings. The Compensation Defence Act 1939, for claims for loss of income, trade or damage due to requisition by the War Department, resulted in a rent of £90 per annum and £13 p.a. for storage of plant. Mr Harte also received £143 compensation for the theft, damage and looting by soldiers.

Before production could start, repairs to both buildings and kilns were carried out, and new potter's wheel-boxes were made by William Simes (builder and carpenter) of Golden Cross.

The new pottery enterprise traded under the name of Dicker Potteries Ltd. and was managed by Mr A. J. Cridge, with a compliment of 9 or 11 employees. In the early days, much of the pottery skills and expertise were down to Cecil Parsons and Francis ("Robbie") Robb, who had been potters there in the pre-war era, also Keith Richardson and Fiona Freeman, whose knowledge aided the introduction of the new alkaline glazes, which had replaced the now illegal lead glazes. Initially clay was dug from land behind the pottery, but later was extracted from the field off Mansers Lane and transported by horse and cart, hired from Mr Jones of Knights Farm.

Once production was under way, the potter's 2-week making cycle was up to 2,500 pieces. At this time flower pots and land drains were also made, which were fired in two of the old kilns (the old bottle kiln was totally redundant). As output was maintained, Dicker crafted art ware once again became very fashionable and was exported around the world to California, the West Indies, New Zealand and Rhodesia.

By 1950, a new building had been erected and an electric kiln installed. Such was the pottery's fame, upwards of 450 visitors were treated to conducted daily tours to observe the pottery being made. So great was this affirmed prestige, the local newspapers (*Sussex Express* in 1928 and more recently, the *Sussex Daily News* in 1950) saw fit to feature articles on the success of the pottery.

Francis ('Robbie') Robb

Sylvia Dalton

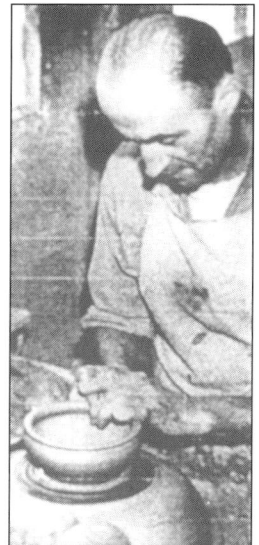

Cecil Parsons

Those who worked at the pottery 1946 – 1958 were

Cecil Parsons	potter	Bill Vidler	potter & kilnwork
Francis Robb	potter	George Read	packer & dispatch
Norman Bridges	glaze room	Keith Richardson	
Fiona Freeman	potter	Roy Hobden	
Sylvia Dalton	handles	John Allen	handles
Leslie Taylor	handles	Peter Smith	handles
Yvonne Wheeler	handles & glaze room		

But the success of the pottery was short lived, for April 1958 brought to an end what was a thriving local industry. This sudden demise came about due to imports of equal quality pottery from Germany and Italy. Subsidies from their own governments enabled foreign manufacturers to produce cheaper pottery, which terminated the Dicker Pottery's ability to remain competitive.

It is not known when the Dicker Pottery was sold, but Sussex Leaf Mould established a business in a contemporary widespan building which superceeds the old glaze store building. This business has since been relocated at Flimwell.

The Old Dicker Pottery was sold to Mr Tony Halpern in the early 1970s, who owned the Forest Row based company Forest Row Plastics. The old

1970s

Dicker Pottery buildings replaced by modern industrial structures

pottery buildings and kilns were demolished by Lower Dicker firm Plant Hire, and Forest Row Plastics moved into modern industrial buildings. Mr Halpern's death around 1986 coincided with Stuart Shepherd's need for larger premises so he moved Shep Plastics from Hailsham to Lower Dicker.

Following Stuart Shepherd's sudden death in April 1995, Mrs Pam Shepherd took control of Shep Plastics. The factory now operates with a staff of 65 on a 24-hour production cycle.

The Timber Yard

Before moving to Lower Dicker, James Carpenter had been listed in *Kelly's* 1870 trade directory as a carpenter effecting his business at The Friths, Muddles Green near Chiddingly. By 1887 the business had been relocated to Lower Dicker, whereupon the directory then listed him as, "carpenter and joiner, builder and contractor; estimates given for wood cutting on any scale, with a portable steam mill and other appliances". The Timber Yard was well established by 1887, which in due course probably prompted James Carpenter to build the house later known as Southdown House, with the brick and tile office and joinery shop located at the yard's entrance.

The Timber Yard's committment to use locally grown oak for the manufacture of farm gates and posts, necessitated James Carpenter's early purchase of a stationary steam engine to power the large rack sawbench, capable of reducing timber to manageable size. (this motive power continued in use beyond 1943). The bandsaw and planer had been powered by a Ruston-Hornsby engine, but later, after Wealden Electricity Supply Company had installed power lines to the area around 1932 were superseded.

A 1917 entry in Ernest Lade's account book shows Nathaniel Carpenter had taken over his father's business, and in *Kelly's* 1924 directory he was listed

The Timber Yard   *circa 1910-1920*

as "builder". House construction helped the Timber Yard's fortunes as they manufactured window frames etc. A house built alongside the Chiddingly road to Nathaniel Carpenter's specifications purported to have had the first bathroom with running water in the neighbourhood, and he would invite any interested person in to view this innovative addition! In the 1930s, he also built houses near Shallow Hollow (commuted by local dialect 'Shaller's olla')which were later called Silver Dene, Buckley, Ashlea and Laurelville.

Following Nathaniel Carpenter's death at Southdown House, the business was overseen by executors, but the building trade became depressed after 1939 due to Britain's wartime commitment. At this point, the business was managed by Len Coates, and the Timber Yard carried on limited joinery work for local farmers.

In 1945, Mr J S Webb took over the business, but four years later it was purchased by a Mr Smith who traded under the auspices of Southdown Timber Ltd. During the 1950s they manufactured drain rods mainly for the GPO, and carried a limited stock of prepared timber for sale. Probably at this time Southdown House was sold. Eventually the yard became known as Bramble Works, but locally was always referred to as the Timber Yard.

Abbott Joinery was founded at Golden Cross by Harold K Abbott following the closure of Jaynanbee Joinery in Hailsham in November 1970.

1976

Abbott Joinery

Staffed by ex-employees of Jayanbee Joinery (John Cottington – manager, Mrs Joan Biggs, Bill Aldridge, Phil Barnes, Charlie Baigent, Steve Bedwell, Donald Hayes, John Hodd, Dave "Bruno" Humpheys, Cyril Hall, Reg Horton, Ron King, Kevin Pankhurst, Colin Palmer, Jeff Mason, Ian Post, Kevin Holland and Roland Thorpe. Window frames and staircases were produced with timber shipped from Finland to London docks. Additional buildings were constructed in the 1970s, and demolition of the old brick and tile office and joinery workshop, and the corrugated saw-shop, extended the yard area to accommodate the factory's growth.

Abbott Joinery   1997

Following Mr Abbott's sudden death in 1979, Abbott Joinery continued under the family's administrative mantle. The field adjacent to the factory had been purchased in 1981, and a warehouse was constructed there three years later.

In 1990, Lester K Abbott obtained the controlling interest in the business, as described in the *Builders Merchants News* in 1991: "the company is now under the guidance of Lester Abbott and Colin Borrer, now occupies some 60,000 square feet of factory space, employing over 125 local employees and produces 150,000 window frames each year". Following the introduction of the u-PVC window, the company commenced production of a new extensive range of window and door frames in 1994, and immediately constructed new office and factory space. The latest phase in the company's expansion occurred when the storage and distribution depot had been procured at Heathfield in 1999.

Rural commerce and employment had nearly always been reliant on agriculture. Other than the tradesmen, there had always been occupations linked with the rural community. The 1841 census shows William Bourne listed as "rat catcher" and Robert Funnell as "collector of bones", a marked contrast in employment in 1871 when David Hayler was listed "chimney sweep", Joseph Meers as "chair bottomer" and Richard Mitchell as "huckster"; whether such work provided full-time employment remains speculative! By 1881, the census mentions Stanton Noakes as "coal merchant" and Lewis Gooderham as "photographer"; it was said by some that the building of what was referred to as Gooderham Cottage (now The Cottage) was a financial catastrophe. It was fifteen years after the 1856 Parliamentary Act, which advocated that local authorities must provide a professional police force. Thomas Mullard was listed as police constable in 1881, so law and order had been secured (at last) in the Parish of Upper Dicker!

Nineteenth century employment in the parish had been sustained by agriculture and would remain so until the conclusion of the 1939-45 war, whereupon, enticed by access of easier travel and probably higher wages, many gained employment in Hailsham factories, such as Green Brothers, Burfields,

1998

South Down Trugs and Crafts (Robin and Peter Tuppen)

Lushingtons and Bowes Seal-fast.

Old buildings which have become used for commercial enterprise on the Dicker, unlike a town, are few. The brick and tile building adjacent to Downsview Farm, Lower Dicker, which had previously been a green-grocers and, for a short time, a second-hand car business, is now used for trug making. Under the auspices of South Downs Trugs, Robin and Peter Tuppen who started the trug business at Horsebridge Farm in 1983, before moving to Lower Dicker. By 1988, eight thousand trugs were being made annually for home and overseas markets, and in that year, were awarded the Gardener/Garden News Trade award for export, and were also displayed at the Chelsea Flower Show. The *Hailsham Gazette* on the 19th July 1989 announced a marriage between two companies, South Down Trugs and Crafts Ltd and Thomas Smith, trugmakers of Herstmonceux. The new company, under directors Peter and Robin Tuppen, and Anne Piper, have now been relocated in Herstmonceux.

The concluding decades of the 20th century have seen a 60% increase in employment in Sussex, the primary sources being manufacturing, construction and service employment, reflected locally by the expansion of Hackhurst Lane and Northfield trading estates, and with 330 now employed by Abbott Joinery Ltd.

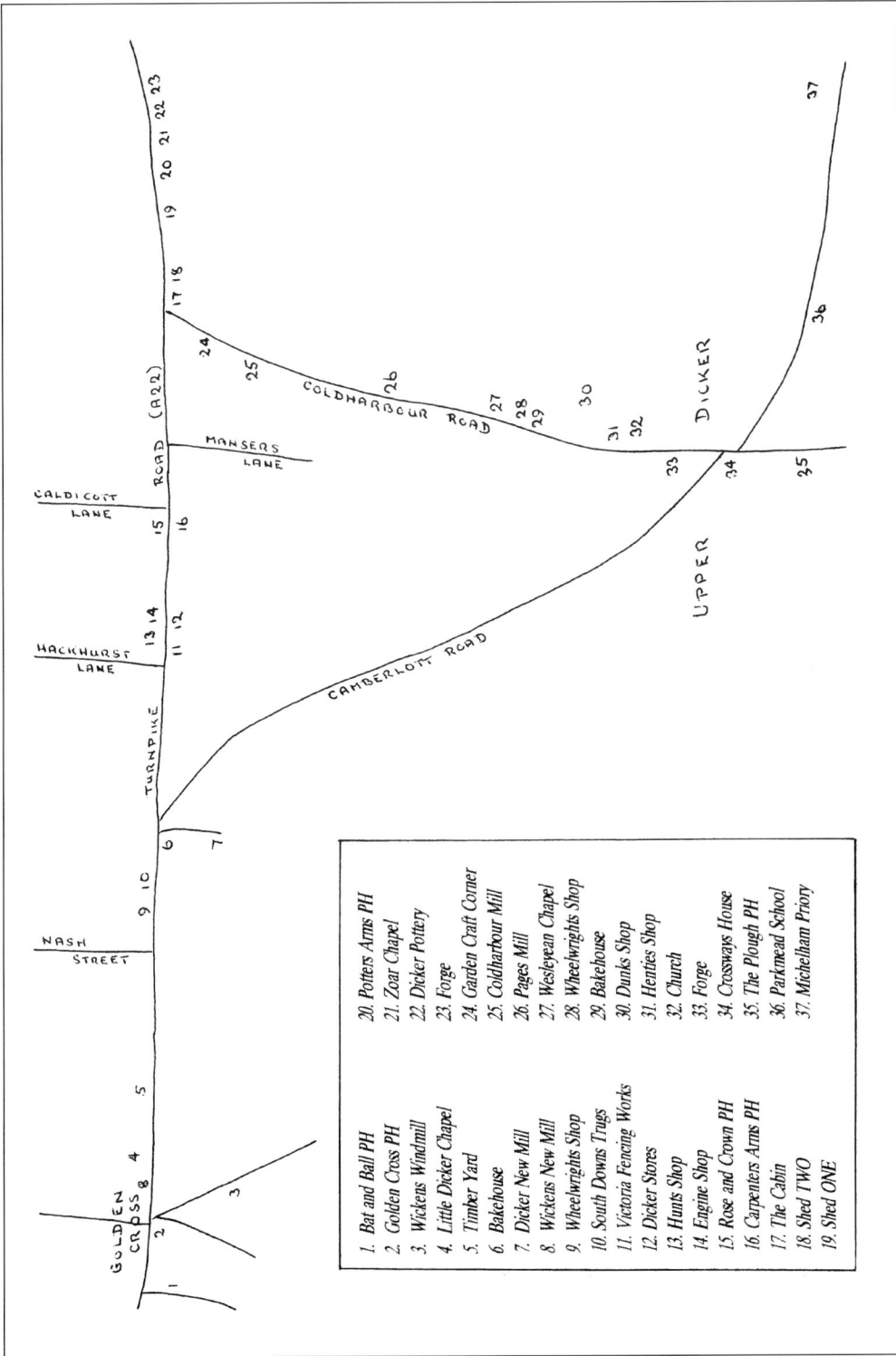

1. Bat and Ball PH
2. Golden Cross PH
3. Wickens Windmill
4. Little Dicker Chapel
5. Timber Yard
6. Bakehouse
7. Dicker New Mill
8. Wickens New Mill
9. Wheelwrights Shop
10. South Downs Trugs
11. Victoria Fencing Works
12. Dicker Stores
13. Hunts Shop
14. Engine Shop
15. Rose and Crown PH
16. Carpenters Arms PH
17. The Cabin
18. Shed TWO
19. Shed ONE
20. Potters Arms PH
21. Zoar Chapel
22. Dicker Pottery
23. Forge
24. Garden Craft Corner
25. Coldharbour Mill
26. Pages Mill
27. Wesleyan Chapel
28. Wheelwrights Shop
29. Bakehouse
30. Dunks Shop
31. Henties Shop
32. Church
33. Forge
34. Crossways House
35. The Plough PH
36. Parkmead School
37. Michelham Priory

Chapter 8

BARE NECESSITIES

The Village Shop

Before the nineteenth century, rural families had generally been self-sufficient regarding the bare necessities of life. However, the rising demand for provisions and other goods which were readily available in towns led to the establishment of the village shop. Comparable with most early village shops, a room within a house was used to accommodate such provisions, no less so the dwelling adjacent to Providence House in Upper Dicker.

Although listed as being owned by William Cowper, the 1841 census states his son William's occupation as grocer and residing next door to Providence House. (This may well make it the first shop premises in Upper Dicker). Subject to a public meeting of the Ratepayers of Arlington Parish in 1843, the assistant overseer deemed that William Cowper Snr and William Cowper Jnr should each be rated at three pounds, also that Isaac Dunk (shopkeeper) would be rated ten shillings.

Having moved from Tunbridge Wells, Isaac Dunk had been involved in the early success of the village shop. By 1855, Ebenezer Dunk had taken the role of sub-postmaster in his father's business and six years later the 1861 census listed him as grocer, draper and postmaster, employing seven men. The expanded range of necessities brought about the need for increased shelf space; every village shop would have had a stock of patent medicines, i.e. Epsom salts, camphor and castor oils, magnesia and zinc ointments. Eventually the shop premises had extended to a butchers shop, hardware, china and glassware department, a slaughter-house sited at the rear of Cowpers Cottages (later misconstrued as Coopers Cottages.), and the village bakehouse.

The expectancy of some shopkeepers that assistants should work unlimited hours, brought about the 1886 Shop Hours Act which stated that an employee under eighteen years of age should not work longer than a 74 hour week. However, the Act did not apply to adult staff, who continued to work long hours. An additional Act in 1911, compelled shopkeepers not to employ assistants for more than a 60 hour week, even though their premises might be open for much longer.

Dunk's Shop, Upper Dicker. (Post Office doorway on extreme left of shop)   *1910-1920*

1910-1920

Following Ebenezer Dunk's death in 1901, John, grandson of Isaac Dunk, became the third generation of grocers at Upper Dicker. Little had changed in John Dunk's initial years as village grocer; provisions were supplied in sacks, chests or boxes, which required weighing and insertion into prepared blue paper cones. Customers brought a jug or glass jar if black treacle was required. Prior to Christmas, a back room was always set aside, festooned with garlands, displaying items purchased for the festive season! Indispensable to the village grocer had been his horse-drawn van which had provided a delivery service to remote farmhouses and dwellings. But poorly maintained lanes to outlying farms resulted in excessive wear and tear to John Dunk's van, so much so that the Blackwell's who resided at a farmhouse down Sessingham Lane were obliged to collect their groceries left at a house at Wick Street. In Ernest Lade's account book, an entry dated 27th September 1927, shows repairs had been undertaken on John Dunk's Ford van, a change in mode of transport. John Dunk remained as the village shopkeeper and postmaster until 1938 when the business, with Reuben Langridge as manager, was sold to Leonard W Wilde. From January 1940, food rationing and complex legislation was

Glen Carr   *1991*

stressful for the grocer as he endeavoured to please his customers. Wartime rationing had ceased by the time the partnership of Hargraves and Turner had taken over the shop and they continued in business until 1971. Over the ensuing six years, the shop changed ownership three times. The forenames are open to debate, so these owners can only be referred to as Messers Blake, Eames and Simpson.

Following the 1855 Enclosure Act, a tract of common land contiguous to Providence House was awarded to William Cowper (minister). It was sold by Mr Blake in the 1970s and became Upper Dicker's village green.

In 1977 Glen and Phyl Carr moved from Woolwich in London and took over the Upper Dicker shop until 1991 when St Bedes School purchased the shop, thus ensuring an unbroken one hundred and sixty years as a village shop.

Isaac Dunk's shop had been well established in the Dicker area by the 1860s, the 1861 census proclaimed Uriah Clarke and Henry Miller had shopkeeping interests at premises that fronted the turnpike road (later known as Lower Dicker).

On the land which later became the Dicker Stores, the 1843 Tithe map and schedule shows a ten-acre field owned by Elizabeth Sarah Smith. Deeds dated 1845 indicate a pair of dwellings had been built, and had been converted into shop premises. Although trade directories do not specifically mention the shop by name, *Kelly's* 1867 directory listed Josiah Moore as shopkeeper at Dicker in the Parish of Hellingly, possibly at the Dicker Stores. By 1874, Josiah Moore had been recorded as grocer and draper, and the shop now stocked items of clothing. Josiah Moore died after being laid low by an illness in 1892. Although the 1895 trade directory listed Henry Curtis as grocer and draper at Lower Dicker, two years later there is Asher G Clarke shown as grocer and draper. The location of the shop is not known.

After a commotion outside the shop in December 1898, Asher Clarke was summoned to appear at the Hailsham Court as witness after Police Constable Bond apprehended Frederick Hamper, drunk while in charge of a horse and cart!

Extract from the *Sussex Express,* dated 17th December 1898:
"HAILSHAM BENCH OF MAGISTRATES
DRUNK!
*Frederick Hamper of Chiddingly, was charged with being drunk on the Dicker while in charge of a horse and cart on December 3rd. – PC Bond stated he saw the defendant in the road, and was not in his opinion in a fit state to drive a horse and cart. He shouted and swore very much, the witness asked him to get down and he did so and could hardly stand. Witness told him to get in the cart and he would drive him home, to which the defendant said he would not let any ******* policeman drive him. He was cross-examined by Mr Kirkland and admitted that defendant was very rough and his coat got torn. Asher Clarke, grocer, Dicker, gave evidence and said the defendant drove up to his shop and called out to him, and went out and was present at the same time as the constable. He said defendant had had a lot of drink, but was not drunk, and he could not say he was sober. Defendant then elected to state his case, as he is entitled to. He said he was not drunk and the constable treated him very roughly, tearing his coat halfway down his back, he had a scar on his nose where he was hurt. He was, in his own opinion, quite capable of being in charge of his horse and cart.*
He was fined ten shillings, including costs."

Following Asher Clarke's departure as grocer at Lower Dicker, the 1907 trade directory confirms Frank Hide as grocer and draper at the Dicker Stores, until the early 1920s. At this point, the directories list Hogben as grocers in 1922-4, and it also shows Job H Neve as shopkeeper at Lower Dicker in 1930.

Dicker Stores, Lower Dicker   1905-1920

A successful application that revised an off-beer licence permitting William Firrell to sell beer in singular bottles from the Lower Dicker Stores, had been greatly opposed at a licensing session held on 2nd March 1927 by Hailsham magistrates. Contention over the application had been submitted on behalf of the owners and licensees of the Golden Cross, Potters Arms, White Hart and Kings Head public houses. Supporting this application had been Donovan Martin, agricultural engineer at Lower Dicker, who said that there were several men in his works who were not able to get home to dinner, and they would appreciate being able to have a bottle of beer.

By 1934, the Dicker Stores had been taken over by Percy Sanders, now listed in the telephone directory as Hellingly 23. Around 1946 Maurice Austen purchased the shop, and instigated a delivery service. On Saturdays local lad Arthur Colbran delivered groceries by way of carrier-cycle to outlying houses on The Mount, Worlds End and Hackhurst Farm.

The shop was later sold to a partnership of Deschamp and Shorter, and then Mrs Daphne Harvey and her mother purchased it in 1963. The shop would always attract passing trade but as with so many village shops, it lost many local customers to the modern superstore. The Dicker Stores still maintains the very image of the village shop.

Opposite the Dicker Stores a building was constructed sometime between

1875 and 1899; the external structure suggests that it may well have been intended as purpose-built shop premises. Trade directories list William Ashdown as a tea dealer on the Dicker between 1895 and 1903, and in 1907 as shopkeeper, so it can be conjectured that he may have occupied these premises. Following the death of William Ashdown in June 1917, *Kelly's* directories show his widow as shopkeeper from 1918 until 1922, the family having committed themselves to nearly thirty years as shopkeepers.

On his return from the 1914-18 war, Arthur 'Mick' Hunt and his wife took over the shop, the 1924 directory listing them as confectioners. Later adopted locally as Hunts Shop, it sold mainly tobacco and cigarettes, sweets, Fryco and Tizer bottled drink, and fireworks for the local November 5th celebrations. At the rear of the shop, Mick Hunt was renowned for his 'straight-back and side' haircuts. Those who braved his clippers and scissors said, "what he didn't cut, he pulled out"! Mrs Hunt continued to run the shop until retiring in the late 1960s.

It was still listed as 'Freehold Shop' premises in the *Sussex Express* property supplement of July 1988, with outbuildings approved for light industrial use, together with spacious single storey accommodation, at a price of £180,000. In recent years, it has been owned by Mr N Graham and used as a centre for Pear Tree Pottery, and more recently by Past and Present, a showroom for period furniture.

Old Mrs Breach sold tobacco, sweets and other sundries from her home at Allander Lodge, Upper Dicker, while William Bridges ran a shop prior to World War I from his home at Boship Green, Lower Dicker, continued later by Mary Bridges until the early 1930s.

Transcendence from open common which had been subject to the 1813 Enclosure Act, a parcel of land recorded in 1843 as two acres Mead (meadow) owned by Radcliffe Lunatic Asylum and farmed by John Noakes. It has been divided and subdivided into what we see today, incorporating two dwellings Thompsons Cottage and Ella's. Subject to the auction of Cold Harbour Farm in 1878, the field listed as Lot 3, states it as being available for building purposes. At the auction held on the 2nd August, Uriah Clarke purchased Lot 3 together with Lot 4, a field with extensive frontage, also suitable for building purposes.

The two buildings located at Lower Dicker, near the Coldharbour Road junction, have served many trades and occupations, and both at some point have been shops. (They will be referred to here as Shed One and Shed Two.)

Appraisal of the 1899 OS map shows Sheds One and Two had been built, also Diamond (later known as Boxtree) and Jubilee Cottages, which as their name implies, were built in 1897, the year of Queen Victoria's Diamond Jubilee.

Leased from Uriah Clarke in 1895, John Thompson, listed as a "poultry appliance maker" occupied Shed One until he met with financial difficulties; the business was taken over by Percy Hide at the turn of the century. Eventually the growth of the business necessitated larger premises which were found in Hailsham. The company became known as Hides of Hailsham.

In the 1930s Shed One had again been used as a carpenter's workshop, as well as a fruit and veg shop, and at some point was described as an "Odd Boot and Shoe Store"! During the 1939-45 war, staffed by auxiliary personnel, it became the local fire station. During the immediate post-war years it became home and workplace of Jim Foreman who made baskets from hazel and willow, pegs and clothes props. When visiting the Potters Arms, it could never be determined who had the most fleas – Old Jim or his dog Ginger!

Over the past twenty years, with alterations and painted exterior, the Shed One has been a base for many businesses, ie DB Signs, Marlborough Miniatures, Clark Roofing and Fairways Preservation, and in recent years has been converted into a dwelling.

Unlike it's counterpart, Shed Two was constructed with a bay window, which suggests it may well have been built as shop premises, although at some point it was used as a collection point for local chicken farmers. Mr Martin who resided at Alberta Terrace, London Road in Hailsham around 1920, ran a small shop selling tobacco, sweets and other commodities.

In the early 1930s, Shed Two was used by a Mr Carey who operated a cycle repair business. By 1937 had become the Snack Box run by Mr J Butcher. During the 1939-45 war the shed had been designated a grain store for Macdougalls at the Horsebridge Mill. The immediate post-war years brought conversion into a private dwelling called Thompson's Cottage.

Jim Foreman, basketmaker   *1950s*

By order of the trustees under the will of Mrs Ellen Vine, nine cottages, the sheds and land fronting the main road at the Dicker, were subject to an auction held in Hailsham on the 26th July 1922. The sale document shows Lot 6 as being comprised of two productive meadows and a brick and tile Store or Shed, freehold and let on a yearly tenancy to Mr J Keeley at £14 12s. per annum. (A pencilled note in the margin of the copy of the sale document seen states it was sold to local farmer Mr Saunders for £240.)

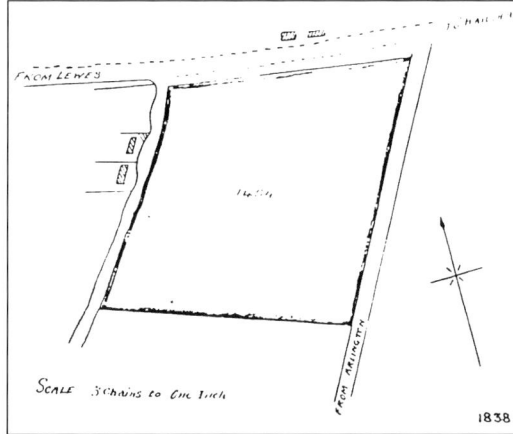

FOOTNOTE The sale map also refers to outline approval for a building that became The Cabin tearooms.

In August 1928 *Sussex Express* property column featured, The Dicker Cabin, a freehold house specially designed for teas and refreshments, situated at the road junction from Upper Dicker, indicating it had been sold privately. Mr and Mrs E Thompson had purchased the house and adjacent brick and tile shed. Throughout the 1930s, The Dicker Cabin was popular with passing motorists and cyclists, but after the war, was a transport cafe, until the 1950s when Bill Swadling converted the cafe into a fish and chip restaurant.

By the 1980s the old Dicker Cabin became one of the many Little Chef restaurants and later became the Jolly Chef. But in September 1991 it was the subject of an arson attack and firefighters from Hailsham, Heathfield and Herstmonceux fought to save it. Extensively repaired it became Raffles pine furniture showroom. From May 1999 it was a showroom for plumbing and heating engineers Alan and Ian Garrett Ltd.

The Radcliffe Asylum also owned an eight-acre (3.24 hectares) parcel of land between Coldharbour Road and Mansers Lane which was auctioned in 1838. Uriah Clarke procured it

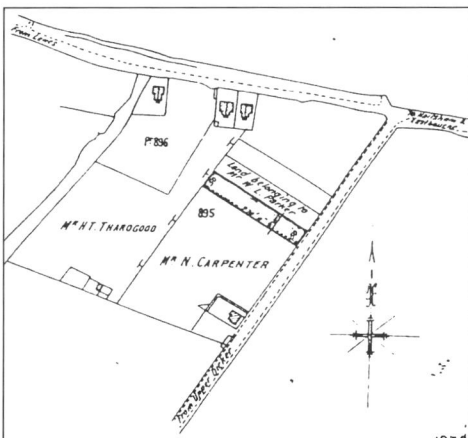

Nos 1-6 Lower Dicker.
1997
Houses built by Uriah Clark – some still retain the cream brick banding and diamond patterns

Court Lodge Flowers

for £300, and sometime after 1875 built six semi-detached cottages, (known as 1-6 Lower Dicker) for local workers' families. The distinctive cream brick banding and diamond patterns still remain prominent features on these houses.

The 1899 OS map shows the eight-acre field, Brick Field, an indication that clay had been or was still extracted for use at the Dicker Pottery. The map also shows Hope Villa had been built, and a building on the southern boundary of the field, later known as Springfield Farm and owned by a Mr Moran. In 1922, the remaining seven acres were sold for £225 to Harry Page of Upper Dicker, and then changed hands again in 1929 when Nathaniel Carpenter (builder) purchased the land for the same amount. Two years later, the field area reduced further, when building plots were sold to Herbert Thorogood in August 1931, and to Albert French and Wilfred L Parker in May 1932. Later that year, a plot was also sold to Joseph Cornford for £42. Around 1933, two more plots fronting Mansers Lane were sold, thus reducing the original eight acres yet again!

A corner portion of land remained undeveloped until acquired as a garden centre. In 1938 *Kelly's* directory it was listed as "Garden Craft Corner" (Ernest A Boon – horticultural sundriesman). The difficult war years meant the site became a waste-land of tall grass and brambles and was sold. Court Lodge was built in 1955 and Mr and Mrs Morgan resided there until 1984. Court Lodge was then purchased by Stuart and Carole Cole who, two years later, started a business selling cut flowers and plants.

The Bakehouse

Bread ovens had been in evidence in homes well into the nineteenth century, and the 1861 census subscribes Sarah Goldsmith as baker of bread, presumably carried out at her home at Dicker Mount. It is not known when the village bakehouse was started. The 1871 census confirms George Thorpe's dual occupation as miller and baker, and the 1875 OS map shows the village bakehouse had been built in front of what is now known as Cricket Field House.

Born at Fairlight and lodging with Stephen and Mary Crowhurst at Ivy Cottage in 1881, Wallace Thorpe had taken on the mantle as village baker.

The bakehouse exerted a great attraction on cold mornings to passing tramps; Molly Mothballs, Biddy Wren, Old Dog Gander and Lucky Dann, if luck came their way, were given a spilt or mis-shaped loaf! The baker levied a small charge to those of the village who brought cakes to be baked in the ovens.

Around 1914 Horatio Bottomley built a new bakehouse and shop adjacent to the church boundary. The tenancy of the bakehouse was taken by John Dunk, the 1918 directory describing his son Harold Dunk as baker, so it is assumed that Wallace Thorpe had retired. Hearsay has it that the old, rather stout baker, now doddery on his feet, insisted on being conveyed in a handcart to the bakehouse, no doubt to pass on his thirty-six years' knowledge of baking bread!

Harold Dunk died from influenza in November 1918 and his brother Walter died six years later. Ernest Guy became the village baker until the bakehouse closed sometime after the sale of Bottomley's estate in 1938.

The new bakehouse-cum-shop had always held a separate tenancy, and its earliest known occupant was Jesse Britcher until the late 1920s, when Harold Thickbroom took over the shop premises.

Harold Thickbroom who had lived and employed outside the realms of the Dicker (even alien to the county), not only became resident but took the tenancy of the shop. Discord ensued in 1930 when Mr Thickbroom applied for a licence to sell bottled beer from the premises, probably contested by Mr and Mrs Willard, licensees of the Plough Inn. The petition signed by 104 people, failed to sway the magistrates at Hailsham's Petty Sessions, who were of the opinion that, "in a very small area with a very small population, there are already adequate facilities for obtaining a drink"!

At the auction of Horatio Bottomley's estate in 1938, the sale document describes the shop as being let to Mr Thomas Henty on a weekly tenancy –

1963
Hentys Stores, Upper Dicker. Gordon and Lilian Manley

£19 10s. per annum, and the bakehouse let to Mr L W Wilde on a quarterly tenancy – £30 per annum.

Born at Barcombe, Thomas Henty who had previously run the Berwick butcher's shop before moving to Upper Dicker. At an unknown date he purchased the shop, which had previously been selling tobacco, confectionary and was the village newsagent, although groceries were stocked later. In 1952, Thomas Henty was joined by his son-in-law Gordon Manley, who had vacated his employ at Bourne and Burgess garage in Hailsham. Mr Henty died in 1963, and his grandson Robert Manley took employment with his father in 1957 at Henty's Stores. The shop probably couldn't support two salaries, and Robert sought new employment in 1964. On his father's death in 1975, he returned to run the shop until it was sold and converted around 1980. As a private dwelling it still retains the name Henties. In 1988 Henties was sold for £175,000.

Land abutting Boship Lane at Lower Dicker and listed in the 1843 tithe schedule as the Old Brickyard, was owned by George Goldsmith. By 1875 houses had been built on the site which became known as The Potteries. The 1881 census records Uriah Clark residing at No 11, later known as Zoar Villa. It is probably around this time that Uriah Clark saw a niche for a hardware shop at Lower Dicker.

In 1891 Uriah Clark was employing his daughter in his small hardware shop next to Zoar Villa. Later Jethro West purchased the property and by 1915 he was a hardware dealer. A horse-drawn van, provided a delivery service to rural villages until the purchase of a Maxwell lorry in 1923. Sometime prior to 1934 Hedley West had joined his father's hardware business, West and Son.

Hedley West continued to provide the 'bare necessities' in the way of paraffin, household sundries etc., delivering locally during the immediate post-war years. In 1967, Zoar Villa and the hardware business was sold to Denis and Elizabeth Upton. The business was not a success and Denis Upton returned to his cabinet making.

The Haywards Heath firm of Upton Furnishers established in 1919 by John William Upton, made oak and mahogany reproduction furniture. John W Upton and Sons continued in Haywards Heath until 1987 when the business was taken over by Denis and Elizabeth Upton and relocated at Lower Dicker. The need for a larger workshop, led to a move to Boreham Street, Hailsham and then Hankham, the old coach-house at Zoar Villa being retained as a showroom. The business is continued by Denis Upton's sons Michael, Richard, Geoffrey and Kevin. With the retirement of Denis Upton and the sale of Zoar Villa in 2001, the showroom for Upton's pine furniture was relocated to a shop in South Street, Eastbourne.

Whereas a village shop had previously sustained the needs of the rural populace, the bakehouse became equally important inasmuch as it had removed the necessity to bake bread at home. A bakehouse existed in the 1890s, when Benjamin Hide was miller and baker. It had been sited near Northfields at Lower Dicker. By 1911, Charles Hide was baker, residing at Northfields. Apparently, when a family member was asked to do the delivery round, they asked which houses were on the round. Charles Hide replied, "every time the horse stops, that house has bread, when he doesn't, they are not our customer"! The Hide family had been both millers and bakers, until Charles Hide sold the bakehouse to Harry Darby sometime before 1930. By 1945 it had been sold to Harry Carter. Carter and Sons expanded the bakery in the 1950s, with vans delivering to most villages, and bread sold from a shop in Hailsham High Street. Eventually the bakehouse closed, and for a time the building was used by Briarhill Antique Furniture until being demolished in 1989. The site then became the Northfields Industrial Park.

Alehouses

'Public house' is the formal name for what had been known as a beer shop, alehouse or an inn, which had quenched the thirst of the hard-working labourer and passing way-farer, probably far safer than drinking tainted well water! Five alehouses have existed on the Battle/Broyle-gate turnpike road which skirted the Dicker Common (A22), and one in Upper Dicker. Long before 1938, when 'haymaking beer' had been sold for ten shillings per $4\frac{1}{2}$ gallon cask, a beer known as Dicker Flint had been spoken of with great affection.

A coaching inn was built in about 1600 on the route from Lewes to

Battle. its proximity to Broad Oak Plain where cricket had previously been played, led to its being known as the Bat and Ball. According to the 1839 Chiddingly Tithe survey, the Bat and Ball had been owned by George Jeffrey and occupied by William Moon. Even though it was in the parish of Chiddingly, newspaper reports refer to it as being 'At the Dicker in Chiddingly'.

Extract from the *Sussex Weekly Advertiser*:
"BROAD OAK FAIR
At the Dicker, in Chiddingly, on Wednesday 29th Jun 1791. 'A Game of Cricket' will be played, for eleven cricket bats, by such persons who may choose that manly exercise and assemble together on the spot by 10 o'clock in the morning; two persons to make their choice each alternately, in order to render the success of the game as equal as possible."

Extract from the *Sussex Express*, dated 19th June 1847:
"GRAND FOOT RACE
On Wednesday last, a foot race of a 100 yards took place for £20 a side, between John Smith, who goes under the cognomen of the 'Regent Street Pet' and Thomas Moon, son of the Mr Moon of the Bat and Ball, which was decided in the favour of the latter. This race which has been in contemplation about two months, has excited a great deal of interest to the probable result, the 'Regent Street Pet' being considered a man of some 'standing', while the other though considered a very fast runner for a short distance, yet has never had to contend with so formidable an adversary, or one who stood so high in the sporting world for swiftness. The spot selected for the race was on the high road opposite the Bat and Ball, on the Lower Dicker. Owing to recent rains the ground was in very bad condition. After a great many false starts, which occupied an hour and a half, the parties got away, and Moon arrived at the winning point about two feet in advance of Smith, doing the distance in about 10 seconds. The race was an admirable one, the betting was even at starting."

Almost with unbroken regularity, the Bat and Ball was the subject of nineteenth century journalistic reports in the *Sussex Express*, mentioning not only the annual Sheep Fair, but felony, fraud, alleged illegal hours and a publican committed to appear at the County Court at Lewes, but also inquest proceedings in 1846, 1878 and 1898 connected with the inn.

Extract from the *Sussex Express*, dated 22nd June 1861:
"HAILSHAM BENCH OF MAGISTRATES
FELONY AT CHIDDINGLY
George Keech, a travelling saw-sharper, was charged with stealing a snuff box valued one shilling from the Bat and Ball public house, Chiddingly, the property of Peter Page, on the 8th of June. Charlotte Brown, servant to prosecutor, said that on the 8th June, prisoner came into the house for a pint of stout between eight and nine in the morning. She had a snuff box in her hand and while she drew the stout, put it down in the tap room. Prisoner stopped about quarter of an hour and when he was gone she missed the snuff box. He was outside the waggon lodge, and she went and asked

if he had it, which he denied.

PC Overton deposed to finding the box on the prisoner who said he did not steal it, he saw it laying and took it.

He was sentenced to ten days imprisonment."

Extract from *Sussex Express,* dated 29th June 1878:

"SUICIDE BY HANGING

An inquest was held at the Bat and Ball on Tuesday before L G Fullager Esq. on the body of Mark Guy. Sophia Guy, the widow, said deceased was aged 58. The previous morning she left him lying in bed at few minutes past eight. She went to work and the deceased was left in the house alone. George Hinkley, brickmaker and farmer, Brookham at Laughton; said deceased's grand-daughter came into him about eleven o'clock on Monday and told him her grandfather had hung himself. He immediately went to the house and found deceased hanging by a bit of cord from a cross-beam in the wood-house attached to the cottage.

Witness cut the cord, the deceased was quite dead.

Verdict – Suicide whilst temporarily insane."

Extract from the *Sussex Express,* dated 11th Nov 1893:

"HAILSHAM MAGISTRATES

ALLEGED ILLEGAL HOURS

William Harmer, Samuel Topping and Harry Goldsmith pleaded guilty to being on licensed premises at Chiddingly on Sunday October 22nd, during prohibited hours. PC Tester, stationed at Chiddingly, visited the Bat and Ball on the day named at 10.30am and found the three defendants in the stable adjoining the inn. A man named Funnell, brother to the landlord of the house, was with them. He had a quart pot in his hand containing beer, and defendant Topping had a glass but witness did not see either Harmer or Goldsmith drink. Harmer in defence, stated he was asked by Funnell on the previous evening, to go to the Bat and Ball on the Sunday to cut his (Funnell's) hair. The beer supplied was given as an equivalent for the job. No money passed.

The Magistrates considered the evidence was not sufficient, and dismissed the case."

Extract from the *Sussex Express,* dated 9th May 1896:

"HAILSHAM BENCH OF MAGISTRATES

ALLEGED FRAUD

Joseph Jenner, labourer, was brought into custody, charged with obtaining by false pretences one bottle of brandy and one bottle of rum, to the value of seven shillings, the property of Bernard Skinner Funnell, landlord of the Bat and Ball Inn. Mr Funnell stated on 13th April about 9pm, the prisoner came to his house and stated he wanted two bottles of spirits, one of rum and one of brandy, for Mr Hope of Gatehouse Farm, who would call on the following day to pay for them. He also stated he was to have a glass of ale at Mr Hope's expense. This was supplied to the prisoner, who took away the two bottles of spirits. William Hope, farmer, stated he had known the prisoner for some time. He had worked for him, but left his employ about March 11th. Witness had never given him authority to obtain spirits or anything else. PC

The Bat and Ball Inn *1900*

William Peddell proved arresting prisoner at Epsom on May 5th, he having been detained by the Metropolitan Police.
Prisoner was committed for trial at the next Quarter Sessions."

From the mid nineteenth century numerous publicans had been granted a licence for the Bat and Ball Inn: Thomas Woodgate, Peter Page, Arthur Shaw, John Hilton, Abel Rooke and Stephen Haffenden.

In July 1906, Mrs Fanny Burgess of Chiddingly, sued William Horscroft of the Bat and Ball public house, for £7 19s. at the county court for the balance of money loaned and goods sold on her behalf. The case was found in favour of the plaintiff, leaving Messrs Tamplin Ltd of Brighton (landlords) in debt and throwing doubt on Hailsham licensing magistrates' renewal of William Horscroft's licence. As Horscroft owed £200 to his landlords, termination of his tenancy was inevitable.

Licence renewal again became the subject of debate and contention in 1909 when eighteen licence applications were reviewed at Hailsham Petty Sessions. At one application Supt.Willard stated that the Bat and Ball no longer bonded to the Sheep Fair and Benefit Association, therefore the public house was no longer required. Even though Samuel Russell, Chairmen of the Parish Council and Mr Nye claimed there were advantages in retaining one of the oldest houses in the district; the authorities' refusal to renew the licence, would

not have been well received by the Bat and Ball's last publican, Thomas Lester.
FOOTNOTE

Extract from the *Sussex Express*, dated 15th October 1909:
"CONPENSATION FOR LICENCES

The Compensation Authority for East Sussex appointed under the Licensing Act of 1904, held a sitting on Monday when the amount of compensation in respect of licences which had been refused was settled. There were twelve cases and in six of these the figures of the Compensation Authority valuer were at once accepted without any material alteration. The total amount of the brewers' claim was £11,762, the valuations for the Authority amounted to £8,112 10s, and the actual sum agreed upon was £8,420.

SUMMARY

Licenced Premises	*Brewers' Claim*	*Mr Page's Valuations*	*Award*
Bat and Ball, Chiddingly	*£930*	*£787*	*£787*
Rose and Crown, Dicker	*£710 14s*	*£622 5s*	*£623*

In more recent times, the Bat and Ball was declared in a 1991 sale description, as a house with great character, with exposed timbers and inglenook fireplace, vaulted beer cellar, guide value £300,000.

Synonymous to local trade, authorities denied logic when granting a licence for a beerhouse that, in the progression of time that would debilitate the trade of the 17th century Bat and Ball coaching inn. The 1839 Chiddingly Tithe survey confirms that a beershop, yard and garden, owned and occupied by John Baxhill, existed opposite the Chiddingly road. On 18th century maps the area was marked as Broad Oak on the Dicker (it was also known locally as Five Ways). It eventually became Golden Cross, the name given later to the beershop.

By 1866 the alehouse the Golden Cross on the Dicker was licensed to James Westgate, carrier and farmer. Following his death three years later, he was succeeded by his son Stephen. The property remained with the family until the 1880s, when the licence was transferred to Frederick Reed, and later to William Herriott.

Robert Calvin Griffin moved to the Golden Cross in 1898, shortly before the closure of the Bat and Ball in 1909, and played host to the annual Farmers, Tradesmen and Labourer's beanfeast.

The 1924 trade directories listed the Golden Cross as being in Chiddingly and no longer proclaimed it as 'on the Dicker' or Lower Dicker.

A parcel of land opposite Caldicott's Lane which was granted to John Minn under the 1813 Enclosure Act, but its provenance as a beerhouse remains unsubstantiated. Long since converted into dwellings, White House Cottages on the Lower Dicker road had been the Carpenters Arms, listed in the 1843 tithe schedule as a beerhouse and yard, owned and occupied by James Harmer.

According to the 1851 census enumerator, James Harmer was a farmer of four acres and Henry Wenham a beerhouse keeper. Henry's father, James Wenham, owned four tenements opposite the Carpenters Arms, which later became the Rose and Crown. Four years later, Stephen Haffenden was listed as beer retailer and farmer; by 1890, seventy-year-old Stephen was still publican of the Rose and Crown after over thirty years.

In 1878 the Rose and Crown was the venue for inquest proceedings, for what was reported as a "Dreadfully Sudden Death".

Rose and Crown, Lower Dicker   1900

Extract from the *Sussex Express,* dated 26th February 1878:

"Yesterday, John Edward Fullager Esq., deputy coroner for East Sussex, held an inquest at the Rose and Crown Inn, on the body of James Wenham, a carter in the employ of Mr Durrant. The deceased, who was sixty years of age, had never enjoyed good health, but for the last three weeks had been much worse. On Friday evening, about seven o'clock, his wife left him sitting in his chair, after telling him she should be back directly to make a plaster for his foot. When she got back she found he had fallen forwards on his knees and was leaning on his hands. He seemed quite dead. He had said to her the previous night, "Ah, missus, I shall not live long." He complained of tightness of breath and pains about his heart. Mr Nicholls, surgeon of Hailsham,

who was sent for, said death resulted from imperfect action of the right valves of the heart. – Verdict accordingly."

At some point after Stephen Haffenden's death in 1891, the Rose and Crown licence was transferred to William Greenfield Haffenden, but almost immediately it was again transferred to Henry Shaw; in 1896, Stephen Sawyer Faulconer secured the tenancy of the inn.

Following what was deemed as 'a common assault' upon the landlord, Thomas Champion was charged with striking Stephen Faulconer after an altercation over a missing pony and trap on the 30th December 1897. The defendant having given a lame reason for the assault, had been fined 5 shillings or in default, 14 days imprisonment. A year later, following the sale of beer outside licensing hours, Stephen Faulconer would himself experience the displeasure of Hailsham's magistrates.

Extract from the *Sussex Express*, dated 12th February 1898:
"CAUTION TO LICENSED VICTUALLER'S.
Stephen Faulconer, landlord of the Rose and Crown, Lower Dicker, answered to a summons charging him with supplying beer during prohibited hours on 30th January. PC Peddell stated that at 10.45 on the morning of the day in question (Sunday), he said he saw a lad come from defendant's house with a basket containing a bottle of ale. Mr W D Peskett contended the beer was supplied to a gentleman who had ridden from Robertsbridge and was a bona fide traveller.
Fined 10 shillings and 13 shillings and six pence costs."

Returning to the possible licence withdrawal of eighteen licensed houses in 1909, an objection was raised over the renewal of the Rose and Crown licence held by Harry James Hunt. Evidence given by Supt. Willard, emphatically submitted there were far too many licensed houses in the district, and that the Rose and Crown should go in preference to the Potters Arms. Mr Thomas Hedley Pitcher, manager of Messrs Harvey of Lewes, pointed out that trade over recent years had increased, and there was also considerable trade in teas. Unmoved by the support shown by Arthur Mutton of the Invicta Cycle Works opposite the Rose and Crown, and by Nathaniel Carpenter (a builder) and Harry Martin (engineer), subject to compensation, the authorities refused to renew the licence.

Extract from the *Sussex Express*, dated 29th October 1909:
"SMOKING CONCERT
What proved to be one of the largest and most successful smoking concerts that had ever taken place in the district, was held recently in a large marquee in one of the fields adjacent the Rose and Crown, the audience numbering about 300. It was inaugurated with the idea of giving the landlord a hearty send off, (the renewal of the licence having been refused at the last licensing sessions), and also securing a sum to hand over to the Princess Alice Hospital.
Mr Walter Scott of Hastings, was the "lion of the evening", receiving encore after

encore, which he most kindly accepted. Mr Hughes of Hellingly was in excellent form, as also was Mr Stacey, who rendered two splendid recitations. Miss Maryan of Hailsham kindly volunteered her services at the piano. In the gentleman's beauty competition (the ladies being the judges), Mr W Hanniford took the first prize and Mr Bob Goldsmith the second, there being thirteen entries. A massive marble clock with silver inscription was presented as a parting present to Mr and Mrs Harry Hunt. A few rounds of boxing were indulged in, Tom Goldsmith beating Sidney Birch by eight points, R Goldsmith, J Carpenter and J Haffenden also tested the leather. At twelve o'clock, "God Save the King" was sung, the concluding an exceptionally enjoyable evening. Mr Arthur Mutton was in the chair and profits amount to £4 for the hospital."

The Rose and Crown became a private dwelling named Verdun House, commemorating the 1916 Battle of Verdun. Mentioned earlier in Hellingly parish magazine as a coal, coke and wood merchant from 1915 until the late 1930s, trade directories listed Charles Hamper as a carman residing at Verdun House.

Situated near Boship Green at Lower Dicker the 1843 Tithe survey shows the Potters Arms was owned by George Goldsmith (snr) and occupied by Henry Bourne. By 1861 Henry Miller was the alehouse keeper and a grocer, two occupations being a common practice with many publicans. Similarly in 1882 Charles Covell was listed as beer retailer and builder; and four years later, Edward Gutsell was both a beer-retailer and a cowkeeper.

In 1876 the *Sussex Express* reported a "Suicide by Hanging". An inquest held at the Potters Arms proclaimed the sad demise of the licensee Henry Miller, who had hung himself in the wash-house while 'temporarily insane'. Stephen Parsons had raised the alarm, Josiah Moore (grocer and draper on the Dicker) returned with the witness and cut down the deceased. Evidence was given that the deceased had not been well for twelve years and latterly had been unable to attend his business.

The Potters Arms again became the venue for inquest proceedings following Emily Hickman's tragic death on 13th December 1894. Her incautious act in the use of benzoline to rekindle a fire had fatal consequences! The deputy coroner Mr E Bedford, returned a verdict of "Accidental Death" from the medical evidence.

Associated with most public houses were the slate clubs which provided monetary assistance during sickness or bereavement, all remaining funds being shared between members at the end of each financial year. Held on 17th December at the Potters Arms, Mr Arthur Mutton presided over the 1912 Slate Club share-out and dinner, where it was said, ample justice had been given to the excellent spread prepared by hosts Mr and Mrs Amos Wenham. Club report read by Mr E Hamper (secretary) had shown receipts of £52 8s. 8d, after sick pay and other expenditure, the 37 members each received £1 0s.

Potters Arms, Lower Dicker   1900

The Potters Arms celebrates the festive season.   1950s
From left to right: Bertha Brockhurst, Mr and Mrs Brockhurst, Jim Foreman

8d, a share of the residual funds. With patriotic toasts honoured, Mr Charles Clark proposed, "Success of the Club", the remainder of the evening being given over to enjoyment of "song and smoke"!

The Potters Arms saw changes of licensee with some frequency at the turn of the 19th century. Following Edward Gutsell's departure, James Goldsmith, George Bridges, Henry Freeland and Amos Wenham were publicans. In 1918 Charles Clark became licensee; a *Sussex County* magazine upholds that he would sing to the accompaniment of his concertina, proclaimed by those who frequented the Potters Arms as the soul of any party!

By 1934, Mrs Kate Elizabeth Keeley had taken over the licence from Charles Clark. Throughout the ensuing war years she served a clientele, many of whom were uprooted by by wartime service; in 1946 the licence was transferred to Bert Brockhurst.

Local Police Constable 'Scud' Skinner's uniformed figure could often be observed in the passage that separated the two bar rooms supping a clandestine pint!

The Potters Arms licence remained with the Brockhurst family for thirty-three years, until Bertha Brockhurst retired as the pub's licensee in 1979, during which time the public house had remained impervious to alteration. In the 1980s when many public houses were refurbished to accommodate a restaurant area, publican Des Pelling worked with Beards of Lewes to change the interior of the Potters Arms. The Potters Arms were able to celebrate in style when Colin Smith won the 1983-4 Hailsham and District darts singles final. However, following brief tenancies of Tony ? , Bernie Bodle and Lionel Glyne, by February 1990 the Potters Arms had been sold to Clifford and Shirley George. It was subsequently refurbished and renamed The Potter, and proclaimed as being rid of the 'darts and sawdust' image; now a free house it provides home-made pub food.

What is now Plough Cottages, was owned by George and Alfred Wood in 1843, and occupied by William Gutsell, who once had a close association with an earlier alehouse in Upper Dicker. The Reverend Filler in his typed manuscript of 1943, *The Dicker Parish – its first hundred years* asserts the pub was called The Wheatsheaf, but this remains questionable until otherwise proven. Referred to in the 1901 census as Old Plough Inn, and listed as two dwellings occupied by William Crowhurst and Ernest Guy, it remains uncertain as to when the old alehouse moved lock, stock and barrel to its present location. But we do know that Levi Gutsell was victualler and tenant of the property "at the upper end of the Dicker Fair Place" in 1799. At a meeting held on 20th September 1826, the Justice of the Peace empowered William Gutsell to keep a common alehouse under the sign of the Plough Inn, whereupon the Commissioners of Excise would permit, "true assize in bread, beer, ale, cyder and all other liquors be duly kept and are not fraudulently diluted or adulterated, that measures be of full size".

The 1831 Rate assessments show that William Gutsell had been rated at seven shillings and six pence against the Plough Inn, he also paid three shillings in return for the use of the Plough Field; with Arlington Parish overseers rated three shillings for Plough Cottage. This suggests the relocation of the alehouse had already taken place.

The Plough would eventually form part of the Southdown and East Grinstead Breweries estate of public houses, and by 1924 was owned by Tamplins of Brighton.

William Gutsell evoked displeasure at Hailsham's Bench of Magistrates in 1861 when publican Eli Colbran of the Royal Oak, Arlington, applied for a spirit licence, believing it to be detrimental to his own spirit trade. Mr Langham supported the application and stated a licensed house was much required, as spirits were not easily obtained in case of illness.

The Plough's function room which was available for licensed social events, had been used for the Cricket Club 'after match' refreshments and for the Hand in Hand Benefit Association meetings. Alehouses had long been a male domain; the Plough was frequented for the weekly cribbage and whist matches, and by 1908 even rifle shooting became an indoor pursuit.

Extract from the *Sussex Express,* dated the 26th December 1908
"RIFLE SHOOTING

A shooting match took place at the Plough Inn on Thursday between Upper Dicker Miniature Rifle Club and Selmeston. The result was a win for Selmeston by six points. This was the first match of the Upper Dicker team, and they are to be congratulated on getting so close to the winners, who have not lost a match since the Selmeston Club was formed.

The following is the score

UPPER DICKER		SELMESTON	
A Gander	33	A Webb	34
W Piper	34	J Carter	34
F Osborne	29	J Hayward	30
A Osborne	31	G Smith	24
E Kingman	32	W Bennett	27
G French	30	F Martin	30
A Page	32	S Wilcox	34
W Rich	30	T Prodger	32
J Batho	32	F Lewis	33
D Cottington	31	W Godby	31
D Gutsell	29	W Ford	32
W Hanniford	29	G Hamper	30
C Clark	23	J Strudwick	30
	395		401

The Plough, Upper Dicker
From left: Percy Ball, miller at Michelham (seated); Mrs Alice Gutsall, licensee; Thomas and
Gerald French, blacksmiths; Bessie Gutsall; Edith Gutsall; Charles Cottington

1905

The Plough.
Charles and Clara Willard, licensees, seated in centre

1920s

On the 25th November 1909, the slate club held their annual supper in the Plough's 'big room', where an excellent dinner was served by Mr and Mrs David Gutsell, with the usual toasts being honoured throughout the evening, club secretary Luther Page would have undoubtedly endorsed another successful year, supported by the members. Three years later, the big room was used for the inquest of a shepherd named George Henry Wheatley who had been found drowned on 27th April in a pond near Wick Street. Evidence was submitted that the deceased had been subject to a severe attack of influenza. There seemed no reason why the 35-year-old man had taken his own life. After the Coroner's summing up, an open verdict was returned by the jury.

The Plough had also been a venue for the Upper Dicker and District Rat and Sparrow Club for their fortnightly meetings in 1912. In March the following year, the *Sussex Express* reported the Club's annual dinner being held in the function room whereupon Mr and Mrs David Gutsell had once again provided an excellent spread, vice-chairman Mr H Wooller presiding over the proceedings. Others present were, Messers J Hare, M R Holman, T Noakes, J Batho, W S Piper, G Dann, T and B Wheatley, A Page, H Akehurst, R Griffin, W T Piper, N Carpenter and H Page; while in a telegram, Horatio Bottomley expressed regret at not being able to be present and congratulated the club on its good work. The control of vermin was deemed important; the Upper Dicker club continued well beyond the 1920s.

The name of Gutsell became synonymous with the Plough Inn throughout the nineteenth century, William Gutsell obtained his original licence in 1826; by 1861 he was both innkeeper and farmer of 35 acres. In 1871 the licence was transferred to his widow Mary Gutsell. By 1881, having resigned his employ as gamekeeper, their son Samuel had secured the inn's licence, followed by Edward in 1900 and four years later by David Gutsell. The transfer of licence to Charles Henry Willard occurred in 1913, David Gutsell having taken temporary accommodation at Osbornes before moving to East Grinstead, severing the family's hundred-year connection with the inn.

Probably for the first time in the pub's history, alterations were carried out when the bar room floor levels were raised. Mrs Clara Willard had a dislike of uncouth language, and offending customers were encouraged to forfeit a fine in the prominently displayed swear-box on the bar. She probably had a greater antipathy to the odour emanating from William 'Dungie' Manser's trousers. Old Dungie, who worked as a farm labourer and resided at Ghyll's Cottages, it was said, "brought his work home and was reluctant to ever have his trousers laundered", hence his nickname and Mrs Willard's revulsion. Following Charles Willard's death in 1932, Richard Grantham secured the tenancy from the brewers Tamplin and Sons, before the licence was transferred in 1934 to Frank Musselwhite, who remained at The Plough until the 1950s.

The Plough had long been owned by a brewery, in the late nineteenth century by Southdown and East Grinstead breweries until Tamplins purchased the business in the 1920s, during the 1950s the Plough sold both Tamplin and Watney ales. The post-war years at the Plough saw firstly the partnership of Reg Fenbow and John Black, then Stan Phillips was publican followed by Maurice Pickering

More recently, many public houses have sought revenue from home-made pub food, and this had been the reason for Les and Margaret Mason's refurbishment of the Plough Inn. The old outbuildings which had been the gent's toilet, stable and cart lodge, were converted into the new restaurant area. Such change to a favoured watering hole gave little joy to some, Bert Dudley and Ern Smith immediately transferred their allegiance to the Woolpack at Herstmonceux.

By the 1980s, the Plough Inn was owned by King and Barnes. Their range of traditional beers on tap satisfied the real ale purist and publican Bill Tobin's till returns.

Towards the end of 1999, King and Barnes accepted a takeover offer by the Faversham brewer Shepherd Neame, and the Plough underwent a £71,000 refurbishment. Sussex County cricketer James Kirtley and Robert Neame officially re-opened the pub in August 2000, with licensee Helen Champion and partner Glen Foord as publicans.

Bootmakers and Repairers

Man's dependency on sound footwear necessitated the village cordwainer. The early nineteenth century cordwainer was listed as a shoemaker or a worker in leather, but later referred to as a cobbler or snob.

Demand on the cordwainer's skills was never more apparent when the 1841 census records six cordwainers working within the bounds of the Dicker; Jesse Salvage, David Smith, John Parker and William Dunk, with George Roberts and Henry Bourne working from their respective homes at Camberlot and Boship Green. Another early cordwainer was James Vine, who, in 1851 worked from his home at Lower Dicker. Both the census and trade directories list many bootmakers who operated over the years in and around Dicker: William Vinall from 1866 till 1878 and Spencer Follington from 1870 till 1903.

Henry Page was recorded in the 1871 census as shoemaker and farmer of 5 acres, residing at Tilehurst. By 1881, his son Luther had joined his father's business based within the bounds of Tylers House, leased from Richard Body (now Bodys Farm). Even though trade directories show Luther Page as boot repairer until 1913, a marriage register entry in 1909 defines him as rural postman; his son, Arthur Page, later became a shoemaker. On his father's retirement in 1925, Arthur Page continued to work as boot and shoe repairer in what may have been his father's workshop, to the left of Pollards Cottage. The workshop was relocated adjacent to his home at 1 Ivy Cottages, where he continued as village cobbler until the early 1970s.

Others who gained employment as boot maker/repairer and based at Lower Dicker, were Jabez Hickman, George Stevens and Arthur Medhurst. From around 1907 until the early '50s, George Stevens operated from a brick and tile workshop between Fir Tree House and Boship Cottages, and at some time had apprenticed both James and Jabez Hickman. Eventually changes in shoe design with compound soles led to the demise of the rural cobbler.

Communication and Services

The Postal Service

The pillar postbox was installed in 1852, and although probably in place well before, the 1875 OS map shows pillar boxes at the Coldharbour Road junction at Lower Dicker and another at Golden Cross. An entry in the 1855 *Kelly's* trade directory informs us, "Post Office – The Dicker", with Ebenezer Dunk as sub postmaster. By 1866, letters for the Dicker were to be directed thus – "The Dicker, near Hellingly, through Hurst Green", although letters for the rest of the parish of Arlington were being forwarded through Willingdon.

Post destined for the Dicker was conveyed from Hurst Green by horse drawn post chaise to Hellingly sorting office and then collected by the local postal messenger. The 1861 census records Luke Coleman as postman residing in Upper Dicker, by 1881 Edwin Roberts was the village post messenger. By 1874, mail distribution had been transferred from Hurst Green to Hawkhurst, and the Upper Dicker Post Office had been upgraded to administer money order and savings bank transactions.

A shoemaker by trade, Luther Page became the village postman in 1885, a situation he kept until his retirement in 1920. At the time of his retirement he recalled that when he took up postal duties, his weekly wage was ten shillings and six pence, and his beat included the road from Horsebridge, Upper Dicker, Michelham, Park Wood and Camberlot Road. On collecting outgoing post, a whistle was blown to inform people of his departure. Collection times at Upper Dicker were 10.25am and 7.45pm, and 10.05am on Sundays. Over a hundred witnessed the presentation ceremony held in the Parish Room in 1920, when Luther Page (of Livingstone Villa, Upper Dicker) received a barometer and a wallet containing £31-16s-3d, in recognition of his 34 years service.

Arthur Page followed his father and adopted the mantle of village postman. Mail which had been conveyed to Hellingly prior to 1938, had been transferred to the Hailsham sorting office and transported by GPO van to Upper Dicker. During his postal duties, Arthur Page witnessed the introduction of both the Postal codes in 1959 and the two-tier scheme of first and second class mail in 1968. His retirement in 1971 brought an end to the village-based postman.

The Telegraph

Ebenezer Dunk's shop at Upper Dicker, was probably the first in the village to have a telephone: UPPER DICKER 1. At a vestry meeting held on 28th March 1887 at the Old Oak Inn, Arlington, the South of England Telephone Company submitted an application for consent to erect a telephone line along the turnpike road. Those present resolved the matter should be deferred. The nearest telegraph office in 1887 was Berwick, and at the October vestry meeting, it was deemed that the matter of erecting telephone poles should be left in the hands of the parish surveyors, with power to give consent if they considered it advisable. Further Parish vestry meetings were held upon the question of the expense and whether this telegraphic instrument was really necessary. Chiddingly's postmaster (Mr J Noakes) received a reminder from the postal authorities that a telegraph instrument would be supplied if the parish would enter into a guarantee to pay £19 incidental expenses. Some at a parish meeting held in September 1894 opposed the expenses, Major Gant stated he, "could get his wires from Upper Dicker office".

By 1934, telephone numbering in Upper Dicker had undergone change: Dunk's shop was now HELLINGLY 34, but very few people had telephones. This was never more apparent than at a Womens Institute meeting in 1937 when Mrs Cane reported that 120 signatures had been obtained on the petition for a telephone kiosk to be erected in the village so that telephone facilities would be available at any time, day or night. The petition was sent to the head postmaster at Eastbourne and later a telephone kiosk was erected opposite Upper Dicker church.

Probably concurrent with East Sussex County Council's 1987 compulsory purchase of a disputed strip of land across Old Forge Garage forecourt, the familiar red GPO telephone-box was removed and replaced with a new one relocated adjacent to the Recreation Ground. The familiar red telephone kiosk at the Coldharbour Road junction succumbed to the same fate on 6th July 1987.

Electricity and Mains Water

Until the advent of these essential services, Lower and Upper Dicker, like other rural villages had been locked in the past regarding domestic lighting, water and sanitation. The arrival of electricity in 1938, was the first service to be introduced. Homes before this date had been lit by paraffin lamp, except

Dunk's Shop and Crossways House which each had a generator. Even though the Weald Electricity Company's 1936 advertisement claimed, "electric lighting that turns night into day", the street continued to be lit by the village lantern (the moon). Firle House became the first house to be connected to this new source of lighting.

Brick-lined wells had long been the daily source of domestic water and it would be several years before houses gained access to piped water. Primarily water would only be available from two stand-pipes, one located opposite Shop Lane and the other opposite Stud Cottages. Although most houses around the Upper Dicker area had their own well, when Horatio Bottomley had the terraced Elm and Stud Cottages built, a shared water supply became the norm. Residents of Stud Cottages, pumped their water from a large rainwater tank beneath the garden of 6 Stud Cottages. Providence House which had two wells, one concealed beneath the kitchen floor, water being raised by a hand-pump near the sink.

Even though older inhabitants advocated that well water tasted better, drought and tainted water did affect some wells. An analysis taken from the water supply at the Park Mead School, in May 1893, stated microscopic inspection revealed the water was of a dirty yellow colour and full of suspended matter, when warmed omitted an unpleasant odour, and was proclaimed unfit for drinking. In 1898, an inspector called the attention of the authorities to

Ghyll's Cottages (now High Barn Cottage), Upper Dicker, the well and privvy still in situ

eight dwellings owned by Uriah Clark, to which there was no adequate water supply. The tenants had expressed willingness to pay more rent if water was made more readily available. with no action being taken by the owner, the authorities deemed it necessary to take out legal proceedings.

Dissension over water shortage in the villages continued throughout the 1930s, and an inspection in the Lower Dicker area deemed the natural supply to wells was brackish, and that a main supply would cost £2,200. Again surveyed in 1938, the Hailsham Rural District Council considered the question of the unsatisfactory nature of the water supply along Lower Dicker but decided that such a mains supply scheme could not be carried out at a reasonable cost. The army's need for wartime water supply to billeted troops in Upper Dicker, hastened the arrival of piped water from mains laid by soldiers along Lower Dicker to Coldharbour Road, and then to the village in 1941. By the late 1950s, piped water had become a reality in most homes.

Sanitation

The introduction of modern sanitation and flush toilets, as with other rural communities, came late in Upper Dicker. The outside privvy, situated a distance from the house, had a wooden seat set above a bucket or cesspit, and so in rain or shine daily excursions down the garden path were a necessity. It aspired to a variety of names, the thunder house, the dike or dunny, the wee house, the throne room and karzi; probably recalled as being basic and uninviting, coupled with the unpleasant task of emptying the bucket or cesspit, the only beneficiary being the garden!

Main sewerage systems had yet to be laid to many rural villages. In houses built after the war, septic tanks were generally used to deal with indoor toilet waste, although plans for a main sewerage system for Upper Dicker were being reviewed in 1960 by Hailsham RDC. Ten years would pass before final approval was given, the sewerage system being completed some time before 1975. The privvy became redundant and was used to store garden tools or pulled down.

Chapter 9

RECREATION AND SPORT

Pleasureground, Parish Room and Village Hall

Pivotal to recreation and leisure pursuits in Upper Dicker, had been the award of the enclosed common land which became the Recreation Ground in 1855. It is likely that the reason for choosing this area was that cricket and stoolball had been played here before that date. At a Parish meeting it was resolved that the Pleasure Ground would be let to William Body for the sum of one pound fifteen shillings, subject to fences being kept in repair and its being used only for grazing sheep. Undoubtedly sheep were used to crop the grass with no added expenditure on the parish funds.

Extract from the 1855 Enclosure Schedule.

"I, Joseph Shoosmith of the Parish of Eastbourne, in the County of Sussex, Land Surveyor.

Whereas the Enclosure of Hailsham Common, Harebeating Green, and the Upper Dicker, and other Waste Lands within the Manor of Michelham Park Gate, situate in the Parishes of Hailsham, Arlington and Hellingly, in the County of Sussex, has duly been authorized under the Provisions of 'The Acts for the Inclosure, Exchange, and Improvement of Land'.

I declare that I have set out, allot and award unto the Churchwardens and Overseers of the Poor of the said Parish of Arlington, all that Piece or Parcel of Land numbered 48 on the said Map, containing Three Acres, to be held by them and their Successors in Trust as a Place for Exercise and Recreation for the Inhabitants of the said Parish and Neighbourhood, and I direct that the fences on all sides of such Allotment shall, from time to time be repaired.

And I have also set out, and do hereby allot and award unto the said Churchwardens and Overseers of the Poor of the Parish of Arlington, all that Piece or Parcel of land numbered 49 on the said Map, containing Two Acres, to be held by them and their Successors in Trust as an Allotment for the labouring Poor of the said Parish of Arlington."

Following the 1894 Local Government Act, all administration and finance relating to the Pleasure Ground was transferred to the newly formed Arlington Parish Council, who decreed all herbage on the ground should be let annually and they should remain responsible for the upkeep of hedges and sheep should be pastured. The herbage was being rented to the Reverend G M

UPPER DICKER CRICKET GROUND. 1904.

Recreation Ground 1905

Social gathering on the Pleasure Ground (possibly Jubilee or Coronation celebrations)

Russell in 1905.

In 1926 when Albert Gander relinquished his tenancy for the grazing, it seems that the Cricket Club took over the ground maintenance paying thirty shillings per annum. The Council also resolved there were no objections to erecting swings for the local children.

Why Eastbourne Gas Company Athletic Club should adopt Upper Dicker as venue for their annual sports outings remains a mystery! On Saturday 17th July 1910, club members and their entourage arrived by charabanc and horse-drawn chaises. Some came by train to Hailsham whereupon sixteen competitors took part in a walking race to Upper Dicker, and the winner F Boniface, who covered the three and a quarter miles to the Plough Inn in 28 minutes, subsequently received a 25 shillings prize. The race was then followed by a cricket match on the Recreation Ground between the office staff and men from the workshop, duly won by the 'pen-pushers' – 74 runs to 42. Tea and refreshments were later served in the Assembly Room at the Plough. This was the club's fifth annual sports outing held at Upper Dicker, and was again deemed most successful. The importance of the Recreation Ground to the village and to others, was shown in 1932 when Arlington Parish Council decreed it should always remain an open space for recreation.

The Recreation Ground became venue for the village's Golden Jubilee celebrations in 1897 for Queen Victoria. A brick Coronation Seat was constructed opposite where Orchard House now stands to celebrate King George VI's Coronation in 1937. Unfortunately, road alterations to Breach's Hill in more recent years have proved detrimental to the seat.

Some of the allotments that had provided for the nineteenth century labouring classes and later sustained the 'Dig for Victory' call during the 1939-1945 war became redundant by 1966 and were made over to a Children's Playground; the pond which had replenished the allotment holder's watercan and served the childhood pursuit of newts and tadpoles, with piped water laid on in 1986 the pond became important to wildlife conservation. In January 1988, Rosemary Collict, who was clerk to the Parish Council, became instrumental in the scheme for more suitable playground equipment and the swings, so long enjoyed by village children since 1926, were replaced in 1989 at a cost of £1,050.

The proposal to create Dicker Copse on vacant allotments had been borne from the loss of many elm trees from disease and the 1987 hurricane, and was vigorously pursued by David Jones and others throughout 1987. In association with Woodland Trust, the planting of the Dicker Copse came to fruition on Friday 2nd December 1988, when pupils from Park Mead School, villagers and others who had subscribed, were actually involved in planting 300 saplings, a lasting memorial to those in the community who created it.

Only when the old school building had been vacated in 1881, did the old schoolroom become the Parish Room. A brief reference was made in the *Sussex Express* in 1891 of its being used as a recreation room, suggesting that some events had taken place, but it was not until 1906 that a named event was reported: a whist and cribbage match. In 1913 the Parish Room was used for a inquest following the tragic suicide of Edward Bannister in a barn at Bourne Farm, Upper Dicker.

During the 1920s, the Parish Room was used for light entertainment, whist drives and the annual children's Christmas Party.

Because of the Parish Room's age, fund raising events were held with the prospect of renovation but, before coming to fruition, tentative steps had been made toward the construction of a purpose-built hall. A fete held at Michelham Priory in August 1927 raised £106 toward the improvement fund or the building of a Village Hall. By October plans had been formulated, the latter scheme adopted as the more practicable, a course of action being agreed to raise the required finance from local events, such as fetes, dances, concerts and whist drives.

Extract from the *Sussex Express*, dated 27th January 1928:
"*VILLAGE HALL FUND*

A meeting in connection with the scheme for erecting a village hall at Upper Dicker, was held on Monday evening, when the financial statement for 1927 was approved. The receipts totalled £150 12s which included half the proceeds from the fete held at Michelham Priory [£106 plus proceeds from other events]. A voluntary subscription scheme of a penny a week which had been started in October 1927, brought in £3 11s. 3d, a balance in hand of £147."

Fund raising events continued to swell the building fund coffers; in 1929 Mr Wright and Mr Dinnes were instrumental in the foundation of the Village Hall Trust, with a committee acting as trustees and an AGM to be held in January.

Extract from the *Sussex Express*, dated 24th January 1930:
"*HALL FUNDS*

Annual General Meeting was held in connection with the Village Hall fund, was held on Monday evening in the Parish Room. The financial statement for 1929 was presented and approved, – the year opened with a balance of £596 3s. 1d; £91 14s. had been used for the purchase of a field for the site of the Hall, (of which Mr R B Wright of Michelham Priory, gave a donation of £32 10s. – the cost of 1 acre.)"

At a general meeting in October 1930, an entertainment committee was elected to organise events that would supplement the fund. With £700 now available towards the building cost and the site opposite the Vicarage already purchased and fenced in, it was decided that the hall should be built during the next summer.

After striving for four years to raise the funds, the Village Hall which had

Village Hall at Upper Dicker
Officially opened on Thursday 29th October 1931

been built by the Ringmer Building Works, was used officially for the first time on Thursday 29th October 1931. Following the opening ceremony, the evening's programme consisted of vocal and instrumental entertainment, and dancing to gramophone music. It was reported in the *Sussex Express* that throughout, Mr and Mrs R B Wright, and Mr S T Dinnes (who had been secretary and treasurer) had been instrumental in the provision of the hall, with the steadfast efforts of the Dicker's inhabitants who had raised £1,050 They were supported by a loan of £290 and a grant from the Carnegie Trust, the final building cost of the Hall being around £1,200.

The Parish Room which had for so long been used by the 'Dicker Dandies', Mothers Union and Womens Institute meetings, and as headquarters of the 1st Dicker scouts, and later in the 1950s as a Boys Club, was no longer needed.

By 1933 a balance of £182 in the accounts was an indication of the Village Hall's success. Described by a *Sussex Express* reporter as "Upper Dicker's Social Centre", the hall had become venue for the annual flower show, various entertainments and social events. The showing of 'Pettitts Popular Pictures', which brought movie entertainment, became a favourite with many who resided in Upper Dicker. The newly formed Dicker Jazz Band shared centre stage with other bands that played at the fortnightly dances.

Dicker Dance Jazz Band
From left: Sidney Guy, H Haffenden, Willie Shoosmith, unknown violinist, Mrs E M Wright

The installation of electric light in 1939 replaced the hall's original oil lamps and twenty years later new heaters pensioned off the old coke-burning stove. In 1979 major structural repairs were carried out by local builder Hedley Moore. During the 1980s the hall underwent modernisation; the existing heating was replaced in 1981 and a new foyer and toilet extension completed by September 1984. Extensive work to its kitchen and storage area amounted to £25,000 and it was completed in 1989. The large mural painted by John Hanson of Upper Dicker in the 1950s was expertly restored in 1986 by Mrs Joan Aggate and Mrs Doris Harris.

Entertainment

The Parish Room previous to the 1920s had encompassed recreational evenings. On the evening of Thursday 19th April 1923 the Parish Room played host to the 'Dicker Dandies', formed by Mrs Tavender of Allander Lodge, Upper Dicker.

Extract from the *Sussex Express*, dated 27th April 1923:
"ENTERTAINMENT AT UPPER DICKER

The Upper Dicker Parish Room was crowded on Thursday evening last week, when a splendid variety entertainment took place, contributors to the long performance are to be congratulated upon the success which attended their efforts. The Dicker Fife and Drum Band, under the conductorship of Mr Jabez Finch, played at the commencement and at the interval.

The first part of the evening was devoted to a farce "Domestic Economy", which kept the audience roaring with laughter. The stage was then converted into a concert platform, with a variety of songs being performed, with Mrs Farrant as accompanist. At the close, the Vicar (Rev G M Russell) thanked Mrs Tavender for arranging the entertainment.

Those who took part were; Messers Jabez Finch, Cecil Parsons, George Oliver, Arthur Page, F Brett, Frank Willard, and Masters Fred Smith and Eric Akehurst. Misses Dorrie, Lulu and Mary Guy, Daisy and Mabel Vitler, Bluebell Rogers, Alice Shoesmith, Evelyn Britcher and Mary Parsons."

The Dicker Dandies had provided light variety entertainment performed to audiences in Upper Dicker, but when Mrs Tavender left the village in 1926, they disbanded. By the efforts of Mr Harry Bramley, a new concert troupe came to fruition in 1927, under the name of the Dicker Ducks.

Extract from the *Sussex Express*, dated 4th March 1927:
"THE DICKER DUCKS"

Two excellent entertainments were given in the Upper Dicker Parish Room on Saturday and Monday evenings to large and enthusiastic audiences by the 'Dicker Ducks'. (The proceeds were in aid of the fund for the cost of placing a roof guttering round the Holy Trinity Church.) 'The Ducks', who looked very effective in orange and black costumes; were Mrs W R Bassett-Smith, Mrs Limburn, Mrs W G Wright,

Miss J Haffenden, Miss W Kingman, Messers H Bramley, A H Clapp and J Finch. Their programme comprised of songs and humorous items, "Musical Men" and a sketch "Lodgings for Single Ladies". The concluding item was the Frothblowers Anthem. Mrs W G Wright acted as accompanist at the piano. During the evening a funny sketch "Uncle Joseph" was presented in good style by six juveniles, Mollie Limburn, Evelyn Britcher, Kathleen Young, Frank Finch, Fred Page and Fred Smith."

Although the Dicker Ducks contributed to numerous concerts in the village and at Hailsham Poor Law Institution, Hellingly Hospital and St Albans' Hall in Brighton, they lasted only two years. Almost a decade would pass before another concert troupe, the "Twinkling Stars" was formed in 1937 by Louise Hunneysett.

Extract from the *Sussex Express*, dated 3rd December 1937:

"ENTERTAINMENT

A new concert party, 'The Twinkling Stars', at Upper Dicker, made their debut at the Village Hall on Thursday last week. Under the direction of Mrs L Hunneysett, they presented a variety entertainment in aid of the fund for giving a Christmas treat to the children of the village. 'The Stars' were, Mr and Mrs F Westley, Mr and Mrs N Pettitt, Mr and Mrs T Hutchinson, Mr and Mrs S Page, Mr and Mrs F Hunneysett, Mrs D Page, Mr R Langridge and Mr S Brett. Several friends and a number of children also took part in the long programme. There was a crowded and appreciative audience. The party's opening chorus was "Calling all Stars". The men members sang "The Fleet's in Port" and the ladies "When the sun says 'Goodnight'". The humorous monologues by Mr Sid Brett were much enjoyed, as was the amusing sketch "The Haunted Bedroom", presented by Scouts, George Lavender, Roy Winchester, Jack Allcorn and Bob Coates. Another funny sketch given by the "Stars" was "Old Maids Matched". The young entertainers included Theresa Fletcher, Jean and Leslie Page (songs), Freda and Rita Parsons, Dorothy, Elsie and Gladys Skilton, and Dorothy Moore (dancing), Alan Page (recitations), Victor Phillipson, Fred Evenden, Nelson and Maurice Pelling. At the close a presentation of a pair of silver cuff links (engraved with stars) was made by the company to Mr Donald Bishop who acted as accompanist".

Contrary to unspoken rivalry by Hellingly's 'Moonbeams' concert troupe, the Twinkling Stars engendered a brand of light entertainment much enjoyed at that time by an appreciative audience throughout the 1940s, their shows always commencing with their theme song *The Stars are Always Shining*. Two concerts were held in May 1945 to raise funds for the forthcoming Peace celebrations. A monologue *Our Village* recited by B Stewart and B Gerry, no doubt involved a great deal of amicable comment after the shows.

Extract from the *Sussex Express*, dated 18th May 1945:

"ENTERTAINMENT

Upper Dicker is already thinking about Peace celebrations, for a fund has been started for that purpose, with a donation of £18. It was raised by the Twinkling Stars

OUR VILLAGE

Now listen all you boys and girls who live at Upper Dicker
For I've a tale to tell you that'll make your eyelids flicker.

Although our village may be small, it's great in other things,
A few years back a man lived here that loved the sport of Kings.

I refer to Mr Bottomley, that man of generous heart,
Who always gave a helping hand to those who were in the cart .

He owned some famous horse too, who won races far and wide,
He's gone alas, but still we look back on him with pride.

We've quite a lot of shops you know, and the Plough — the village pub,
And Mr Wild at the Post Office supplies us with our grub.

Mr Akehurst at the cycle shop, who is always blithe and gay,
Will mend your cycles and your prams, he's got such a winning way.

A useful man is A G Page, he's a snob and a postman too,
He'll bring your post and mend your shoes, what more can a poor man do.

Now Frankie Page is known to all, and knows how to do his stuff,
He'll move your furniture carefully, and never treat it rough.

Then there's old Grandad Blackford, and although he's eighty-six,
He does a spot of gardening, but he just won't cross the Styx.

We've Ernest Guy the Baker, and although he's seventy-one,
He cycles round with his jolly old bread, and of course he takes the bun.

Eighty years old is Harry Smith, he looks just like a gaffer,
And now I'll tell you something else, we've nicknamed him old Snapper.

Young Sid Smith, the son of Snap, comes round to us twice daily,
With milk — and listen — sometimes eggs, which makes us whistle gaily.

Now Mr White, our Willie, is good at laying bricks,
In fact he is so jolly good, he must know all the tricks.

Now Jabez Finch you all must know was twenty-five years a miller,
Fancy milling all those years, you must go all a dither.

Our little church — the village pride, nestles neath shady trees,
Where we may go to worship and to our Maker bend our knees.

Dave Smith, the Verger in our Church, a true and trusty man,
Will find your pews and also books, he'll help you all he can.

We won't forget that little shop that's owned by Mr Henty,
He's got your papers, odds and ends, and all good things a-plenty.

Oh you lucky, lucky people, there isn't a thing that jars,
And then at last, and hope not least, you've got TWINKLING STARS.

concert party by capital variety entertainments they gave on Thursday and Friday last week at the Village Hall. There were crowded appreciative audiences on both occasions. The arrangements were made by Mrs Hunnisett, who was the producer, and effective costumes were worn by the party, who comprised of juveniles and adults. The company took part in a patriotic finale in which Allied Forces were portrayed.

Taking part in the concert programme were; Messers B Stewart, B Gerry, J Bland, A F Woodward, C Harmer and S Page. Mrs S Page, Mrs Westley and Mrs Hunnisett. Margaret and Christine and Alan Levett, Ann Gerry, Violet Knight, Rose Houghton, Peter and John Langridge, Nelson and Maurice Pelling, Eileen Mills, Dora Shier, Bob Colman, M Blake and Rosemary Westwood."

Throughout, the Twinkling Stars had raised funding for the annual children's Christmas party but also for the many

The Twinkling Stars

wartime funds for the Armed Forces. Their decline, as with previous troupes, caused a vacuum of regular staged entertainment in the Village Hall until the advent of the Upper Dicker Dramatic Society's pantomime *Jack and the Beanstalk* in January 1979.

Extract from the *Upper Dicker Newsletter No 11*, dated January 1979:

"'Jack and the Beanstalk' provided the best laugh of the year and warmest congratulations go to the Dramatic Society for such a spirited amateur performance, so well supported by stage craft. The Producer, Mrs Elaine Paul, wishes to thank all those who helped, by giving a great deal of time and effort to the production."

A meeting between the headmaster of Park Mead School and local parents led to the emergence of the Dicker Players, and mainspring to regular entertainment in the Village Hall; pantomimes became a regular feature on the village's social calendar. But during the 1980s the group moved towards plays and the ever popular annual cabaret. Within a decade the Dicker Players had become a polished amateur dramatics group; in Eastbourne's 1996 Arts

The Dicker Players: 'Bedroom Farce'.
The cast: Chris Fuller, Christine Armitage, Lol Briggs, Lynda Harvey, Clive Hale, Sue Talmadge,
Tony Saunders, Kaye Collins, directed by Chris Fuller

Festival, they won the drama section with their production 'Blue Remembered Hills'. The group are credited with many plays: 'Big Bad Mouse' (1987), 'Too Soon for Daisies' (1989), 'The Gypsy's Revenge' (1990), and Alan Ayckbourn's 'Bedroom Farce' in 1988 when it became necessary to squeeze three bedrooms on the hall's diminutive stage. Many local amateur thespians (too numerous to name) have contributed to the Dicker Players' success.

Dicker Egghead Brains Trust

One of the village's more inspired ideas was the provision of a trophy to be awarded to the winner of quiz competitions. The Dicker's Egghead trophy was carved by Robert Gardner, and the competition initiated by Sven Pettit (of Body's Farm) in 1979, with quizmaster David Pike. Teams were attracted from neighbouring villages, as well as Upper Dicker. The 1980 and 1981 competitions were won by a St Bedes Staff team, and the following year by a team from Arlington and Dicker Womens Institute. The Plough eventually sought out their brainiest team, but they never did receive the accolade, "Dicker's intellectual ale-drinkers", but the Village Green team (Jim Flowers, Iris Brewer, Pauline Goldsmith and Frank Howard) became Egghead champions in 1983. The most successful team over the thirteen years of the competition had been Arlington, winners three times, shared the title with Chalvington in 1985, and were beaten finalists in 1987. Throughout the 1980s, the annual competition flourished but the retirement of David Pike as quizmaster in 1992 saw the demise of the Egghead competition. Joint-winners Hellingly and Wilmington were the last to win the Egghead trophy.

Mothers Union and Woens Institute.

Upper Dicker Mothers Union was formed in 1924 and the Womens Institute three years later. Mrs Bassett-Smith had been instrumental in structuring the Mothers Union, with meetings held monthly in the Parish Room. The group's active involvement in the village was demonstrated by efforts to raise money through a series of whist drives with a view to purchasing a piano for the Parish Room.

Extract from the *Sussex Express*, dated 23rd January 1925:
"WHIST FOR PIANO
The second whist drive arranged by Mrs Bassett-Smith and members of the Mothers Union, in aid of a fund in obtaining a piano, a whist drive was held on Thursday last week, Mr Thomas Henty was MC.
The fund now stands at £15."

The Upper Dicker branch of the Mothers Union attended a Deanery festival in Alfriston, and a large rally at Brighton where the group discovered that they were the only branch without a banner. This prompted one to be made with their chosen 'Maddona Lily' central to the design.

Newspaper reports describe annual charabanc outings to Canterbury, Bournemouth, Oxford, Windsor and Hampton Court, Mrs Cohen on many of these excusions, providing the refreshments and sweets.

From its inception in September 1915, the Womens Institute movement in the United Kingdom had drawn numerous villages into the organisation. Upper Dicker's group was formed in 1927, with Arlington four years later, providing housewives an opportunity to share in a wide variety of activities outside the home. Initially, monthly meetings were held on a Wednesday, overseen by the group's first president, Mrs R B Wright of Michelham Priory. At the 1931 AGM, it was decided that future meetings would be held in the new Village Hall.

Extract from the *Sussex Express*, dated 18th March and 17th June 1932:
"WOMENS INSTITUTE
An interesting talk on 'Old Sussex Industries' was given by Miss Fowler-Tutt of Lewes, at the monthly meeting on Wednesday at the Village Hall. Miss Fowler-Tutt exhibited articles made from flint, specimens of pottery and trug baskets. The President (Mrs S T Dinnis) was in the chair. A discussion took place regarding the venue for the

summer outing, Southampton, Windsor, and a biscuit factory at Reading being
suggested. Owing to the small attendance, it was agreed to leave the final decision
until the April meeting. The competition was 'Something new for something old',
winners were Mrs H Haffenden and Mrs Winnie Nash.
On Thursday 10th June 1932, members of the Upper Dicker Womens Institute went
by motor coach to Southampton for their annual outing. A visit to one of the large
liners at Southampton was much enjoyed."

Throughout the 1930s and postwar years, annual outings took place to
London (1930), Southampton (1932), and again to London in 1933, where
the great departmental stores and Piccadilly Underground station, was said to
have claimed their attention! No doubt on their return, the trip inspired tales
of the bustling great metropolis and trains that ran through holes in the
ground!

From 1929 until the war years, Michelham Priory's great barn and
grounds were the venue for Upper Dicker Womens Institute's annual produce
shows, and the Federation's Historical Pageant in July 1936, reported in the
Sussex Express, "motor coaches and cars brought hundreds from far and wide to
enjoy the merry making." (The pageant had attracted 4,286 over the two days.)

Following their September 1939 meeting, members were to prove that
the Institute's activities were not all 'jam and Jerusalem', as with other villages
they were to provide knitted garments and raise funds for the armed forces,
evacuees and hospitals.

Extract from the *Sussex Express*, dated 22nd September 1939:
"WOMENS INSTITUTE
Mrs R B Wright (president) was in the chair at a meeting at the Village Hall on
Thursday last week. There was a discussion on what activities the Institute could
undertake during the war. It was decided to hold weekly needlework working parties
at Michelham Priory to make garments which would be of use to evacuees and
hospitals. It was hoped members unable to attend the meetings would undertake
similar work at home. The tea hostesses were Mrs G H Akehurst, Mrs Dadswell and
Mrs F Tatnall."

The Upper Dicker Women's Institute had responded well to its wartime
role, but by April 1945 it had ceased to function as an active group. A year
later, with Mrs Elvey as president, the Institute was reformed. Minutes from
meetings held in 1948 show that Mrs Lilian Creasey became president and Mrs
M Shier had organised whist drives in aid of many charities. It was also agreed
that all correspondence and bills prior to 1946 should be destroyed. With
improved membership and a healthy bank balance of nearly £27, Upper
Dicker's Womens Institute once again flourished. However, by the late 1950s
falling membership gave rise to fears the group may cease to function; as press
officer, Mrs G Parker's appeal for new members had been unsuccessful, and in
1962 Upper Dicker and Arlington amalgamated, with monthly meetings held

Womens Institute Outing
From left, back row: Mrs Dadswell, Mrs Colwell, Mrs F Smith, Mrs Haffenden, Miss M Haffenden,
Mrs Shier, Mrs Cleeve, unknown, Miss N Bishop, Mrs Sidley, Mrs Elvey, unknown
Middle row: Mrs Evenden, unknown, Mrs Dudley
Front row: Phyllis Dadswell, Ray Dadswell, David Colwell, Elizabeth Colwell, Dora Shier,
Michael Sydercombe, Mrs Sydercombe, Roy Evenden

at alternating venues.

At the 1988 AGM, Mrs M Ticehurst (president) summed up the meeting by stating that the group had enjoyed a successful year, with a membership of 40; a favourable future was assured.

The once popular Womens Institute became subject to changing ideals. The Arlington and Upper Dicker Womens Institute came to an end in 1993.

Extract from the *Sussex Express*, dated 18th December 1998

"LUNCH

I was very pleased to know that some members of the old Arlington and Dicker WI, which broke up some years ago are continuing to have a monthly meeting in the form of a coffee morning. These meetings are always held at the home of a past member and the second Tuesday of each month. On 8th December, nine ladies attended a Christmas lunch at the Yew Tree Inn."

1st Upper Dicker Scout Troop

Following Robert Baden-Powell's experimental camp on Brownsea Island in 1907 cementing his ideas for a scouting movement for boys from every walk of life, and his publication *Scouting for Boys* in six fortnightly parts, boys were quickly attracted to scout troops all over the country and by 1910 over a 100,000 had joined.

In 1925 an attempt was made to start a scout troop in Upper Dicker by Donovan Martin and Owen Lavender, where 8 or 10 boys were drawn to meetings at the Parish Room. Frank Finch recalled they were issued with the wide brimmed scout hat and staves but were soon disappointed that after only six months, the troop was disbanded. During this period, a day trek to Wilmington Giant was organised, borrowing old Mr Breach's handcart to carry the equipment: although exhausted, the boys enjoyed the day. The Scout Association confirm that the troop disbanded before it and the leaders had a chance to register with Headquarters. Three years were to pass before Miss E C Cornford became instrumental in the troop's revival in 1928.

Extract from the *Sussex Express*, dated 17th February 1928:

"Following the service at Holy Trinity Church, Upper Dicker on Sunday morning, there was enrolment service for the Upper Dicker Troop of Boy Scouts. (Scoutmaster Miss E C Cornford.)"

Extract from the *Sussex Express*, dated 14th September 1928

"DEDICATION

At the Parish church on Sunday morning, a Union Jack flag presented to the 1st Dicker Troop by Mrs Jefferson Cohn, was dedicated by the Rev W R Bassett-Smith. In addition to the local troop under Scoutmaster Miss Cornford, there were also contingents from Horeham Road [later Horam] and the 1st Brighton Troops."

The 1st Dicker Troop became affiliated to the Horeham Road and District, and was registered with the Scout Association on the 28th August 1928.

The 1926 scouting handbook gives the price of uniforms: shirt, navy shorts (referred to as knickers), regulation scout hat, hose (long socks), belt, lanyard, whistle and knife, cost 15 shillings and 9 pence. Those who joined the scout troop, were proud to wear the uniform, even though Stan Henty recalled the dark green flannel shirt wasn't at all friendly to his skin! The 1st Dicker Troop opted to wear a yellow neckerchief, initially with Fox, Woodpecker, and Auk patrols, and as more boys joined from both Lower and Upper Dicker, Peewit patrol was added. A Wolf Cub Pack was formed in 1932 that provided similar activities for younger boys, with Bernie Butcher as cubmaster.

Outdoor activities beckoned as boys strove to gain badge awards, whether in pursuit of a cook's badge in front of the Parish Room or life-saving badge in the cold water of the Cuckmere River, near Alfriston lock; both Stan Henty and Jack Allcorn recalled badge-work had been an activity they enjoyed.

In 1929, Fred Page, then a patrol leader, became one of those selected to represent the Sussex contingent at the third World Jamboree held at Arrow Park, Birkenhead.

During the troop's existence, camps were held at Groombridge, Steyning, at Glynde near Mount Caburn, in the grounds of a large house at Uckfield, Hayling Island and the Isle of Wight in 1936 and 1939. They travelled by rail to the more distant camp sites but in the main Mr Harry Page's lorry conveyed the troop's equipment.

The annual sports of the Horeham and District Scouting Association was

1st Dicker Scout Troop   1930
From left, standing: Martin Manley, Roy Winchester, Fred Clapson, Fred Page, Bernie Butcher,
Ken Richardson, George Lavender, Stan Henty
Seated: Raymond Dinnis, Jack Allcorn, Gordon Manley, Miss E C Cornford, Rev W R Bassett-Smith,
Lilian Henty, unknown, Bob Pratt
Front row: Les Page, unknown, Les Winchester, Dave Fletcher, Harry Page, unknown, unknown,
John Peckham

the subject of intense rivalry to win the coveted Challenge Shield; having been runners-up in 1933 and third in 1936, the 1st Dicker Troop were winners in 1935.

Extract from the *Sussex Express*, dated 11th October 1935:
"*SCOUTS CELEBRATE*
To mark their success in winning the Challenge Shield by gaining most points the previous week at

the annual sports of the Horam and District Scout Association, and being awarded the Jarvis Cup for general progress and proficiency, the 1st Dicker Troop held a games night at the Parish Room on Thursday last week. Their guests were scouts from the 1st and 2nd Hailsham. Refreshments were served."

On Sunday 3rd May 1936, as part of the Empire Day parades, nearly 170 scouts and cubs of the Horam and District Scouting Association descended on Upper Dicker for their annual Empire Day church parade. After the service the scouts and cubs marched to the Recreation Ground, where they formed up and were inspected by the Bishop of Lewes (the Rt Rev H M Hordern).

The interest in scouting attracted many boys to join the 1st Dicker troop: George Lavender, Gordon and Martin Manley, Fred Clapson, Ray Dinnis, John Peckham and Don Butters, as well as Len Coates, Bob Pratt, Rodney Colbran, Roy and Les Winchester, and Jack Allcorn from Lower Dicker; no doubt many others were part of the Dicker Troop. Miss E C Cornford who had been instrumental in the troop's foundation, left the village in November 1937, and Fred Page became scoutmaster, with Miss Lilian Henty as cubmaster. With funds raised from varying events and donations, the troop continued to gain good support from the village, and in 1932 Mr Frank Stephens was presented with the 'Supporters Badge' for his sterling work.

Curtailment of scouting in Upper Dicker came soon after the troop's summer camp on the Isle of Wight, in August 1939, when they had been joined by six other troops at Shanklin. Stan Henty recalled the weather as being very hot, with visits to many parts of the Island. Jack Allcorn and Les Winchester remembered a novel game of cricket played by torchlight. None would have visualised that the many ships in Portsmouth harbour would soon be committed to a wartime role; the aircraft carrier HMS *Courageous* anchored nearby, would be torpedoed in September and sunk with the loss of 516 lives.

According to the Scout Association archivist, no registration had been recorded after 1939, so it may be assumed that the war years saw a decline in scouting enrolment and leadership. Over fifty years would pass before Andrew Finch's endeavours re-established scouting in Upper Dicker.

1st Claverham Scout Group

Andrew Finch's determined effort to re-establish a Cub Pack in Upper Dicker came to fruition after a prospectus in 1994 to judge whether sufficient numbers would once again sustain a troop in the area. The 1st Claverham Group, using the Village Hall as headquarters, held their first meeting on Friday 22nd April 1994. Adopting the proposed purple-coloured scarf, the newly formed Beaver Colony and Cub Pack were overseen by Steph Roberts and Paul Ashby. Within a year a scout troop for the older boys was established under the guidance of scout leader Kevin Roberts. With Richard Partridge as

The 1st Claverham Scout Group *1998*

chairman of executive committee and the infectious enthusiasm of Group Leader Andrew Finch, the scouts enjoyed numerous scouting activities and camps. Unfortunately there was a shortage of leaders and Andrew Finch's sudden death in 1997 effectively brought an end to the group. The 1998 annual general meeting noted that numbers had not been as great as was hoped, but scout leader Fred Barrett had maintained a varied and exciting programme for the scouts of Eagle, Falcon and Wolf Patrols. The 1st Claverham scout troop ceased to function in 2000.

1st Dicker Brownie Pack

Probably no other Brownie Pack had a more illustrious setting for their meetings than the 1st Dicker Brownie Pack. Miss Nancy Wright who had previously been Tawny Owl with the 2nd Burgess Hill, used her parent's Michelham Priory home as headquarters, and was instrumental in the founding of the 1st Dicker Brownie Pack in 1929. Pack meetings were held on Saturdays in the Priory's historic gatehouse, but during the winter months moved indoors to the house. Edna Blackwell and Dorothy Moore recalled climbing the stone spiral staircase to the room allotted for meetings, each Six had their own large stone window seat and the vast priory grounds were used

Dicker Brownies in the grounds of Michelham Priory   *1930s*

for activities. For a brief time, Miss Elizabeth Wright had been enrolled as Tawny Owl, but vacated this role in 1932.

Extract from the *Sussex Express,* dated 26th June 1931:

"GIRL GUIDES AT HORAM ROAD

Nearly 300 guides and Brownies with their Guiders, attended a rally in the beautiful grounds at Tanners Manor, on Saturday afternoon, by kind permission of Mr and Mrs Hassell. The weather was favourable.

The Guides and Brownies present were from, Heathfield, Cross in Hand, Horeham Road, Hellingly, Warbleton, Hailsham, Dicker and Waldron.

A play, entitled 'The Gipsy Laddie' was given by Cross in Hand and Heathfield, and Guides and Brownies of the district gave a sketch entitled 'The House the Guides built'. A tent pitching competition was won by Hellingly Troop. The rally which was a great success, concluded in the early part of the evening with the singing of the National Anthem."

Church parades were held regularly in the Parish Church, on Sunday 24th May 1936, the Dicker Brownies were part of 150 Guide and Brownie contingent at the Empire Day Parade at Chiddingly.

Unlike the Dicker Scout Troop, whose activities were reported frequently by the local press, the Brownies' activities went unreported, little is therefore known about them. The 1st Dicker Brownie Pack was disbanded in December 1938.

Cricket

The Dicker had long been associated with cricket, a reference to "Creag" in 1300 may well be cricket's predecessor. Records exist of a match played in 1550 at a school in Guildford, evidence of a form of cricket long before 1677, when the treasurer to the Earl of Sussex recorded, "Paid to my Lord when his Lordship went to the crekitt match ye Dicker." While it is uncertain as to whether this was a single or a double wicket match, cricket has been played on the Dicker for over 300 years. During the seventeenth century, there were fears that the game may influence impious waywardness, and some sought to put the game down! In 1654 seven parishioners of Eltham in Kent were fined for playing cricket on the Sabbath, and thirty-two years earlier six men were prosecuted for playing cricket in Boxgrove churchyard.

By the 1750s cricket was being played regularly at "Broad Oak on the Dicker" (near the junction of A22 and B2124 roads – adjacent to the old Bat and Ball coaching inn, location of this early cricket venue can still be accurately pin-pointed).

Extract from the *Sussex Weekly Advertiser*, dated 23rd June 1788:

"On the 26th June, cricket will be played on Broad Oak between the Gentlemen of Alfriston and the Parish of Chiddingly, with four men, any two of which may be selected from any part of the county. The wickets to be pitched at ten in the morning, a great many spectators are expected."

Eighteenth century cricket at Broad Oak Plain (now Golden Cross) had seen the change from a two stump wicket to three, and by 1790 bats were straight as opposed to being curved. Matches were by invitation between neighbouring parishes, with wagers on their outcome. Scores were kept by cutting notches into a stick, hence today's 'notching up a good score'. Cricket became increasingly fashionable, and clubs grew up all over the country. Annual fixtures began to take place, and spectators would walk some distance to see a game; diarist Thomas Turner's interest in cricket led to a journey to see his favourite game being played on the Dicker.

The first match played in the 19th century at Upper Dicker was one played on 7th May 1807 between the Gents of the South and Gents of the North, probably players drawn from north and south of the parish of Arlington. In 1837 "Lamberts Instructions to Scientific Cricket Playing" state some cricket laws, including Rules 34 and 43: "If any player stop the ball with his hat, the opposite party shall have five runs added", and "No umpire shall be allowed to bet".

The *Sussex Agricultural Express* gave notice that a forthcoming match between gentlemen residing on the Downs against those of the Weald was to be played on the Upper Dicker on Thursday 24th May 1838. In 1872, a newspaper report names the members of the village team: J W Body, G

Thorpe, S Gutsell, P Barnes, J Gosden, D Whitbourne, D Gutsell, A Parsons, R Gutsell, C Carpenter, L Gutsell, J Barnes and W Guy.

Extract from the *Sussex Express,* dated 3rd July 1880:

"CRICKET

ALCISTON AND SELMESTON UNITED vs UPPER DICKER GRASSHOPPERS

This match was played on the new cricket ground (kindly lent by Mr G H Elphick) on Saturday last. Stumps were drawn at 5.30pm, and the party adjourned to the Barleymow Inn, where Host and Hostess Harvey had provided a bountiful repast in their usual good style. After the cloth was cleared, songs and toast became the order of the evening, and a most pleasant day was spent by all. The following score, –

SELMESTON AND ALCISTON – F Carter b E Gutsell 0, F Burrows b L Page 3, C Piper c Page 0, G H Elphick c Page b E Gutsell 6, C Carter thrown out F Deadman 8, John Hymans st S Gutsell 1, George Hufflect c G Deadman b E Gutsell 3, John Westgate b E Gutsell 0, C Wickens b E Gutsell 1, H Potter not out 0, H Collingham c and b E Gutsell 0, Extras 2 – Total 24.

UPPER DICKER GRASSHOPPERS – L Page b Elphick 1, B Goldsmith c and b Carter 2, E Gutsell c Hymans b Elphick 13, R Hill b Elphick 4, F Deadman lbw 0, George Deadman c Westgate b Elphick 0, S Gutsell c H Potter 16, W Crowhurst c Carter b Elphick 1, A Smith b Hymans 2, G Gutsell not out 1, George Colbran c Carter b Elphick 0, Extras 8. Total 47.

Second Innings – Selmeston and Alciston 35 – Upper Dicker 55."

A match played in 1887 at Hailsham, where both teams had struggled to make more than 30 runs in the first innings, Dicker players had scored 186 for 7 wickets in their second innings leading to a decisive win over Hailsham. In 1891, a letter to the *Sussex Express* from the Upper Dicker Cricket Club shows they were open to play any challenger.

Extract from the *Sussex Express,* dated 19th December 1891:

"NOTES FROM UPPER DICKER

The hon. secretary of our cricket club has succeeded in getting us a splendid new pitch made. Now you first class teams, send in your challenges. We can play you all, but shall have to play the best, now that we have a pitch like a billiard table to play on. What a mistake that the Australians are not coming this year. We wanted a three day fixture with them!

Prospective – Pavilion on the cricket ground."

Anyone doubting their prowess would have to think again when in 1892 Dicker gave a good account of themselves against Heathfield Park.

Extract from the *Sussex Express,* dated 26th July 1892:

"Dicker contested a game with the Heathfield Park Club on Tuesday. The visitors winning the toss went first to the wickets, but were all dismissed for 26, owing chiefly to the deadly execution of B Goldsmith with the ball, who took five wickets for nine runs. S and E Gutsell batted in their usual good style (28 and 20 respectively), and Luther Page soon made his dozen by brilliant play."

Although it was reported in 1891 that the cricket pitch had been levelled, it was not uncommon for the outfield to remain uncut, batsmen who hoisted the ball into the outfield's long grass were able to secure an extra run or two as fieldsman searched for the ball. By the end of the nineteenth century, the Upper Dicker Cricket Club had became well established, playing local adversaries Chiddingly and Chalvington, amongst other teams. In the 1890s the team was captained by Luther Page, with stalwarts B Goldsmith, Fred Norton, Harry Page, Albert Gander, David and Edward Gutsell, D Smith, Will Brett, J Warne, J Wheatley, H Akehurst, W Crowhurst, H and S French forming the nucleus of the team. Jabez Finch, who played for Chalvington and would later play for UDCC in 1899, took nine wickets in a game against their old Dicker adversaries.

Playing for a challenge cup presented by Mr J H Batho (of Alfriston) in 1906, Dicker along with Alfriston, Chalvington, Glynde and Selmeston, became founder members of the Cuckmere Valley League. Although winning their first match against Selmeston by a comfortable margin, five years would pass before Dicker were proclaimed champions of the Cuckmere Valley League.

Extract from the *Sussex Express*, dated 26th May 1906:
"UPPER DICKER vs SELMESTON

This match was played at Selmeston in the Cuckmere Valley League on Saturday, Upper Dicker winning by 107 runs, thanks to the splendid batting of T Watson, who scored 103 not out. His innings included three sixes, six fours and six threes. For the winners, C Clarke took three wickets for two runs.

UPPER DICKER		**SELMESTON**	
W Piper, c Haffenden, b Westgate,	0	G Westgate, ht. wkt, b Watson,	23
A Page, b Potter,	15	J Hayward, b Batho,	3
T Watson, not out,	103	S Haffenden, c A Page, b Batho,	0
F Renison, b Potter,	6	R Turner, c Batho, b A Page,	5
H Page, b Piper,	6	C Cross, b Batho,	1
C Clarke, c Hudson, b Piper,	4	B Hufflet, b Clarke,	16
F Manser, c Turner, b Honnisett,	8	H Potter	0
J Batho, not out,	8	W Honnisett, b Clarke,	0
Extras	8	H Honnisett, b Watson,	3
Total (six wickets)	160	L Hudson not out,	0
(F Oliver, H Lavender and J Finch		P Piper, b Batho,	0
did not bat)		Extras	2
		Total	53"

At the cricket club's 1908 annual dinner at the Plough Inn, a cup was presented to Luther Page for the best bowling average and T Watson received the Lord Michelham Cup for the fourth consecutive year for batting. It was expressed that as Mr Horatio Bottomley had promised to donate a bat to the winnerof the batting trophy.

Typical prices paid in 1908 for almost every cricket requisite was reflected in Watson's advertisement in the *Sussex Express*: bats 7s. 6d or as used by C B Fry 13s. 6d, stumps 3 shillings, leg guards 8s. 6d, batting gloves 5s. 9d a pair and cricket balls from 1s. 9d to 4s. 9d.

By the end of the 1911 season, Dicker had become champions and played the Rest of the League at Selmeston's Recreation Ground, concluding with a dinner at the Barley Mow.

The team's journey to London in September 1913 had probably been the furthest the Dicker team had ever travelled and resulted in an undignified defeat when eight batsmen failed to score a single run.

Extract from the *Sussex Express*, dated 19th September 1913:

"On Saturday, members of Upper Dicker Cricket Club journey to London to play Mr Houston's Eleven, the match taking place at Manor Park, Wanstead. The Dicker team left Berwick Station by the 9.12 train, Mr Bottomley (president of the club), very kindly getting a saloon carriage put on and paying expenses to London. The team was

Upper Dicker, winners of the Cuckmere Valley League   *1911*
From left, standing: David Gutsell, Harry Page, Bert Pitcher, Bert Page, Bert Gutsell, Dick Winter
Seated: Thomas Routledge, Arthur Page, Jack Batho, Charlie Clark, Tom Wheatley
Front: Luther Page, Frank Oliver

met at Victoria by Mr Houston, they journeyed by motor bus through the City to Wanstead, where a capital lunch was in readiness for them. Mr Houston's XI went into bat and scored a 120. The Dicker team on going into bat were all dismissed for the paltry total of 10 runs (only J B Batho and B Page scoring any runs.) On going in a second time the Dicker managed to score 92 runs, (A Page 40 not out). The team reached Berwick about 11.30pm."

Extract from Arlington Parish Council Minutes, dated 17th April 1914:
"Resolved that the Council have no objection to the extension of wood cricket pavilion on the Recreation Ground."

Transport to earlier matches had been by Harry Page's Maxwell lorry. Such style would only have been eclipsed by Mr Bottomley's (no expenses spared) pledge of a saloon railway carriage. Far, far removed from this was when team members elected to walk to neighbouring Chalvington's ground.

World War I brought a temporary cessation to the village game, which by the early 1920s had seen Firle, Chiddingly, South Heighton and East Hoathly enter the Cuckmere Valley League. Over the ensuing decade Dicker won the league in 1919 and again in 1923, 1926, 1927, 1929 and 1930. Competitive league cricket brought about numerous keenly fought encounters.

Extract from the *Sussex Express*, dated 7th September 1923:
"UPPER DICKER WIN LEAGUE

Upper Dicker have secured the championship of the Cuckmere Valley League. The issue was in doubt right up to the last match, which was on Saturday between Upper Dicker and Firle on the former's ground. Firle were half a point ahead of Dicker prior to the game and Dicker won the match by 10 runs, (58 to 48), so putting themselves half a point in front. There was an exciting finish, Upper Dicker requiring four runs to win when their last man went into bat."

Dicker began to emerge as the team to beat; the 1927 averages indicated a core of batsmen who could score runs, bowlers Joe 'Pecker' Brett, Ern Guy and P Guy had taken 233 wickets.

1927 AVERAGES*

	runs	most in innings	average		runs	most in innings	average
Frank Page	489	91	20.37	E Guy	102	17	6.37
P Guy	217	28	9.86	C Parsons	100	21	5.88
Ern Smith	157	40	9.81	F Blackwell	87	16	5.80
J C Thorpe	89	27	8.09	A Harmer	92	28	5.11
J Brett	157	29	7.47	E C Hamper	79	22	4.64
B Guy	74	14	7.40	E Akehurst	17	7	2.83
Ed Smith	154	19	7.33				

*(Also batted – S Guy, G Pettitt, L Cleave, W Hutchinson, G Finch, A Page, Fred Page and J Lee.)"

Uper Dicker. Winners of the Cuckmere Valley League   *1929*
From left, standing: Bill White, Edmund Smith, Eric Akehurst, Frank Blackwell, Alfred Harmer, Frank Page, Ted Hamper, Wilfred Page
Seated: 'Brub' Hare, Joe 'Pecker' Brett, Percy Guy, Arthur Page, Ernest Smith
Front: Ernest Guy, 'Ike' Parry

After his sojourn at 'His Majesty's pleasure' which came to an end in 1927, Mr Bottomley was guest of honour, when he presented the CVL cup to Dicker's captain Frank Page, completing a season when the team had won 11 out of 12 league games.

An important element of the game had been umpires David Gutsell, Tom Smith, Dick Winter and Bill 'old bugger' White. Using the initials of the Upper Dicker Cricket Club, the players would re-assign them as 'Uncle Dick can't come', whenever Dick Winter was unavailable as umpire. Old Bill White gained his nickname during his playing days: after misfielding the field would resound to "old bugger"!

The year 1929 had probably been Upper Dicker's best season when the team won 13 out of 14 league games. At the concluding fixture against the Rest of the League, the Rest were dismissed for 61, and the champions, for whom A Parry hit out lustily to make an undefeated 93, won with a total of 193 for six wickets. Even though Dicker had won the league in 1930 for the fourth time in five years, the club suffered one of its worst defeats in league cricket.

Extract from the *Sussex Express*, dated 12th September 1930:
"CUCKMERE VALLEY LEAGUE
SELMESTON 73 – UPPER DICKER 17
In this match at Selmeston on Saturday, the home team inflicted a surprise defeat on the champions, thanks to excellent batting of J Westgate, backed up by some good bowling. For the Dicker, E Guy took six wickets for 28 runs."

Impervious to Upper Dicker Cricket Club having been champions seven times, the committee elected at the 1932 AGM, not to enter the Cuckmere Valley League in the forthcoming season, and to have only friendly matches. Although they played against one or two stronger teams, Upper Dicker won 11 matches of the 19 played, with their seasoned players, A G Page, Frank Page, Edmund and Ern Smith, Bert, Percy and Ern Guy, 'Pecker' Brett, A Taylor, E C Hamper, Fred Page, E Piper and F Blackwell.

In the days when cricket could not be played on Sundays, bank holiday matches were a feature of the season's fixtures. In a game against Brightling Park on Whit-Monday (2nd June 1933) Dicker scored 224 (W Longley 47, A G Page 40, Frank Page 32, E Piper 31, Ern Smith 25, P Piper 25 and P Guy 13) and 34 for 2 wickets, in reply to Brightling's two innings of 93 and 159. Concluding the 1933 season under captaincy of Ern Piper, 20 games out of 28 had been won, and the Michelham Cup was awarded to Frank Page for the best batting averages.

During the 1930s friendly fixtures were played. At a Parish Council meeting in 1937 it was declared that the Recreation Ground rent would be reduced from 30 shillings to two shillings and six pence per annum. During World War II fixtures were replaced with scratch matches. The changing order of cricket came when clubs began to consolidate a team outside the bounds of the village. At the bank holiday game played on 7 August 1939 when Joe 'Pecker' Brett secured his 100th wicket of the season, the team were J M Askew, A G Page, C J Bremner, F Blackwell, E Piper, Frank Page, C D Bremner, C H Everall, L Page, E Everall and J Brett.

In 1947, Dicker became one of the founder members of the competition for the Oakshott Cup and subsequently beat their arch-rivals, Hellingly, to win the cup in it's inaugural season, (the team were Joe Brett, Ernie Croxton, Bert Guy, George Lavender, Arthur Page, Frank Page, Fred Page, Eric Petch, Gerry Matthews, 'Paddy' Tracey and Walter Matthews).

Pre-war stalwarts Frank Page, Joe 'Pecker' Brett and A G Page were joined by Eric Petch, E Croxton, George Griffin, Tom Winter and George Winter, and by younger players Richard Wise, Maurice Pelling, and later by Brian White and Graham Holter.

In 1948, Arlington Parish Council granted the club permission to extend the pavilion, and cricket could now be played on Sundays. It was said old

Ernest Guy was most indignant when he heard that his son-in-law, Frank Page, intended to play on Sundays. Cricket on Sundays may well have caused alarm to the aging Reverend Elvey and his dwindling congregation. Although prompted to send letters regarding the Sabbath's observance, the reverend gentleman could still be observed watching cricket on a Saturday afternoon.

With the introduction of a gang mower in the early 1950s, batting averages showed a marked improvement, probably in part due to the absence of team censure when balls were lost in the outfield's long grass. John Kilkenny's 146 in about 90 minutes was the clubs highest individual score. In contrast with county cricket grounds, one visitor remarked, "the ground resembles a potter's mis-shaped saucer". Cricketer-cum-groundsman Les Page put in many hours of pre-match time on the pitch.

The annual cricket dinner which had always been integral to every cricket season was held at varying locations. In the early days it was at the Plough Inn, the Parish Room and the Village Hall, but in the immediate post-war years, as with match refreshments, Mrs May Shier had overseen the serving of many of the cricket dinners in the Village Hall.

In 1966, the club were given permission by the Parish Council to extend the pavilion and in 1971 they approved the request to rope off the cricket pitch to avoid damage when not in use. It was also agreed in July 1974 to support the club's application for a new pavilion in view of the forthcoming cricket tercentenary in 1977.

Two tercentenary matches were played against the MCC and Sussex CCC XI on the 20th and 21st August 1977, celebrating cricket "on the Dicker" since 1677. Richard Wise captained Dicker on both days against formidable opponents; the bowling averages of Brian White, Ron Cousins and Les Page were severely savaged as Sussex hammered 22 sixes in an innings of 305 for 7 wickets. Inclement weather brought a premature end to this impressive festival of cricket, and the event was commemorated by a bat autographed by all who played that weekend, now displayed in the "Old Oak" at Arlington. A hand-crafted weather vane made by Les Page and a Maple tree planted by Sussex captain Tony Greig also mark Upper Dicker's link with the tercentennial celebration.

Over a 10-year period, Graham Hobden became the club's most consistent batsman, supported by Mick Baker, Nigel and David Hawkins, Jim Davies and other team members. The 1975 season was crowned by the dual success of Graham Hobden who made over 1000 runs and Brian White who had taken more than a 100 wickets, the first time this double had been achieved by club members.

Through a strong nucleus of players in the 1960s and '70s, the Club had remained competitive in both friendly games and earlier rounds of the

Annual Cricket Dinner held at the Village Hall *1950s*

Upper Dicker
From left, standing: John Page, Terry Brown, Richard Wise, Jim Davis, Mick
Baker, Ray Tookey, David Hawkins
Seated: Peter Message, Nigel Hawkins, Ron Wickson, Les Page, Len Hesling

Oakshott Cup, but the final remained elusive. Following recovery in an earlier round against Waldron, success came when they beat Heathfield Park in the 1985 final. The team were, – Mike Ticehurst, Julian Guthrie, Richard Wise, Graham Holter, Brian White, Ken Tucker, Peter Whitby, Ron Cousins, David Hawkins (capt), Paul Edwards and Steve Carpenter.

Extract from the *Sussex Express*, dated 5th July 1985:

"LONG WAIT IS OVER

Dicker ended a long wait when they received the Oakshott Cup from Mrs Oakshott at Hellingly on Tuesday. They last won the 20 over competition in 1947 but were worthy winners of this season's final against seven times winners Heathfield Park. David Hawkins hit 51 as Dicker made 116 for 5 wickets and then restricted Park to 87 for 7 wickets."

At a Parish Council meeting in 1985, St Bede's School were granted permission to play cricket on the Recreation Ground, in return for help given in the maintenance of the pitch.

In 1991, it was agreed that Upper Dicker Cricket Club should seek to rejoin the Cuckmere Valley League. Sponsored by Peter Owen's Hailsham based business, the club was styled 'Dicker Butterfly'; Peter Owen's youth programme led to teams being entered in the East Sussex Junior League. At the conclusion of the 1998 season, Dicker Butterfly became Cuckmere Valley League (division two) champions. (The team were, Matt Horton, David Tradewell, Ian Bradley, Tim Tutt, David Hawkins, Rhys Terrington, Max Weller, Roland Gardner, Simon Owen (capt) Paul Terrington and Peter Sanders.)

Stoolball

Stoolball had been played by those of the fair sex long before it became fashionable for them to display an ankle in public. As early as 1564, protests had been made to authorities that stoolball and other games were being played on the Sabbath. The Reverend W D Parish (Vicar of Selmeston) refers to stoolball in his book, *A Dictionary of the Sussex Dialect* published in 1875, "An old Sussex game similar in many respects to cricket, played by females". Stoolball clubs were establised in many villages, which not only "provided good exercise for young ladies who might otherwise become lazy, but also promoted kind, social communication among all classes". The game of stoolball which had been referred to "as cricket up in the air", not only became popular with the fair sex but with men and boys. At a match played in Lewes in 1909, it was reported, "eight pairs of trousers played against ten petticoats".

The Upper Dicker Ladies team's earliest reported matches were against Hailsham and Firle Ladies in 1921. Those who played were, M Guy, L Page, R Harmer, Mrs A Page, Mrs Goddard, D Smith, N Guy, S Pearman, M Smith,

Upper Dicker Stoolball team   *1920s*

From left, standing: Tom Henty, Flo Pettitt, Bessie Kingman, Jane Haffenden, Maidie Izzard,
Dolly Smith, Mrs Henty, Mabel Guy.
Seated: Winnie Kingman, Rose Harmer, Ethel Kingman, Lulu Guy, Edith Helyer.

A Shoosmith, S Guy and N Smith. At the 1922 AGM it was decided that
friendly matches were to be arranged with other clubs, and Miss L Page and
Miss R Harmer were elected as captain and vice-captain.

Upper Dicker became one of the founder-members of the Cuckmere
Valley Stoolball League in 1926, and successfully secured the championship in
its inaugural year. At the match played at Dicker on Tuesday 20th July, the
team gained an easy victory over Alfriston. The team were Mrs D Page, R
Harmer, L Guy, M Guy, Mrs Helyer, Mrs F Smith, W Kingman, F Pettitt, Mrs
E Moore, Miss Haffenden and A Shoosmith.

Extract from the *Sussex Express*, dated 1st October 1926:
"UPPER DICKER WIN LEAGUE TROPHY
Upper Dicker cricketers won the Cuckmere Valley League Trophy this season, and the
ladies of the Upper Dicker Stoolball Club has also been successful in securing the cup
of the Cuckmere Valley Stoolball League, a new competition this season. They went
through the season without losing a league match. To wind up the season, the Club
played a match on their own ground on Thursday last week with a team representing
the Rest of the League. The Dicker Club and friends entertained both teams to tea at

the Parish Room, after which, the Rev J T Burns [Rector of Berwick], the donor of the Cup, handed the trophy to Mrs F Smith, captain of the Upper Dicker Club. On behalf of the Club, Mrs Smith presented Mr Thomas Henty a silver mounted walking stick in recognition of his services as umpire during the season."

The 1928 final of the J Thompson-Burns Challenge Cup played at Glynde between Berwick and Upper Dicker, became titanic in the extreme with 269 runs being scored in two limited one-and-half-hour innings, Dicker being victors by one run. Upper Dicker – W Kingman run out 51, B Kingman 12, F Pettitt run out 0, L Guy 32, Mrs D Page 16, R Harmer 3, Mrs F Smith run out, R Hare run out 1, A Grant 5, extras 13, total 135. M Oliver and J Haffenden did not bat.

By 1934, Upper Dicker team had resigned from playing in the Cuckmere Valley Stoolball League, but continued to play friendly matches against other village teams until the war brought a halt to stoolball activities.

Post-war annual meetings held in Park Mead schoolhouse show that a new generation had embraced a love of the game and acknowledged that team members Mrs Green, Mrs Turner, Mrs J Kilkenney, Mrs A Page, Mrs J Fletcher, Mrs D Osborne, and Misses Ann Parker, Iris and Dora Shier, Kathleen and Betty Verrall, Elsie and Margaret Crittenden, Cathrine Fairall, Angela Manley and Susan Finch, had formed the nucleus of the 1950s team.

All semblance of a village-based team had disappeared by the 1980s when a team adopted Dicker's sobriquet and recreation ground for their home matches, and successfully competed in the Red Triangle League and Cup competitions, achieving the double in 1987.

Football

By 1908, the game of football had spread to most villages, the first established game played at Upper Dicker was in 1906.

Extract from the *Sussex Express*, dated 10th February 1906:

"UPPER DICKER vs EAST HOATHLY

East Hoathly visited Upper Dicker on Wednesday last, to play the return match, and again had the satisfaction of winning (4-1). There was a good display of football on both sides, but the winners appeared to show a better combination and defence. Mr Ralph kindly acted referee. One of the players suffered a broken collar-bone. E Penfold, S Bailey (2) and C Potter scored for the visitors and F Lavender knotched the home team's only goal.

UPPER DICKER – A Page (goal), T Wheatley and J Batho (backs), W Hanniford, J Bryan and F Thompson (half backs), Rich, Stephens, Clapson, Bridges and Lavender (forwards)."

Tyldesley and Holbrook placed an advertisement in the *Sussex Express* in 1906s for football requisites indispensable to the game: shirts 20 shillings a dozen, knickers 1 shilling and 9 pence a pair, boots 5 shillings and 4 pence and goal nets, 40 shillings per set.

Extract from the *Sussex Express*, dated 26th February 1909:

"FOOTBALLERS AT TEA

On Saturday, the football match between the Hailsham Athletic Club and Eastbourne YMCA, was played on the Hailsham ground, when the home side won by several goals. The Eastbourne players afterwards cycled over the Hide to the Plough Inn at Upper Dicker, where Mr and Mrs D Gutsell served an appetise tea, before their pleasant cycle run home."

The Hailsham Junior Football League being formed in 1919, Dicker United entered the league the following year and after beating Hailsham II six goals to nil in their first match, probably had sights set on winning the Champion's Shield donated by Horatio Bottomley in 1920.

Dicker United photographed behind Park Mead School
From left, standing: Teddy Cox, George Newnham, Tom Wheatley, Arthur Page, Bill Wright, Frank Page, Fred Griffin, Jimmy Hare.
Kneeling: 'Tich' Crickmere, Fred Knott, Cliff Keeble, Jim Harris, Gurr.

In only their second season of league football, Dicker United and Polegate Comrades had contested the 1921-22 league championship until the season's final whistle. Polegate champions, with the Upper Dicker team runners-up: F

Page (captain), A Page, C Keeble, F Eynott, E Guy, J Crickmere, C Parsons, G Newnham, Ern Smith, W G Wright and A W Jones. Although judged as a successful season, it had been shrouded in controversy when a motor vehicle which had conveyed the Uckfield team and supporters, was tampered with.

Extract from the *Sussex Express*, dated 30th December 1921:

"A DICKER INCIDENT

TO THE EDITOR OF THE SUSSEX EXPRESS

Sir, I noticed you published in your issue of December 23rd, the 'contemptible occurrence' in regard to my motor lorry whilst waiting to convey the supporters of the Uckfield football team from the Upper Dicker match.

Whoever the culprit is he could not have stooped to a more degrading action, causing considerable expense to the owner and to the benefit of nobody. Had he stolen the lorry one could have claimed insurance but as it is, about £15 has to be found by the owner to cover this dastardly action. Although rumours are afloat that the Upper Dicker Football Club were paying for damages, up to the time of writing the only compensation I have received is a report that they have put it in the hands of the police.

Yours truly, W Toye."

The team had a disastrous 1922-23 season; there had been matches cancelled due to a deficit of players leading to a forfeiture of points. Only three league matches were won which probably induced a knock-on effect of a three year defection from league and cup football.

Revived in 1926, Dicker United once again joined the Hailsham League and associated Gwynne and Charity cup competitions. At the conclusion of the 1926-27 season, Dicker became league champions and finalists in both the Gwynne and Charity cups, being beaten by Herstmonceux and Pevensey in respective finals played at Hailsham. Postscript to Pevensey beating Dicker 5-0 in the Charity Cup final had been a condolence card sent to a Dicker player – "In loving memory of DICKER UNITED, who were run over and squashed flat by PEVENSEY, on Easter Monday April 18th 1927." Dicker United team were: A Page, F Page (captain), F Nicholls, E Smith, G Proffit, P Baker, J Fissell, C Pelling, E Rose, E Akehurst and E Izzard. Dicker United 1926-27 league statistics were: played 20, won 16, drawn 2, lost 2; goals for 107, against 27, points 34.

After defeat by Hailsham in the 1929-30 Charity Cup final, league and cup honours for Dicker United were but a distant aspiration. At the club's AGM held on 18th Aug 1930 in the cricket pavilion, the committee agreed to enter the Hailsham League, with Ernest Smith (captain) and Ben Wise (vice captain) for the forthcoming season. It was a disappointing season with only four wins, two drawn matches and nine defeats, and perhaps led to Dicker United abstaining from playing league football from 1931 until the 1938-39 season.

Dicker football field compared favourably with many other village pitches, but had a tendency to cant from one goal mouth to the other, and was muddy during inclement weather. Matches had previously been played on a pitch adjacent to Park Mead School and a field at the end of Henties Lane, and one adjacent to Upper Dicker's Village Hall. The team strip had varied from Bottomley's racing colours (vermillion and black, halved with white sleeves), to blue and white stripes, and the post-war blue shirt and white shorts.

Prior to the start of the 1938-39 season, Upper Dicker Football Club had gained entrance into Division Two of the Hailsham League, and the team were to prove worthy runners-up to the league champions, Magham Down. In the league's Junior Cup they were beaten finalists, two goals to one. (The team were: J Allcorn, P Cleeve, R Hobden, N Wheatley, F L Page, C Harmer, D Fletcher, S Guy, R Ashford, R White, G Matthews, R Francis and Frank Page.)

Extract from the *Sussex Express*, dated 1st August 1947:
"HAILSHAM LEAGUE

The first annual meeting of the Hailsham and District Junior League since the outbreak of the war, was held on Friday at the Coffee House, Hailsham. Eleven clubs signified their intention of joining the league, it was agreed the annual subscription would be raised from 2 shillings and 6 pence to 10 shillings per club. (The clubs were, – Hailsham, Polegate, Herstmonceux, Polegate British Legion, Jevington, Magham Down, Chiddingly, Ashburnham, Horam, Upper Dicker and Dallington.)"

Extract from the *Sussex Express*, dated 26th September 1947:
"THE HAILSHAM LEAGUE AND THE TRANSPORT PROBLEM

The transport problem arising from petrol shortage, was mentioned at a meeting of the Hailsham League on Friday. It was decided to award medals to the runners-up, as well as the champions."

The team's 1947-48 season began and ended in defeats; newspaper reports also frequently described the pitch as being waterlogged and unplayable, with some fixtures being played on opponents' ground. The season's results showed that Upper Dicker had played 22 games – won 3, drew 3 and lost 16, – goals for 38, against 96 – league points 9.

Extract from the *Sussex Express*, dated 25th June 1948:
"PREPARING FOR THE WINTER GAME

Upper Dicker Football Club are already thinking about next season and arrangements were made at the annual meeting last week in the Village Hall, Mr A G Page presiding. The accounts showed a balance in hand of £34 14s. 10d. The Chairman said the club were not very successful on the field but they were in a satisfactory financial position, and if all pulled together, the prospects for the coming season were very bright. There was a discussion on the present playing pitch and it was resolved to re-seed if possible. Efforts are to be made to secure the use of another field for the next season. The committee elected David Fletcher captain for the coming season and Leslie Page vice captain."

During 1949, considerable expenditure had been made on the ground and provision of equipment. During the 1950-51 season centre forward Eb Izzard scored 43 goals out of 116 for the team. The following season the club were winners of the Frank Moore Cup and finished third in the Hailsham League (Div II) – statistics: played 28 games, W20 – D2 – L6, goals for 93 – against 56, 42 points.

Upper Dicker Football Club (winners of the Frank Moore Cup)   *1952*
From left, standing: Gordon Manley, Reg Fox, Sid Guy, George Newnham, Vic Evenden, Bill Newnham, Les Page, Fred Page.
Kneeling: Dennis Hobden, Fred Evenden, Michael Sydercombe, Reg Evenden, Nelson Pelling, Eb Izzard.

Extract from the *Sussex Express*, dated 2nd May 1952:
"FRANK MOORE CUP

For the first time since the revival of the club after the war, Upper Dicker have gained a trophy. They won the Frank Moore Cup on Saturday after a sporting game on Hailsham recreation ground.

During the greater part of the first half, Upper Dicker were the attackers. The East Dean defence had plenty to do but F Fuller in their goal, had good shots to deal with. After 30 minutes R Fox injured an ankle, and although he resumed on Dicker's right wing, he was only a passenger. The only goal of this period was scored eight minutes from kick-off by Upper Dicker. The ball was sent over from the right and E Izzard beat Fuller with a good shot. After the interval, East Dean showed up much better, and R Evenden the Upper Dicker goalkeeper, was tested on a number of times, East Dean levelled the scores midway through the half. R Sands was fouled just outside the penalty area, and from a free kick J Brown shot into the top of the net. This set back rallied Upper Dicker and Fuller had some busy periods. From the right, E Izzard sent the ball across the front of the goal and D Hobden drove the ball over the line. East Dean made several raids in the closing stages but were kept out. The donor of the Cup, Mrs Allcorn of Heathfield, presented the trophy to Upper Dicker captain F Evenden."

Albeit against a depleted team, conceivably the greatest goal tally ever scored on the present ground, was in the 1961-62 season against Hooe II on Saturday 10th March 1962. An ardent village cricket supporter was heard to remark, "Dicker have scored 23 without loss of a single wicket".

Extract from the *Sussex Express*, 16th March 1962:

"HAILSHAM LEAGUE

UPPER DICKER 23 – HOOE II 3

Hooe II went to Upper Dicker on Saturday with only 9 men owing to a last minute demand by their first team. Dicker obtained their seventh double figure and highest score of the season. They opened the scoring after five minutes but Hooe soon levelled. Seven goals were added by Dicker at regular intervals, and just before half time, Hooe scored again, (8-2). Dicker's total had reached 15 about twenty minutes from the end, when Hooe got their third, eight more were put in by Dicker. Their marksmen were, – P Grammer 10, B Taylor 6, M Gosden 3, R Wise 3 and T Frith."

An unexpected sequel to the conclusion of the 1963-64 season had been the Club's intention not to enter a team in the following season's Hailsham League competition, which would end Upper Dicker's long association with the league.

An attempt in 1973 to resurrect the football club lasted two disastrous seasons in league competition but at a meeting held and chaired by schoolmaster Mr Roy Steadman in 1979, it was agreed to rejuvenate the disbanded Dicker football club. Following pre-season fund raising and training, they entered a team in the Sussex Sunday League, and enjoyed moderate success.

In recent years the Village Hall football ground has been used by Sunday League team The Plough.

Cycle Speedway

Post-war Speedway attracted thousands back through the turnstiles, and gave many boys their first experience of the sport, inspiring the fledgeling sport of cycle speedway. Oval tracks modelled on their counterparts at Wembley, New Cross, Belle Vue and at Eastboune Eagles' track at Arlington, were built on inner city bomb sites and any other vacant piece of land. Track bikes were made from spare parts scrounged or bought for a few shillings and a length of inner tube formed a starting gate.

Inspired by visits to watch their favoured Eastbourne Eagles race at the Arlington track, Roy Lancaster, Ron Medhurst and Ron Winter's response in 1947 had been to form a cycle speedway team called the 'Red Hearts' and appropriate the old wartime emergency airstrip on Milton Hide, near Upper Dicker, as a track.

From its inception in 1946, cycle speedway attracted many, and established leagues with rules and fixtures implemented by a board of control. Local teams adopted names like Battle Bulldogs, Broad Oak Aces, Sidley Cyclones and East Hoathly Hornets. By 1949, the Red Hearts had vacated their Milton Hide track and were holding matches on waste ground adjacent to the old Back Lane at Lower Dicker. In response to this move, Upper Dicker Lightnings took over the track at Milton Hide before they too moved to a new track opposite Hentie's shop in Upper Dicker.

1949

Lower Dicker Red Hearts at the Back Lane track
(Due to adverse sunlight, the photograph had to be taken inversed.)
From left: Michael 'Ticker' Parker, John Langridge, Gordon Page, Ron Medhurst

Extract from the *Sussex Express*, dated 2nd September 1949:
"CYCLE SPEEDWAY COMES TO DICKER
If you should see a lad wearing a white cloth breast shield on which is a large blood

red heart symbol, he will be a member of the Lower Dicker Red Hearts. This is the name a group of lads have adopted and they are enthusiastic exponents on the cycling speedway.

At present there are 16 members, their ages range from 13 to 18 years, Roy Lancaster is the captain. The Red Hearts started with a track on Milton Hide, Arlington about two years ago, but they have now made a track on the old London road between Horsebridge and Hackhurst Lane, Lower Dicker. Here on most evenings of the week the lads are practising on their stripped bicycles, no brakes or mudguards, trying to increase the speed at which they can skid round the bends. The circular track is 95 yards (87.6 metres) and the record of 32 seconds for three laps is held by both Ron Smith and Ellaby Martin.

The first match that the Red Hearts had was on Easter Monday at East Hoathly, where by beating the local Hornets, they won the Challenge Cup. They went on to St Leonards for their next match but were beaten by Baldstow Boomerangs 62 points to 46.

On Saturday (28th August), the Red Hearts had their first meeting on their own track, and they obtained revenge against Baldstow, winning 63 points to 45. Top scorers for the Hearts were, – Roy Lancaster 16, Ellaby Martin 11, John Langridge 12, other members of the team were Ron Smith, Gordon Page, Doug Cox, Ron Medhurst and Pete Langridge."

Although cycle speedway had been slow to capture the media's attention, the Red Hearts attracted large crowds to their Back Lane track. High-spirited spectator noise and close proximity to a large house, eventually led to a confrontation with the owner. Despite this, the owners donated the Bruford Best Pairs trophy. Closure of the Back Lane track became inevitable, and a new track was built on vacant ground at Horsebridge near MacDougall's Flour Mills; the team was renamed the Hellingly Lions.

The Lions competed in the 1950 News Chronicle Team Championship and the East Hoathly Challenge Cup which they won, and they raced against the Edinburgh Tourists in July, which attracted a record 350 spectators. Two matches were also contested against arch rivals, with Dick Wise top scorer for the Upper Dicker Lightnings on both occasions. Once again track location and the team's success, courted controversy!

Extract from the *Sussex Express*, dated 4th August 1950:
"CYCLE SPEEDWAY TRACK CRITICISED

The little track at Horsebridge, made and used by Hellingly Lions Cycle Speedway Club, came into some criticism at a meeting of Hellingly Rural Council. In a report, described the track as a public danger, situated on a narrow winding road, people watching proceedings stood on the road, some holding bicycles, occasionally cars drew up, – making conditions very dangerous indeed. The whole thing took place during church hours and was highly objectionable."

Hellingly Parish Council gave permission for a track to be built on the

Lower Dicker recreation ground, which had previously been gifted to the parish in 1926 following a road accident in which a boy was injured while playing in the road.

Extract from the *Sussex Express*, dated 20th August 1926:

"RECREATION GROUND ON THE DICKER

Children living on the main road on the Dicker, now have an excellent recreation ground in which to play and elderly people have a pleasant spot in which to sit. Mrs M E Mason of Temple Court, Reigate, purchased the land, with 300ft frontage to the main road situated between Coldharbour Road and the Dicker Stores, on the south side of the road; has been laid out with trees, seats, a see-saw, double entrance gates, and a large felled tree for the youngsters to clamber over. Mrs Mason has offered the land to the Parish Council with a free conveyance and there were no conditions attached to the gift, except the land should be preserved as an open space or recreation ground."

Following construction of their Lower Dicker track, Hellingly Lions joined the Hastings and District League in 1951, and what now must be perceived as the cornerstone of the Lions illustrious cycle speedway history. During the 1950s the Lions' team had been champions of both the Hastings and Seddlescombe Leagues, "News Chronicle" Sussex champions, winners of the Criterion Cup and Bown Cup, the East Hoathly Challenge Trophy and RAFA Cup, as well as individual championship trophies won by Ellaby Martin, Ron Smith, Ron Medhurst, Gordon Page and Peter Smith.

In 1956, floodlighting was used at the Lower Dicker track for the first time when they rode against London-based teams, Western Broadsiders and Weston Stars.

Early funding and support for cycle speedway had always been difficult. Track bike maintenance necessitated visits to a cycle shop in Hailsham affectionately known as 'Quank and Pweddle' due to the owner's speech impediment, and transport to away matches always presented a drain on limited resources. The removal of rear seats to accommodate the team's bikes in one of Ben Wise's coaches meant there was no problem with transport to the numerous away matches. A financial crisis that plagued Hellingly Lions in 1953 was surmounted by Mr A D Jarvis of Hailsham, champion of many youth organisations in East Sussex, and Mr George Kirby who had been elected chairman at a general public meeting held at the Kings Head, Horsebridge. The meeting and media coverage not only brought about public awareness of this fledgling sport but ensured Hellingly Lions' immediate future, and previous financial problems and loss of track sites were now a distant memory.

By 1959, Hellingly Lions had joined the Southern Premier League, and a year later had entered the British League. At the start of the 1963 season, £50 had been spent on track improvements and repairs at Lower Dicker and a new

Hellingly Lions 1953
From left, standing: Norman Martin, Ellaby Martin, 'Mog' Richardson, Peter Smith, Roy Lancaster, Peter Champion, Ron Winter, Geoff Harris.
Kneeling: Bill Hollebon, George Hollobon, Bernard Smith, Ron Medhurst

set of team colours purchased, and five riders had purchased new track machines, costing almost £150. Tom Killick won both the Sussex Individual Championship, and the Easter Trophy at the Brighton Scorchers track (which had previously been won by Lion's George Hollobon), Hellingly Lions defeated South London Rangers in the final of the BCSF Gold Cup at Bournemouth.

Extract from the *Sussex Express*, dated 20th September 1963:
"LIONS WIN GOLD CUP

The climax to the major team competition of the British Cycle Speedway Federation was reached on Sunday when Hellingly Lions and South London Rangers met in the final of the knockout Gold Cup on the track at Iford Lane, Tuckton, Bournemouth.

Lions sprang a surprise by winning 57 points to 50, for the Rangers had only been beaten once this season in the British League, and the Lions were their victims in two of the encounters. Lions reached the semi-finals stage of the Gold Cup in the previous three seasons. Rangers became the first holders in 1959 and in 1961 were beaten in the final.

As anticipated, it proved a hard fought 18 heat match, a cracking pace being maintained throughout. The Lions took the lead in the third heat with score at 10-7, gained a five point advantage at the sixth and at the interval the score was 29-24. On the resumption, Rangers struck back strongly, and were in front 37-34 at the twelfth heat. In the next heat, the Lions wrested the lead from them and retained it to the end. Tom Killick and John Myles, mainstays of the Lions throughout the season, scored 12 and 11 respectively; George Hollebon and Mick Green each contributed nine, Roy Hazeldene (age 15) youngest member of the team 8, Ron Smith 5, Pete Smith 2 and Mick Martin 1.

The cup was presented to Lions captain Tom Killick by Tony Lewis, speedway star with Poole Pirates. The individual members of the team received pennants."

The demise of many Sussex teams meant the end of locally based leagues. Outside of friendly matches, Hellingly Lions had been compelled to enter a British League, which resulted in longer journeys to race against South London Rangers, Bournemouth Viscounts, Thurrock Racers and Drayton St Leonard Vampires based in Oxfordshire. The defeat of Beckenham Monarchs (64-44) in the Sussex Invitation Cup in October and winning the prestigious Gold Cup brought to an end another satisfactory season for the Lions team. During the winter months a new track surface was laid and a new electric starting gate installed. The 1964 season saw the Supporter's Trophy won for the first time by a Hellingly rider (Tom Killick) and John Myles defeated British champion Ray Chivers in a run-off to win the Champion of Champions trophy on the Hawbush track. In September of that year, Hellingly Lions toured Holland competing in a series of challenge matches. The popular impact of cycle speedway in the 1960s was demonstrated by the press coverage in national newspapers.

In 1970, Hellingly Lions left the British League and underpinned the forthcoming season with entry into the Southern League. They became League Champions after beating Hawbush Hammers 60-47 on Sunday 22nd August (scorers – T Killick 12, J Myles 11, B Weaver 10, D Davidson 9, R Smith 8, G Hollebon 5, L Cox 3 and S Killick 2). The Hellingly Lions again captured the limelight in 1976 when they won the Southern League (Group B) Shield.

Prior to the 1979 season, the *Sussex Express* headline "THE END FOR LIONS", would have brought consternation to cycle speedway's followers. Due to a shortage of riders, disbandment became a serious threat. Following an influx of new riders from a training school held a week before the Lion's match against Beckenham, the Lions sustained a comfortable win in the first match in the new Radio London sponsored league. It was at 'Festival of Sport' held at Southwark, London that Hellingly Lions became the victors in a challenge match against Beckenham Monarchs. The season which started ominously, ended with a heavy defeat by Uxbridge Pirates.

The dearth of riders continued throughout the early 1980s. The 1981

Hellingly Lions 1977
From left, standing: Sam Killick, Tommy Killick, Peter Hamper.
Front row: Alan Boniface, Graeme Smith, David Ford, Charlie Killick, Alan Field

season which had seen them as the league's wooden spoonists, was followed by a season when the Lions only competed in challenge matches. In 1985, the club left the Southern League and entered the British (South East) League. Despite seasons of uncertainty, some team members had been successful in individual events: Darren Prodger had won the Daily Mirror sponsored Southeast region's 1991 Schoolboy Championship; in 1984 Gary Walder won the London Individual Junior Championship and in 1987 Martyn Hollebon became the Daily Mirror Schoolboy Champion, and a year later became the youngest rider to represent England.

On Saturday 2nd May 1987, Hellingly Lions celebrated their 40th season as a cycle speedway club, by beating Hawbush Hammers 91-88, to finish third in the British League (Division three). They were elevated to Division Two due to league restructuring, and with determined and competitive riding by Gary Walder, Tommy Killick, Eddie Ridley, Darren Prodger, Martyn Hollebon,

Hellingly Lions   *1996*
From left, standing Darren Prodger, Zac Parsons, Martyn Hollebon, Steve Collins, Eddie Ridley.
Kneeling: left to right, Phil Holford, Nathan Streeter, Gary Walder

Clive Kidman, Alan Boniface, Matthew Honeyball, Simon Curtis and Mark Cornford, the Lions were runners-up in 1988 and 1989, and won the southern League Cup in 1989.

In the 1990s the Lions continued to compete in the British League until moving to the Southern Premier League in 1998; following a good start to the 1993 season, hopes were dashed of the runners-up spot when they lost 90-88 to Headley Hawks. In 1994, the Lower Dicker track hosted a semi-final of the British Open (Senior) Championship, a year later Hellingly Lions beat Leicester in the Under 21 team final. Following the Lion's first tour in Poland in 1997, there was a winter of uncertainty due to depleted team numbers. Although the Lions had been beaten at home by Exeter Aces, Horspath Hammers and Poole Pirates, the Lions could take heart from their 1998 season. Two major results stand out: winning a last heat decider against a strong Polish side and the shock British Team Cup victory over Wednesfield Aces, before losing to Stoke in the quarter finals.

A disappointing 1999 season resulted in finishing in the league's basement and electing to compete only in challenge matches the following year. Hellingly Lion's survival was much due to manager George Hollebon's stubborn 'never-say-die' attitude and hours dedicated to the track's appearance Experienced riders Martyn Hollobon, Eddie Ridley, Gary Walder and Zac Parsons form the nucleus of today's team and open practice sessions encourage new riders. In 2003, Hellingly Lions had the distinction of not only being the sole surviving Sussex cycle speedway club but the oldest in the United Kingdom. After beating Manchester-based Bury Comets on 31st August the Lions were crowned National League Champions in front of one of their largest crowds. The team were: Martyn Hollobon, Neil Hollobon, Eddie Ridley, Zac Parsons, Joe Plumstead, Barrie Geer, Jamie Cheshire and Alan Boniface.

Chapter 10

THE BOTTOMLEY ERA

One perplexing question: why in 1889 had Horatio Bottomley come to prefer the rural setting of Upper Dicker for his country retreat rather than any other place? Had Bottomley journeyed through this idyllic corner of Sussex by chance, opted to purchase and build on to Crossways House, a diminutive cottage with three acres of land, which in 1881 had been occupied by 72-year-old farmer Henry Cousens from Selbourne in Hampshire? As the name Crossways House suggests, it is situated where four roads converge and central to the village. Bottomley, with no advance consideration or deliberation over expense, built a palatial country residence which he later named The Dicker. At that time, local inhabitants probably frowned upon this large red-brick house built in their midst, and viewed it as an excess for one man, with no conception of what impact Bottomley would have on their rural village.

Horatio Bottomley, during his chequered lifetime, had been a politician, lay lawyer, journalist, newspaper proprietor, racehorse owner, financier and patriotic lecturer; he was born in March 1860 in Bethnal Green, London, second child of William and Elizabeth Bottomley. By 1865, Horatio and his sister Florence had been orphaned following the death of their father in 1863 and their mother two years later. Although Florence was fostered out, Horatio was not nearly so lucky, and was eventually sent to Josiah Mason's Orphanage at Erdington, a few miles from Birmingham, where it was said he made the best of an orphan's lot. At the age of fourteen, having tired of his orphanage existence, he absconded and ran away to nearby Edgbaston and sought refuge with an Aunt Caroline. At an age when most boys were already working, he entered employment as an office boy with a firm of builders in Birmingham, but almost immediately resented being a general factotum. Eager to be nearer to where his sister Florence lived, he returned to London and gained employment with a firm of engravers but again found little aptitude for the work, and became an errand-boy for a haberdasher that specialised in fringes imported from France. Even this failed to appease young Bottomley's urge for something more demanding. His introduction to a solicitor in the City, gave him his first understanding into the ways of law procedures, and a realisation of a natural flair for legal matters. A shorthand course at Pitman's College ensued and at seventeen he became a shorthand clerk with a reputable solicitor off The Strand in the city. As an exemplary employee and with his astuteness as a first-rate law reporter, in 1883 the firm of solicitors took him into partnership, changing the name to Walpole and Bottomley.

While living in Battersea, he fell in love and had married Eliza Norton in 1880. Being a partner in a reputable firm of solicitors should have secured the future for the young Horatio and Eliza, but business aspirations led him into the world of journalism and to start a newspaper; his venture was the Hackney Hansard, shortly followed by the Battersea Hansard. Financial difficulties were thwarted by a merger and he went on to acquire a small chain of newspapers. After further mergers, in 1885, he formed the Catherine Street Publishing Association to parent his chain of newspapers. Later with other business associates, and with a view to financial gains, he reformed the company calling it the Hansard Publishing and Printing Union. In April 1889, the Hansard Union was given a Stock Market floatation and entered the market with a capital of £500,000 but eventually disreputable dealings would send the Hansard Union on a downward spiral to financial disaster. Even though Bottomley secured more capital, rumours were rife in the City regarding the Hansard Union's pending disaster, it became known as the 'Bottomley Swindle'. In the short space of two years, out of a capital of a million pounds, £600,000 could not be accounted for! Although it had been said Bottomley had taken over £100,000, nobody knew where the money had gone, and following the Official Receiver's findings, it was decided to prosecute those thought responsible for the Hansard crash. The case against Bottomley and his associates was deemed as a cast-iron one; after a lengthy trial in 1893, in which Bottomley conducted his own defence, he was found not guilty of fraud. Even though praised for his own brilliant defence, it was suggested he become a barrister, but Bottomley still believed the quickest way to a fortune was to become a company promoter. Already forced to file a bankruptcy petition in 1891, Bottomley would always lack the fundamental qualities for success in business.

Incidental to the inception of the Hansard Union in 1889, had been Horatio Bottomley's purchase of Crossways House in Upper Dicker. The 1889-90 Land Tax schedule already showed Horatio Bottomley as owner of the property. A meeting of the Parish Overseers noted that extensive building work was taking place and value re-assessment was deemed necessary.

Extract from Arlington Parish Minute Book, dated 2nd November 1889:

"Resolved that Crossways House, Upper Dicker, have the assessment raised by the Overseers from £17 gross to £30 gross viz: £26 for the house and buildings, and £4 for the land."

Construction would have continued apace while Bottomley's funds allowed, and local brickyard owners rubbed their hands in anticipation of vast orders of bricks and tiles, unaware of the dubious way in which it was to be funded. At the time of the enumeration of the 1891 Census, Eliza Bottomley's parents were living at Crossways House and her father, Samuel Norton, was employed as caretaker, possibly indicating that building work at that time temporarily denied the Bottomley's of living there.

Apart from his desire for untold financial wealth to support his extravagant lifestyle, it was acclaimed his greatest ambition was to become a Member of Parliament. In 1887 he had stood for the Liberals in the Hornsey by-election but was defeated by a narrow margin by 'Inky' Stephens.

Extract from the *Hornsey Park Journal,* dated 15th August 1889:

"Mr Horatio Bottomley, the Liberal candidate for North Islington, begins as it were his political campaign in a week or two, by holding meetings in the division. So as to thoroughly pursue his candidature he has given up his house at Clapham, and has taken a large house near Islington. The same gentleman, the other day purchased a beautiful residence in a fashionable resort in Sussex."

The reporter seems to have been unfamiliar with the topography of Sussex, and the fashionable resort was, in fact, the small rural village of Upper Dicker!

Although North Islington had invited Bottomley to become their Liberal candidate in the forthcoming general election, due to bankruptcy in 1891, he was forced to resign his parliamentary candidature. This also brought a brief intermission to his overriding passion to extend his country mansion in Upper Dicker.

The discovery of vast quantities of gold in Western Australia in the 1890s would be the lifeline that rescued Bottomley's bereft financial status from the doldrums. Managing to borrow £2,000, Bottomley grasped the opportunity and installed himself as promoter of Westralian mining shares. As investors sought every available share that came on to the market, unscrupulous people were all too ready to float another company to satisfy demand. In just one year Bottomley had floated 23 companies with a capital of ten million pounds, resulting in an enormous profit; in three years he became a very rich man. The *Financial Times* ran a supplement entitled 'Men of Millions', in which Bottomley was named among the magnates.

Bottomley's reconstituted affluence induced a flurry of building activity at Upper Dicker, eager to extend his country residence and cement his desire to build houses to replace some he thought were old and not in keeping with the ideals of his adopted village. By 1899, the old pair of dwellings opposite Pollards Cottage were pulled down and replaced with what became known as Firle House and Carlton House, and Nos 1 and 2 Ivy Cottages. All within the grand design of Horatio Bottomley's grandiose ideals, Crossway Cottages were

Crossways House, Upper Dicker *1890*

The Dicker, palatial residence of Horatio Bottomley Esq *1906*

built, followed by eight terraced houses abutting the two older Elm Cottages. His weakness for spending money in an endeavour to provide modern houses for his workers, were enhanced by ornate green wrought-iron railings and gates. The village roadside verges were planted with coniferous and deciduous trees. Even the old dwelling situated on the corner of Camberlot Road, which he probably deemed as an obtrusive eyesore, succumbed to demolition and was replaced by an orchard. He thought nothing of engaging a taxi in London and instructing the driver to take him to Upper Dicker.

Although he had no real knowledge of racehorses, Bottomley had a genuine passion for the 'sport of kings'. Racing always gave him an excuse to gamble, where he frequently won and lost large sums of money. His career as a racehorse owner started in 1898, with racing colours of vermillion and black halved with white sleeves. He always boasted to the press that his horses were being trained to win both the Grand National and the Derby. The acquisition of Clifton Farm and other land on the periphery of the village enabled Bottomley to build his elaborate racehorse establishment and The Dicker Stud. This was augmented. by an area known as The Gallops where his horses were measured for speed, and a private racecourse near Camberlot Road used for his own private race meetings for his house guests. Managed by Jimmy Hare, The Dicker Stud engaged Dick Fletcher, 'Snowy' White, James Parsons and many others as stable lads. Through his fondness for the local ale, Bottomley's farrier, Charles Pearman was sacked nearly every Friday after a liquid lunch at The Plough but always reinstated when he arrived for work the following Monday! The purchase of horses through his trainer, Harry Batho of Alfriston, brought numerous successes: winning the Stewards Cup in 1899 with 'Northern Farmer', 'Wargrave' won the Ebor Handicap in 1902 and the Cesarewitch in 1904. Some horses such as 'Le Blizon', 'Spendour', 'Gentle Ada', 'Count Schomberg', 'Hawfinch' and 'Adansi' became household names. Bottomley the ever incurable optimist, always expected to win, horseracing was to cost him thousands of pounds a year.

Applauded as the poor man's champion, he supported many worthy causes, and organised excursions for the poorer people of South Hackney and gave Christmas parties for hundreds of children. His burning ambition to become a Member of Parliament and overwhelming benevolence, sealed his candidature for the working class constituents of South Hackney. Bottomley's parliamentary aspirations came to fruition in 1906 when he was elected Liberal member for South Hackney.

Although there had been those who opposed his presence in Westminster due to his unscrupulous past, once within the inner sanctums of the House, he never lost an opportunity to speak or raise questions. By 1908 he had received more press notices than any other back-bench member. Some accolade should be afforded to Horatio Bottomley as suggestions put before the House were later to find their way into the statute book. In 1906 'Bottomley's Betting Bill' must have been irksome to some bookmakers, despite the fact that in the past he had helped to line many a bookmaker's pocket.

Bottomley's continued infatuation with journalism manifested itself in his purchase of *The Sun* in 1902 (not to be confused with today's tabloid), an evening newspaper he believed could be revitalised by specialised narration which would bolster a languishing circulation. The

Horatio Bottomley Esq

circulation improved, but it failed to make a profit, and Bottomley's dire financial plight forced him to sell the newspaper to another proprietor. Forever the optimist, despite the fact he was very hard up, he rebounded with the launch of a new weekly paper called *John Bull*, which would be printed by Odhams. With a circulation of over half a million, Bottomley declared *John Bull* as the pinnacle of modern journalism! Even with its phenomenal success, Bottomley was still plagued by money troubles. In 1906 alone, he had been served with forty bankruptcy petitions but still he remained attached to his extravagant lifestyle. Continued improvements on his Upper Dicker country house, his weakness for companionship of the fairer sex, and horseracing constantly thrust him towards financial dissipation. Probably persistent with his belief that affluent times would return, Bottomley's quest to find new sources of revenue, resulted in

Mrs Eliza Bottomley

Dicker Stud   1920s

Stable lads at the Dicker Stud

an unscrupulous floatation of company shares worth precisely nothing, in the John Bull Investment Trust and the John Bull Agency. Bottomley's third and most sordid money-making phase came to an abrupt end in 1911, when charges were brought in the Curtis versus Bottomley trial. By 1912 Bottomley's financial position was deemed hopeless, and owing to his second bankruptcy, he was forced to relinquish his seat in the House of Commons.

By this time his once diminutive cottage had been extended and transformed to grandiose proportions, with spacious guest accommodation, a library with ivory inlaid panelling and a billiards room, where Bottomley delighted in showing off his skill on the green baize. The domestic offices comprised a kitchen with double oven range, larder and butler's pantry, cellar and stillroom overseen by his butler Louis Flower and cook Mrs Beyfus, with six indoor domestic servants. Bottomley's sumptuous idealism procured the comforts of his London flat into his Upper Dicker residence: hot and cold running water, and a private source of generated electric light with central heating in every room. By 1910 the impressive garden was as opulent as the house; flower borders were surrounded by wide lawns and shaded by trees, sloping down to an ornamental lake and thatched tea room. Within the grounds were stabling and garage premises, a heated conservatory, a tennis court, and a kitchen garden with glasshouses maintained by six gardeners, Edwin Izzard (head gardener), Fred Stone, Fred Tatnall, Percy Parsons, Alfred Hodges and William Piper.

With the grand ambiance of Crossways House and superficial opulence of the landed village squire, Bottomley renamed his country residence The Dicker. Denied his seat in the House of Commons, the postcards sold in the village shop would have required alteration, deleting 'MP' after Bottomley's name to render them correct. Driven out on excursions along the Dicker byways by his coachman Thomas Routledge, Bottomley's notoriety would have preceeded him as bystanders uttered, 'That's Horatio Bottomley'! Benevolence to families and sports clubs had endeared him to everyone who lived in Upper Dicker; he was still on speaking terms with the Reverend Russell – after all, he had presented the church with a new bible and lectern in 1897!

Bottomley still lived in The Dicker even though it had been transferred into the name of his son-in-law Jefferson Cohn. By the autumn of 1912 the weekly circulation of *John Bull* had reached one and a half million and his horse had won the Cesarewitch. Bottomley remained confident he could muster the £233,000 that would annul his bankruptcy and enable him to return to Westminster as MP for South Hackney.

The assistance of a certain Mr Reuben Bigland led to the formation of the John Bull sweepstakes, with a prize of £15,000. The first one was the 1913 Derby and with total receipts of £270,000, once again Bottomley was 'in clover' and making money hand over fist! Other sweepstakes were to follow in 1914, the Grand National, F A Cup and the Derby, but Bottomley along with many other people, failed to anticipate the shattering effects of the 1914-18 war. The war effectively brought an end to Bottomley's lucrative lotteries, clouded by irregularities and deception!

At fifty four, Bottomley had felt the war would open another door of opportunity. he told his friend Henry Houston, who had been his political secretary, 'whatever my faults and failings in the past, I will start again with a clean slate and expurgate old associates and everything that has gone before'. Rumblings of war had brought about Eliza Bottomley's return to The Dicker after her long convalescence in the south of France, but by now he had fallen in love with actress Peggy Primrose.

Even though Bottomley had scooped thousands from his last money-making venture, he was still in the red. Through a series of newspaper articles and the use of *John Bull,* which had in the past debunked people in authority and critcised events believed not in the public's interest, he secured an enormous income through journalism and patriotic lectures. Bottomley excercised an unbridled patriotism throughout the war, with lectures and recruitment meetings; some believed his services would have been better utilised by the government. Still a bankrupt with debts of £233,000, his extravagant lifestyle continued to be a constant drain on his financial resources.

A short while after the Government had introduced the new War Savings Certificates, Bottomley's own War Stock Combination scheme was announced in *John Bull.* The readers responded magnificently, and within a month had subscribed over £80,000 in the scheme. Heavily oversubscribed, unlucky subscribers were given a chance to invest in another of Bottomley's schemes with the winning numbers published in *John Bull,* but not the winner's names. Bottomley was again operating the same racket as he had done with his racing sweepstakes in 1914. Strange as it might have been to some people, he had been fortuitous to have his bankruptcy annulled and he returned as member for South Hackney to the House of Commons.

No doubt buoyed by his return to Westminster and regained affluence, Bottomley was delighted to offer the grounds at The Dicker for the village's victory celebrations.

Extract from the *Sussex Express,* dated 25th July 1919:
"MR BOTTOMLEY ENTERTAINS UPPER DICKER
The inhabitants of Upper Dicker were very fortunate for the expenses of their celebrations were most generously borne by Mr H Bottomley MP, and he also threw open the grounds at Dicker House, where the proceedings of the day took place. A cricket match in the morning between the married versus the single ex-service men, resulted in a win for the former by eight runs. In a barn on the estate at one o'clock the ex-service men and their wives, numbering nearly 70 were entertained to a

capital dinner. Mr H Bottomley who presided, proposed the health of the men and welcomed them back from their successful campaign. Others present at the dinner, included Mrs Bottomley, their daughter (Mrs Cohn), the vicar (the Rev G M Russell, who was chairman of the Celebrations Committee), Mr C E Morrison (of Camberlot Hall), Major Morrison and Lieutenant Morrison. At 2.15, the grounds were opened to the whole parish, and a fine programme of sports for adults and children was carried out. A company of about 400 sat down to tea, and the prizes were given by Mr C E Morrison, and were presented to the successful competitors in the sports by Mr Bottomley at eight o'clock. Mr A Page had acted as secretary to the Committee."

In 1919, Horatio Bottomley had expressed his desire to purchase the Parish Room with a view to extending the building or to build a new Memorial Hall, which would stand as a lasting memorial to the fallen of the village in the First World War. Although Lord Sackville and the Reverend Russell entered into the spirit of this kindly offer, an earlier 'trust property' proviso terminated further negotiations, and Upper Dicker was denied a new village hall.

Financial disaster was never far away. When the government issued Victory Bonds at £5 each, making them too expensive for most people, Bottomley decided to launch his Victory Bond Club that would offer the small investor a chance to buy one fifth bond shares for £1 with a chance to win a fortune!

Unfortunately Bottomley's hastily drawn up prospectus was to fall short of it's promises and obligations. Mismanagement and hopeless organisation could not cope with the Victory Bond Club boom, receiving cash at a rate of over £100,000 a day, which surpassed even Bottomley's expectations. Ex-servicemen, maiden ladies and domestic servants began to realise that the Victory Bond Club had been a colossal swindle, and masses of subscribers demanded the return of their capital, which they were entitled to do. The lack of organisation meant many subscribers failed to be reimbursed, whereas some were overpaid.

Again Bottomley pressed the self-destruct button; with no free capital of his own he purchased two failing newspapers for £41,500, and took a lease on St Martin's Theatre financing stage shows in an attempt to make Peggy Primrose into a leading lady. If the truth were known, she had neither the talent nor experience.

The Victory Bond Club lurched toward financial disaster, and fifty thousand subscribers who had been rash enough to invest in Bottomley's newly contrived Thrift Prize Bond Club realised that their money was only to keep him afloat. At the same time as newspapers covered his unscrupulous share trading, Reuben Bigland publicly exposed Bottomley as a swindler, who had duped poor subscribers of their savings and fraudulently converted them to his own use. It was inevitable that Bottomley would be subject to a receiver's investigation and eventual committal for trial at the Old Bailey.

Committed before Mr Justice Salter following 24 indictments of fraudulently converting funds from the War Stock Combination scheme, the Victory Bond Club and the Thrift Prize Bond Club, Bottomley's trial opened on 19th May 1922 at the Old Bailey, which alleged a defalcation of £170,000 from invested funds. Conducting his own defence, his endeavours to persuade the judge and jury he was not the villain people made him out to be, held no sway with the court. Found guilty, Mr Justice Salter sentenced Bottomley to seven years penal servitude. A man who had aspired to journalism immediately became front-page news in both national and provincial newspapers.

Extract from the *Sussex Express*, dated 2nd June 1922:

"HORATIO BOTTOMLEY

The news of the result of the trial of Mr Bottomley was received at the little village of Upper Dicker, where he was the local squire, with profound regret. It was over thirty years ago that Mr Bottomley purchased a house there and had it enlarged, and has ever since then used it as his country seat. Attached are many acres of ground and garden, and just before the war he had a race course of over a mile in length laid, he also erected extensive racing stables. Mr Bottomley built numerous cottages for his work people. On Sunday, Mr Bottomley had motored down and visited his wife and daughter (Mrs Cohn), at The Dicker, and commenced the return journey to London soon at six o'clock in the evening."

The Upper Dicker populace were stunned by their benefactor's incarceration. Charabancs which had brought daytrippers to the village where Horatio Bottomley lived were less frequent, even though Clifton Farm laid claim to the final resting place of the German submarine *Deutschland* (albeit only the conning tower section). The submarine which had fulfilled her wartime role and was subsequently handed over to Britain after the armistice and exhibited around the country, was eventually acquired by Bottomley for £15,000 of Victory Bond Club subscriber's invested money. Tragically, while being dismantled at Birkenhead in 1920 an explosion of gas cylinders resulted in the deaths of five apprentices.

At the time of Bottomley's incarceration, with little money to pay wages, hardly any staff remained at The Dicker or at the Dicker Stud, both manager Jimmy Hare and head stablelad Jack Crichmere contemplated their future once the horses had been sold.

Extract from the *Sussex Express*, dated 21st July 1922:

"MR BOTTOMLEY'S HORSES SOLD

By order of the Receiver (Mr Ernest James FCA of London) in the action of J H Hare (trainer) versus Mr H W Bottomley, in the Chancery Division of the High Court, the stud of bloodstock at Upper Dicker Stables, was sold by Messers Langlands and Sons of Epsom, on Monday afternoon. There were 17 lots, ten horses in training (including several winners of many races), 5 brood mares and foals, a stallion and a colt. There were very few buyers present, top price was paid for "Narcesh" 630 guineas. The sale raised £2,000."

Extract from the *Sussex Express*, dated 11th April 1924:

"MRS BOTTOMLEY SUED

COST OF WORK ON DICKER ESTATE

In the Kings Bench Division on Monday before Mr Justice Branson, a case was heard in which Mrs Eliza Bottomley of Crossways House, Upper Dicker, wife of Mr Horatio Bottomley, was defendant.

A claim was brought by Mr Alfred Durrant, trading as A Pettitt and Son, Builders and Contractors, of Alfriston, to recover £5,180 18s. 3d, alleged to be the balance of an account for goods sold and work done for the defendant on The Dicker estate between June 1913 and June 1922.

Giving evidence the plaintiff, who was represented by Mr A S Comyns Carr, said that since 1911 he believed all accounts had been rendered in Mrs Bottomley's name. Before he issued the writ, Mrs Bottomley offered to do what she could to help him. The proceedings, he said, were not being taken out of any animosity to Mr and Mrs Bottomley, he had to do it to cover himself.

From 1912, accounts for work done on The Dicker estate were rendered by Mr Elliott (estate manager) in the name of Mrs Bottomley. After Mr Elliott ceased to be manager of the estate, Mrs Bottomley had given orders for work done since that sued for. Only on Saturday last, Mrs Bottomley told the plaintiff that the case had come on to the list rather suddenly, and she had hoped to settle it before coming to trial.

Mrs Bottomley said she had never authorised Elliott to give any orders for work on the estate, nor did she authorise her husband to give orders for the erection of new cottages. She had never received an account in connection with any of the work sued for, nor had she made any payments in connection with the work. Cross examined by Mr Comyns Carr, Mrs Bottomley said she had received the ground rents of the cottages. Mr Pettitt recalled that the cottages were first occupied by employees at Mr Bottomley's racing stables, as a result, the cottages erected had become her property. By allowing the cottages to be built, Mrs Bottomley had ratified the orders given by Elliott, as her agent and in her name. His lordship therefore gave judgement for the plaintiff for the amount claimed, with costs."

The cottages, which became known as Stud Cottages, were built at a time when Bottomley was again fighting to stave off creditors with dwindling financial resources. Construction was to take five years to complete and they were affectionately referred to within the village as Bankruptcy Row. In March 1923, Bottomley had been declared bankrupt for the third time.

Bottomley had been recognised generally as unscrupulous and devious when it came to funding his own ideals and aspirations. He was moved from Wormwood Scrubs to Maidstone Prison where he had become a model prisoner, befriended by warders and prisoners alike. Mr Harold Thickbroom, who superintended the prison's printing and book binding shop where Bottomley worked moved to Upper Dicker on his retirement and undertook the role of tobacconist and confectioner. Also beguiled by Bottomley's generous charisma, Jack Morris who had served time for his wife's manslaughter, gained employment as the village's roadman and resided with Mrs Pettitt at Devon Cottage opposite the Recreation Ground.

Rumours circulated long before Bottomley's release from prison, and folk in the small village of Upper Dicker had talked of a gala reception, houses decorated with flags and banners, and Hailsham Town band to welcome him home. In view of his good conduct, Bottomley's clandestine release from Maidstone Prison on 29th July 1927, had caught the villagers off-guard.

Extract from the *Sussex Express*, dated 5th August 1927:

"MR BOTTOMLEY'S RETURN

HOW UPPER DICKER WELCOMED HIM

Upper Dicker was roused to a state of great excitement on Friday, when it became known that Mr Horatio Bottomley had returned home to his country residence 'Dicker House'. Mr Bottomley was sentenced to seven years' penal servitude at the Central Criminal Court on 29th May 1922, and had served just over five years of that period. His arrival at Upper Dicker was quite unexpected by the villagers, the general impression being that he would be released from Maidstone Goal next Tuesday.

At 8.50am, on Friday, a large blue saloon Rolls Royce motor car of which the sole occupant with the exception of the chauffeur, was Mr Bottomley, drew up at the front door of "Dicker House". Mr Harry Haffenden, one of the employees on the estate, who happened to be walking along the road at the time, was the first to see his old employer, and quickly spread the news of his home-coming through the village. Mr Bottomley was welcomed at the door by his wife and Mrs Cohn, his daughter, who had been notified by telephone a short while before.

Flags soon made their appearances in the village, being displayed out of cottage windows, tied to garden railings and hung on trees. A large Union Jack was put out from the balcony over the front door of "Dicker House". Throughout the day, there were large numbers of people in the vicinity of the house, including many London Press representatives and photographers, who hoped to get a glimpse of Mr Bottomley, but they were disappointed. Groups of school children carrying flags, and sightseers, brought out from Eastbourne in motor coaches, swelled the throng. Mr Bottomley was not seen in the village during the weekend."

After it became more generally known of Horatio Bottomley's homecoming, cars and charabancs conveyed scores of curious sightseers out to Upper Dicker, in the tentative hope that they may glimpse the notorious Bottomley, or at least see where he lived!

Extract from the *Sussex Express*, dated 30th September 1927:

"MR BOTTOMLEY'S FETE

UPPER DICKER RESIDENTS ENTERTAINED

To celebrate his homecoming, Mr Horatio Bottomley entertained all the residents of Upper Dicker to a fete in the grounds of his residence "Dicker House", on Saturday afternoon and evening. The guests numbered over 300, the majority of whom were Mr Bottomley's tenants. Mr and Mrs Bottomley received the guests, and with their daughter Mrs Cohn, were present throughout the proceedings. The fete was capably organised by Mr A H Clapp (agent to the Dicker Estate), the various events following upon one another without an interval and interest was not allowed to wane. Except for one shower, the weather was fine. Those who were paying their first visit to Mr Bottomley's residence greatly admired the fine house, the extensive grounds and the large lake with it's island summerhouse.

The Hailsham Town Band conducted by Mr Percy French, played selections on the tennis courts. A programme of sports was carried out during the afternoon. No one was successful in climbing the greasy pole. (The prize winners were as follows – Egg and Spoon, Mabel Guy; 60 yards flat race for married ladies, Mrs Crickmere; 60 yards flat race for single ladies, Lulu Guy; Pick-a-back battle, C Pettitt and B Davis; Blindfold tandem race, Eric Akehurst and Winnie Kingman; Cycle Obstacle race, A Hills; 100 yards flat race for men, Eric Akehurst; Potato race for ladies, Mrs Fletcher; for men Louis Cleeves, Pole pillow fight, C Pettitt; Sack race, R Fletcher.)

A sumptous meat tea was served in a large marquee, at which Mr Bottomley resided. After the repast, the host expressed the great pleasure it had been to him, his wife and daughter to welcome the residents of Upper Dicker there that day. On behalf of the guests, Mr F Pettitt thanked the host and hostess for their welcome and hospitality.

A concert followed in another marquee, which included several popular items given by Eastbourne artistes. Then came dancing on the hard tennis court which was illuminated with fairy lights. The Hailsham Town Band provided the music. The grand finale was a display of fireworks at nine o'clock, being set off from the bank of the lake."

Despite rumours that the caterers for Mr Bottomley's 'welcome home celebration' had not been paid, his rapturous return had taken immediate effect. Men still doffed their caps in passing and the villagers still feted him as their 'benevolent squire'. Imprisonment had neither dulled his own social acceptance nor his oratory prowess whenever the opportunity presented. Saturday 17th September 1927 saw Bottomley to play host to over a hundred Eastbourne pensioners at an informal gathering in the grounds of Dicker House, and later in the day he was an interested guest and spectator at the cricket match on the Recreation Ground between Upper Dicker (champions of the Cuckmere Valley League) and The Rest; tea, the trophy and medals presentation followed in the Parish Room.

Following a series of newspaper articles for a substantial fee of £12,000, Bottomley believed he could restore his depleted

UPPER DICKER
FÊTE.
(To celebrate Mr. Bottomley's Homecoming.)

ADMIT BEARER

To Grounds of The DICKER HOUSE,
Saturday, September 24th, 1927,
AT 2 P.M.
ENTRANCE AT SIDE GATE.

coffers but his reputation had gone before him. The failure of his planned grand lecture tour, the demise of Bottomley's latest newspaper venture called 'John Blunt' and the settlement of damages and costs of court action for libel brought by Sir Arthur Conan Doyle in October 1929, had forced Bottomley into bankruptcy for the fourth time. Consequential to this last bankruptcy, Bottomley lost his cherished Dicker mansion and estate for ever, to his son-in-law, Jefferson Cohn in defrayal for many unresolved debts. Although Bottomley had hoped to pay all his outstanding debts in full, in 1930, he had neither the revenue or resources. Debts amounting to £112,048, including £109,984 outstanding from his 1922 bankruptcy proceedings and a claim for £50,000 in respect of income tax, were never settled!

The village were stunned by the tragic death of Alfred Clapp on the morning 7th February 1930, whilst rabbit shooting on the Dicker estate, and then Mrs Eliza Bottomley's death the same afternoon. Practically all the villagers were present at the two funerals held at the Holy Trinity Church, Upper Dicker, the same six employees on the estate acting as pallbearers: Messers R Fletcher, T Finch, E Izzard, H Haffenden, F Page and P Parsons.

A short while after her mother's death, Mrs Florence Cohn who had resided at the White House, Upper Dicker, married Charles Gilbert Moreland at Eastbourne Register Office and moved to a new life in South Africa.

Bottomley had always sought and enjoyed the company of the fairer sex, but as his world teetered and crumbled, it was Peggy Primrose who had become the 'love of his life', who gave solace and companionship when most had turned their backs on him. The loss of his beloved Dicker House and the humiliation of coming to the end of his resources, had left him a broken shell of the man he once was. Following a heart attack, Bottomley's health deteriorated. Peggy Primrose remained his constant companion while he was in the Middlesex Hospital, where he died on the 26th May 1933.

News editors worldwide sensed the magnitude of his death, and from the Yorkshire Post, the Herald in Melbourne to the New York Times, they gave instant print coverage on the life and times of Horatio Bottomley.

Extract from the *Daily Mail*, dated 29th May 1933:
"On the death of Horatio Bottomley, reflected –
What opportunities he had, but how sadly they were wasted. His gifts were brilliant. He had personal magnetism, eloquence, enthusiasm and power to convince. He might have been a leader at the Bar, a captain of industry, a great journalist. He might have been almost anything, but for one fatal defect, known for a better word as "kink", which misdirected his efforts."

Extract from the *Daily Express*, dated 27th May 1933:
"Upper Dicker is a village of mourning; 'the Squire' has passed on.
For nearly forty years, up till the death of Mrs Bottomley in February 1930, the squire and his wife had lived at The Dicker, a large mansion standing in well wooded

Residual of staff who worked on the Dicker Estate in 1930
From left, standing, unknown, unknown , Ted Izzard.
Seated: Horatio Bottomley, Edwin Izzard, Tom Wheatley, Will Crowhurst, Louie Flowers.

grounds in one of the most beautiful parts of the Sussex Weald. To the villagers Bottomley was a hero, and his ups and downs in the financial world, and even his conviction, failed to shake their faith in him. When he returned from prison in July 1927, every flag that could be found was put out. At one time he owned practically the whole village, including a private race-course, and large racing stables.

At the present time 'The Dicker' is occupied by Major Maurice Cohn, a brother of Capt. Jefferson Cohn, the former husband of Mr Bottomley's daughter, Florence."

After Horatio Bottomley's funeral at Golders Green Crematorium, his ashes were scattered by Peggy Primrose on the gallops at Alfriston, where many of Bottomley's racehorses had been trained. The inhabitants of Upper Dicker felt bereft of their patron, many overlooked his disreputable past, and remained perpetually loyal to his name.

Even though Clifton Farm and some estate houses had previously been sold, the death of Major Maurice Cohn in May 1937 brought about the sale of the remaining portions of The Dicker Estate at the Crown Hotel, Hailsham, the following year. The conclusion of the sale held on Wednesday 23rd November 1938, when Dicker House, the Dicker Stud and enclosures of pasture, Stud Cottages, the detached house known as Shermans, The White House and the shop/bakehouse were sold, effectively brought an end to the 'Bottomley Era'.

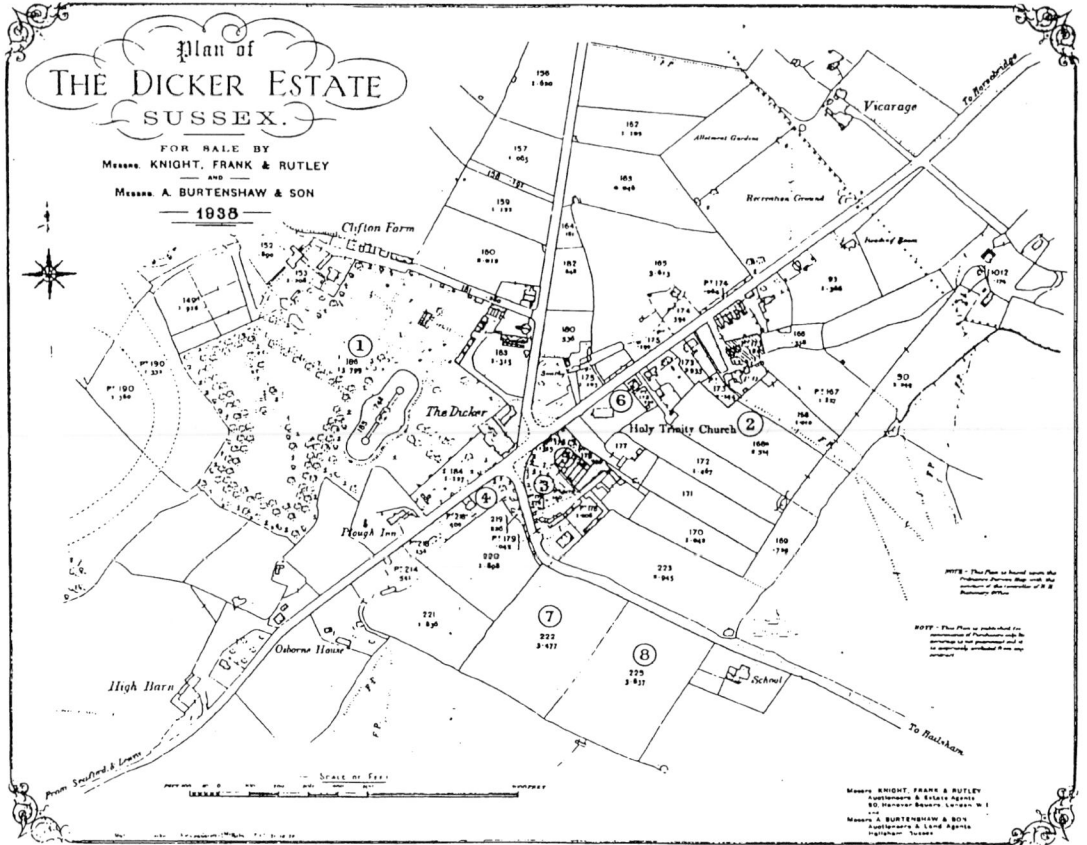

Reference to Lot numbers and associated property or land

Lot 1	*The Dicker, freehold residence with 17 acres of gardens and grounds.*	*Lot 4*	*Shermans*
		Lot 5	*The Stud Cottages.*
Lot 2	*The Dicker Stud and stables.*	*Lot 6*	*Shop and Bakehouse.*
Lot 3	*The White House.*	*Lots 7 & 8*	*Enclosed pasture.*

Chapter 11

A VILLAGE IN WARTIME

For those who had witnessed the horrors of the 1914-18 war, another world war would have been beyond comprehension. Most people blinkered themselves against the possibility of yet another war with Germany. Upper Dicker's populace were probably cocooned in the belief that nobody would drop bombs on them, thoughts in 1938 were more about the cricket season, dances held in the Village Hall or the current film showing at Hailsham's Pavilion cinema. But modern aerial warfare would make this one different. The *Sussex Express* reported in 1938 that "the importance of hurrying on with the work of air raid precautions and emergency fire brigade measures in view of the present international situation was imperative", and confirmed 40,000 respirators (gas masks) for the district had been delivered and were stored at Polegate.

Chief Warden Mr John Duncan of Oldways House, Upper Dicker, informed members of Arlington Parish Council at the October meeting, that all Air Raid Precaution arrangements had been implemented and gas masks issued. The necessary wardens had been enlisted and taken up their duties in the village.

With air raid precautions and other emergency measures in mind, Sussex Constabulary increased its force by one inspector and five sergeants. At Hailsham's Petty Sessions, Eric Bick, George Early and Thomas Wickens (of Chiddingly), Arthur Page (Upper Dicker), Don Martin, William Pearce and Percy Piper (Lower Dicker) were sworn in as 'part-time specials' (Special Constables) and were thanked for offering their services.

Aimed to test the efficiency and skills of different emergency services, the Civil Defence exercise held in July 1939; with simulated incidents caused by enemy bombers at Heathfield railway Station, a serious fire at Burfield's factory, another fire in Church Lane at Ninfield, and other bomb-related incidents at Wilmington, Herstmonceux and Rushlake Green. The success of the exercise re-assured the local populace all was in hand if the 'balloon went up'!

On Tuesday 6th June 1939, members of the Women's Institute enjoyed their annual summer outing to the Military Tattoo at Aldershot, whilst on Friday 30th June, the Church Sunday School children travelled by coach for their summer treat on Eastbourne's seafront (soon to become a restricted area fortified by dannert wire and anti invasion obstacles). Many were drawn to Bertram Mills Circus touring Sussex, on Saturday 12th August, and spectators had been captivated by the flying skills of German acrobatic star Vera von Bissing at Wilmington's Air Pageant. Even though an uneasy peace prevailed the social calendar was under threat.

Government directives galvanised people's awareness of public safety in the event of war. Dicker citizens became pre-occupied by the requirements imposed by blackout restrictions, and rushed to the shops to purchase blinds, curtains and blackout paint to prevent windows from emitting light at night. The blackout dramatically transformed the nocturnal landscape: the village had no street lighting and no re-assuring friendly lit window to guide the wayfarer – how was old 'Shoppey' Akehurst expected to walk home from the Plough on Saturday night? Vehicle drivers were permitted initially to use only sidelights, and this brought dangers and a sharp rise in road accidents, many with fatal consequences. The *Sussex Express* reported, "A road accident occurred near Golden Cross (on the Dicker road) during blackout on Saturday (8th July 1939), when Arthur Holloway of Nash Street, Chiddingly, was struck by a car causing fatal injuries and died in Princess Alice Hospital, Eastbourne."

The government's evacuation of two million people from London meant Upper Dicker's Reverend R C Filler would have more than parochial duties to think about. As Assistant Billeting Officer for the parish he was responsible for compiling a survey of houses listing number of rooms and occupants suitable to accommodate evacuees, prior to the proposed mass evacuation from cities thought vulnerable to bombing. On the strength of the survey, the parish's Chief Billeting Officer Mr W Pickard, could expect to receive 150 evacuees at the three reception centres, Upper Dicker Village Hall (60 evacuees), Arlington Hut (55) and Milton Court (30).

Within the fire service, part-time auxiliaries provided increased manpower for sections in rural locations. The brick and tile constructed shed adjacent to Pensons Grove Farm was designated as Lower Dicker's 'fire watch headquarters', affiliated to Hailsham Fire Brigade. Dicker's part-time auxiliaries were men of reserved occupation or too young for military service, divided into three squads, giving continuous nightly fire watch cover for the immediate area. The light, manually-operated pump conveyed behind Tom Adams' car, was basic and rudimentary. Fire practice was carried out at nearby Dicker Pottery where enthusiasm outshone fire-fighting skills, and where starlings and sparrows were assured an involuntary bath in the name of practice. More serious fire drill instruction came when they linked up with the Hailsham brigade.

At night, when German bombers droned overhead on their way to

London, Tom Adams' over-zealous nature at times countered common sense, and he would have had Dicker's auxiliaries present at every incident in the county! Les Winchester proclaimed later, he had only joined for the free issue wellington boots, but it was said Tom Adams had volunteered to evade his wife's sharp tongue and constant castigation.

LOWER DICKER FIREMEN

Thomas Adams	Rodney Colbran	Aubrey Dann
'Jock' Fowlie	Alan Funnell	H French
John Izzard	Robert Izzard	Edward Lancaster
Reuben Medhurst	Alan Parsons	Ernest Smith
Alfred Staplehurst	Leslie Winchester	

Defending home and village against fire from enemy bombing captured the imagination of men and women of Upper Dicker. Volunteers formed a band of fire watchers, and patrolled the village in pairs on staggered two-hourly patrols, from twilight till dawn. Armed with only stirrup pumps and buckets, and a limited source of water from wells, their night-time vigil would have been more important than valour. The danger from incendiary bombs had long been realised before the advent of war. Due to its location and visual prominence over the surrounding landscape, Coldharbour Mill was also used for fire watch duties.

UPPER DICKER FIRE GUARD

Rev R C Filler	Mr Colman	John Duncan
Mrs Fletcher	Frank Finch	Miss N Gander
Mrs Gray	Mrs D Page	Mr E Stephens
Albert White	Miss K White	

Embraced by thoughts of another war and one that brought fears of bombing, Dicker residents responded to the call for volunteers, bringing a sense of community togetherness. By sheer coincidence Hailsham's Pavilion cinema had been showing *All Quiet on the Western Front*; nothing could have been further removed from the present uneasy peace which prevailed. Fred Tatnall who lived at Plough Cottages, had been gassed and witnessed the carnage of the 1914-18 war, and was able to reflect on the travesties of another war.

On Saturday 2nd September 1939, the distinctive wail of Hailsham's air raid siren would have been heard as it was tested for the umpteenth time. Upper Dicker cricketers were playing against Chalvington on the Recreation Ground, and Holy Trinity's lone church bell heralded the wedding between Lilian Henty and Gordon Manley. Village events were eclipsed by the arrival of sixty evacuees the day before.

The Village Hall was the centre for Upper Dicker's intake of evacuees from the New Road School in Rotherhithe. For some this was a great adventure but for others, frightened by this strange environment, Dicker was a strange place away from London's East End. Overseen by Reverend Filler and aided by ladies of the village, the evacuees were billeted with families in and around the village; for twelve of them their adoptive home would be Stud House; twenty evacuees were placed in the grand *mise en scene* of Michelham Priory. The evacuee influx was a prelude to the invasion of Poland and Britain's declaration of war with Germany on Sunday 3rd September, and it had more than doubled the village's young population.

Extract from the Park Mead School log, dated 18th September 1939:

"School re-opened today having been closed an additional two weeks owing to the outbreak of the war and arrangements having to be made for the number of evacuees. A number of boys, a few girls and infants from New Road School, Rotherhithe, are using the school with four teachers. At present the Headteacher (Miss E M Rogers) of this school has her own class in the north classroom (formerly used as dinner and playroom), the three Rotherhithe Masters use the south classroom with five dual desks and borrowed tressle tables and chairs, both sets of infants are using (Mrs Farrant's) the Infant room. Room for all is very limited, especially in the Infant room and lobbies."

The evacuation had witnessed 2,756 children, and 1,727 mothers and infants accommodated within the bounds of Hailsham's Rural District; the influx taxed both billetters and schools. Even though a billetter received from the state ten shillings and six pence for the first child, they failed to comprehend the cultural shock of an evacuee thrust involuntarily into an alien rural village. Park Mead's headmistress, Miss E M Rogers, complained about lack of space and constant noise in classrooms, and later recorded in the School Log that "books and furniture used by the London School are in a much worse condition than before". Evacuee contact with country ways produced bewilderment: water drawn from a well and the privvy down the garden where boldness was required on a dark winter's night. When told that manure was put round rhubarb, an evacuee proclaimed they had custard with theirs! For two Rotherhithe boys billeted at Michelham Priory, seated awaiting tea at a large family table for the first time, one observed to the other, "Cor blimey, same pattern on all the blinking cups and saucers". Dicker was indeed a world far removed from Rotherhithe.

The war became the sole topic of conversation; the Parish Council agreed to purchase a quantity of sand for use in event of fire caused by 'aerial activity' and kept at Upper Dicker. Identity cards and ration books already issued, householders were advised to prepare a refuge room, tape windows against the effects of bomb blast and adhere to the blackout restrictions. Cyclists were still found flouting the law; Ernest Baker of Chiddingly was apprehended at 7.30 by PC Edgar Heard at Lower Dicker, and subsequently fined ten shillings for

Evacuees billeted at Michelham Priory

Spring 1940

not having a rear light.

Young men being called for military service had cast a hesitancy on the forthcoming football season, but war or not, Dicker sustained a resemblance of social normality. Barriers between evacuees and local children were dismantled by rural pursuits of conkers and a game called 'golden rod' which involved a stick and cow-pats. Evacuee John Young was captivated by the countryside and wildlife, and his first experience of seeing a hoar-frost. There was an evening of staged 'entertainment' on Thursday 30th November (1939), in which some evacuees took part. The Christmas party for both evacuee and local children on Friday 29th December, given by Mr and Mrs R B Wright of Michelham Priory and weekly whist drives, bore witness that some village social life remained unaffected.

Hailsham's air raid siren tested at 10am on 6th January 1940 gave little solace to those living in the area; Lilian Madge of Lower Dicker, regretted her carelessness after apprehension by PC Edgar Heard for cycling without lights and colliding with a passing motorist at Horsebridge. She was subsequently fined £1. Mrs Pratt took issue with the local constabulary after a haystack at Boship Farm had been damaged by a mysterious fire, assuming children were to blame.

In January 1940, Sussex witnessed the most severe weather conditions in decades when the county was blanketed with up to eighteen inches of snow, isolating towns and villages. Immense snowdrifts blocked both Coldharbour and Camberlot roads; the wholesaler's lorry and Southdown bus were denied access to the village, Mr Kelly's antiquated canvas-roofed charabanc would have certainly sputtered disapproval at the snow-covered roads. Park Mead School log recorded only 13 pupils were present on 29th January, and the coke supply had been almost exhausted. Tortuous road conditions delayed the funeral of Mrs Bertha Dudley at Upper Dicker on 25th January; snow also impeded those who had braved the elements and enjoyed an evening of cinema films presented by Mr John Duncan in the Village Hall. All press coverage of the weather was censored for fifteen days for fear it would be of value to the enemy; if Hitler had intended to invade, an abundance of shovels would have been necessary. The spectacular ice-storm that followed, encased the landscape in ice, telephone poles and wires snapped under its immense weight, birds were frozen to branches, the weather would have outdone the war as the main topic of conversation!

Food rationing was introduced in January 1940, with Britain's need to be more self-sufficient regarding home-grown foodstuffs. The County War Agricultural Committees were reinstated and the Womens Land Army (Land Girls) reformed. The 'Dig for Victory' campaign encouraged food production from gardens and allotments, and the Rev R C Filler sanctioned that the

1941-42

Black Barn Farm, Lower Dicker
From left: Phyllis Morton, Fred Medhurst, Viv Morley, 'Gypsy' Morton

vicarage garden be divided into seven plots for village use.

Whilst most farms on the Dicker remained with farmers, the War Ag based at Lower Dicker controlled and managed Pekes Farm at Chiddingly, Black Barn and Boship at Lower Dicker, Primrose and Caneheath Farms at Arlington, as well as Nate Wood and Coppards fronting the Polegate road. The local War Ag workforce numbered about a dozen at any given time, including Fred Medhurst snr, Charlie Hamper and eighty-year-old Omar Grant, who had come out of retirement to help the war effort.

WAR AG WORKERS BASED AT LOWER DICKER

Colin Ballard	Jack Burgess	Raymond Coates
Harold Ford (foreman)	Charles Hamper	Robert Henley
Omar Grant	John Izzard	Fred Medhurst snr
Fred Medhurst	Phillip Parkinson	Sidney Roberts
Lionel Roberts	Fred Roberts	Stanley Smith
David Stephens	Harry Winter (foreman)	Thomas Winter

Land that had laid fallow or neglected for years came under the plough, great swathes of the South Downs carried their first crops since Saxon times. A greater abundance of wheat, flax and sugarbeet were grown under directives from the county's head office at Lewes, but not without the danger of being attacked by marauding enemy planes or unforeseen accidents. Both old Omar Grant and Fred Roberts died from work-related accidents.

As volunteers or conscripted recruits, the Land Girls who were paid the statutory twenty eight shillings for a 48 hour week, bolstered the shortage of manpower, and turned many city girls into useful farm hands. Those who made up the Dicker WLA contingent came from London, Brighton, Huddersfield and Leeds, as well as local girls like Peggy Hoad. For better or worse, Dorothy Ball from London, volunteered for the

Threshing gang at Pekes Farm
Front, centre: Dot Ball

WLA when she received papers to work in a Coventry factory. Fortunately her posting away from bomb-torn London to Lower Dicker contributed to romance and marriage to a young War Ag tractor driver, Fred Medhurst.

Supplied with a yellow and black painted bicycle (affectionately referred to as Wasps) maintained at Harry Martin's garage, became a mobile workforce and sent from farm to farm as required, frequenting a variety of work from dung carting and spreading, potato planting to stooking wheat sheaves.

Both Upper Dicker Men's Club and the Village Hall committee held the last of their winter events in April 1940. The cricket club after a decisive victory over Hellingly by 88 runs to 45, were resolute that the war would not impede the forthcoming season. For those who read the *Sussex Express*, "The government's promise to pay compensation at the end of the war to owners of property damaged by enemy action", had different interpretations as German armies moved through the Low Countries into France. Fears about the possibility of an invasion led to the formation of the Local Defence Volunteers, to assist in the defence of the country. The response was immediate and overwhelming.

Extract from the *Sussex Express*, dated 17th May 1940:
"*VOLUNTEERS IN QUEUES*

There has been an immediate response all over the country to the broadcast appeal by Anthony Eden, the new War Minister, for local defence volunteers. The force, which is entirely voluntary and unpaid, will be used to defend the country against parachute raids, and the volunteers will serve in their own localities. Enrolment began in all police stations in the county on Wednesday morning, they included many ex-servicemen and also young men aged 17 to 20 years."

From a sense of duty they wanted to help defend the country in its hour of need, young lads from the Dicker area, along with John Clark, Frank Page, Arthur 'Mick' Hunt, and Fred Tatnall (veterans of the 1914-18 War), joined the 20th Sussex (Hailsham) Home Guard Battalion. The five platoons of E Company's recruitment from the Hailsham area, included men from Lower Dicker in No 7 (Hellingly) platoon and volunteers from Upper Dicker in No 20 platoon. High Barn's elevated location and unimpeded sweep of the Cuckmere valley and proximity to The Plough Inn, made it an ideal observation post and headquarters with easy access to liquid courage. Mr Wilfred Peerless owned High Barn, and become the platoon commander. In its early days nightly patrols from 7pm till dawn, with only an armband with initials LDV stencilled in black and a stout stick or shotgun sufficed for Dicker's irregular force. There were many invasion false alarms in 1940 and Sergeant Fred Tatnall had to rescind his last order to the searchlight unit behind the Village Hall, because what he had, in fact, observed in the twilight gloom were grazing cows not Germans! On June 13th 1940 an order was given that church bells would only be rung if the village was under attack, the

Reverend Filler reaffirmed to Mr Peerless that Holy Trinity's bell would remain silent. With uniforms and a consignment of rifles, Dicker's part-time volunteers assumed a more soldierly appearance. Concerted training ensued, even though training manuals had not been allocated. Michael Hayes' inability to march in step with the rest of No 20 platoon or his inability to understand basic rifle instruction, made him a danger to more than the enemy. Sid Finch accidentally discharged a bullet into the barn's roofspace while undergoing rifle instruction,and a soldier billeted at Starnash Farm had a narrow escape when a LDV member shot at him, after he learnt his wife was providing him with more than just 'home comforts'! Even with scant military skills, Dicker platoon in a simulated assault later on Michelham Priory defended by Canadian soldiers, gave a good account of themselves.

The evacuation of troops from Dunkirk and fall of France, heightened fears of invasion along the Kent and Sussex coastline. Upper Dicker witnessed soldiers of the Cornwall Light Infantry and Devonshire Regiment move into the village. Crossways House and Michelham Priory were requisitioned by the army. Mrs Latham had kindly placed two rooms at Robin Post, Hailsham, at the disposal of the troops for rest and recreation. On the 24th June 1940, Miss Rogers recorded in the school log that most of the evacuee children had been transferred to Wales. Ironically Hailsham's Pavilion cinema was showing *When Tomorrow Comes* at the time it was reported that bombs had fallen on a Sussex village, fortuitously the only casualties being a pony and some poultry. Mr Pettitt who had watched the plane and searchlights in action, had believed it to be practice. Arlington and Hellingly parishes as with so many others, became part of the Home Front.

Under the guidance of Mrs Kent and Mrs del Court, assisted by Mrs Dinnis, Kate White, Mrs May Shier and daughter Violet, Gwen Goldsmith, Blanche Sindercombe, Mabel

Home Guard volunteer Stan Pelling

Haffenden, Dolly Austin and Eva Arron, the Parish Room became a soldiers' canteen and was open every evening for recreation and refreshments. Apart from additional allowances to cater for the soldier's refreshments, rationing and shortages continued to blight what was readily available, but when Tom Henty secured the opportunity to purchase a vast amount of cigarettes before a price increase, soldiers queued at the shop to obtain a share at a cheaper rate.

Inundated by military vehicle activity, with khaki clad soldiers now billeted in the village, Pollards Cottage was requisitioned and occupied by six dispatch riders (referring to the cottage as 'The Hovel' due to neglected state). Local girl Jean Page found her needlecraft skill in demand, with requests for their 'Red Rose' insignia badges to be sewn onto battledress tunics.

Invasion was imminent, and Sussex had been fortified with pill boxes, tank blocks and barbed wire. Pill-boxes were constructed to form a defensive line along the rivers Ouse and Uck, two were built at Lower Dicker to aid defence of the A22 road bridge near the Boship roundabout. Tank blocks were sited around the perimeter of Hailsham, indicating a concentrated defence of the town that would impede the enemy's progress. Steel cables suspended from tall poles were evident across fields that bordered The Mount and Prices Farm, and across fields near Park Mead School at Upper Dicker. It was hoped that they would deter an airborne invasion. The LDV, sardonically referred to as 'Look, Duck, Vanish', were officially renamed the Home Guard. Upper Dicker platoon played an important role patrolling the coast road between Pevensey Bay and Cooden. The government's remuneration for use of a bicycle having been denied, nevertheless it was much more agreeable than patrolling on foot!

The summer of 1940 witnessed the new peril of aerial activity over the Hailsham area, with machine-gun fire, vapour trails and exploding bombs almost a daily occurrence. Anderson shelters were made available, but two local men constructed their own shelters. Frank Smith of Boxtree Cottages used a redundant car-body buried in the garden as the main structure, and Eddie Lancaster built a concrete shelter at the rear of Lindyville at Lower Dicker (which in 1991 was still there).

Eastbourne's first taste of war came on 7th July 1940 when a lone German bomber dropped bombs on Whitley Road, destroying nine houses and damaging sixty – one person was killed and twenty two injured. Ten days later explosions were heard when seven bombs fell near Cralle Place, Cowbeech and another twelve fell on farmland at Vines Cross. Hailsham experienced bombing for the first time on 16th August 1940, when a bomber dropped four bombs on the town, causing one casualty. With German bombing raids on London, invariably some that were not dropped on the capital, were despatched around the Sussex countryside on their way back. Throughout August explosions could be heard around the Hailsham area. As always the Bat and Ball Fair was held at Golden Cross where A Burtenshaw and Son conducted the sale of store and dairy cattle; cancelling it would have given disgruntled farmers a chance to discuss what the war was doing to their farming.

Relentless aerial combat over Sussex continued as Spitfires and Hurricanes fought a desperate battle with German planes, in what would become known as the Battle of Britain. Press censorship was imposed and posters warned people that 'Careless Talk Costs Lives', a Sussex Express headline stated "NAZI RAIDER DOWN IN SUSSEX", referred to a Messerschmitt Bf 109 severely damaged by Pilot Officer J McClintock which made a forced landing in a cornfield at Berwick.

Extract from the *Sussex Express*, dated 16th August 1940:

"NAZI RAIDER DOWN IN SUSSEX

During Tuesday's (13th Aug) air battle over the Channel and along the coast, a Nazi raider was driven down in a cornfield. The pilot was captured by two railwaymen. The airplane, a Me 109 came out of the cloud, the undercarriage was not lowered and it crashed, landing in a field near the railway line. There was a number of bullet holes through the fuselage, their positioning being a tribute to the accurate marksmanship of the British pilot. The two railwaymen Messers F Hurst and A Matthews, were working about 80 yards away at the time, and they observed the sole occupant jump out and commence to run immediately his plane came to a stop. He hid in the corn, but they went to the spot, closed with him and held him prisoner until the military arrived, who took him into custody."

Vapour trails and gunfire over the Hailsham area were evident of the RAF's supreme and gallant struggle against German fighters and bombers. Pilot Officer B G 'Stapme' Stapleton of 603 Squadron flew as a fighter pilot throughout the Battle of Britain. At a meeting with him in 2002, I learnt about his exploits and death-defying moments as a Spitfire pilot in the battle. On the 5th September 1940 Pilot Officer Stapleton shot down the infamous German, Oberleutenant Franz von Werna, who after escaping as a POW in Canada became the legendary 'one that got away'.

Known as Black Saturday, 436 were killed and 1,600 seriously injured on 7th September after London's East End and dockland were heavily bombed. As the evening descended, hundreds of fires mirrored Dante's inferno, witnessed fifty miles away at Lower Dicker.

Throughout September, a siren somewhere wailed warning of the approach of German planes, ARP warden Arthur Hamper made it known he still had not been issued with a 'tin helmet', schoolboys with outstretched arms emulated aerial battles around Park Mead's playground, as Hurricane and Spitfire pilots continued to fight a desperate battle against overwhelming odds in the skies over South East England. Eastbourne suffered from sporadic raids on the 15th and 16th September: twenty-three HE bombs were dropped in the vicinity of Hailsham and Hellingly, and on the 19th Maynards Green had a fortuitous escape when 500 incendiary bombs were dropped. PC Max Soffner reported on the 27th that fourteen 50kg bombs fell in the Horam area.

The splutter of an aircraft engine starved of fuel drew Don Martin and Ern Smith's attention when a Hurricane flown by Pilot Officer J Urwin-Mann made a forced landing in a field at Perrylands Farm, after an unsuccessful patrol over London. In 1991, Mr Urwin-Mann wrote to the author, "On the day (13th Sept) when Brian Considine and myself were patrolling I spotted Ju 88 about to enter cloud over London, I gave chase, entered cloud but was unable to locate the Hun a/c again so I descended through the cloud and suddenly found myself surrounded by a balloon barrage, in a great panic about turned and climbed through the cloud to 25,000 feet. By this time, I was running out of petrol and made a somewhat hurried descent and landed in a field south of Hailsham. An army section let me have some petrol in 4 gallon tins and off I went again to arrive at Tangmere for lunch."

The day five German airmen were interred in Hailsham cemetery, 27th September 1940, had also witnessed some of the most dramatic aerial battles over the area. German Messerschmitt 110s pursued at tree top height. Pilot Officer Percy Burton's Hurricane was embroiled in aerial combat with one, out of ammunition and determined to down his adversary, so he rammed the German plane as it flew over Hailsham. Both Hurricane and Messerschmitt crashed, killing Pilot Officer Burton as well as his adversaries.

September had seen the RAF gain the upper hand, Hitler cancelled Operation Sealion, his planned sea-bourne military invasion on Britain.

Organisers in the majority of parishes were working hard on behalf of Hailsham's Spitfire Fund; Mr George Dann donated £8 and patrons of the Potters Arms had given £3 to bolster the Dicker contributions. On Sunday 13th October members of Upper Dicker and Hellingly Home Guard attended the morning service at the Holy Trinity Church.

Indiscriminate bombing continued throughout October and November, bringing a sprinkling of bombs to most parishes. One HE bomb and 17 incendiary bombs were dropped over Berwick, a single bomb exploded behind Martin's Garage at Lower Dicker causing damage to nearby properties and on 1st November 1940 ten incendiary bombs fell in the vicinity of Upper Dicker. The Womens Institute ladies continued to organise weekly whist drives that would fund knitted garments for the forces. Apprehended at Hellingly on 8th November for no rear light, Henry Peach of Upper Dicker, required ten shillings to pay a judiciary fine! Dicker had welcomed back Sidney Guy and Charlie Lambert from Dunkirk but were to learn that John Lawrence from Starnash was a POW in Germany. On Friday 8th November, the funeral took place of 70 year old William Matthew (the oldest member of the Dicker

Platoon), seventeen members of the Home Guard escorted the cortege to the church.

Spitfire P7920 flown by Sergeant M Lee escorting returning Wellington bombers on 22nd December had engine failure and force-landed in a field at Park Wood Farm. He was uninjured and was conveyed to 219 Brigade Headquarters at Crossways House, Upper Dicker. PC Edgar Heard and members of the local Home Guard mounted guard on the damaged Spitfire until the military arrived.

In spite of wartime restrictions and rationing, the threat of invasion and dangers from bombing, the Slate and Tontine Club share outs helped fund the austere 1940 Christmas. The Dicker populace had adopted the mine-sweeper trawler *Guide On* and donated a Christmas parcel to the crew. Through Mrs Kent's benevolence nearly fifty village children enjoyed their belated Christmas party at her Bourne Farm home on Saturday 4th January 1941, when Mr Harry Kent distributed gifts from a large illuminated tree. For Mr and Mrs Fred Hider of Ghyll's Cottages, it had been a bleak and sad festive season, when their seven year old daughter Betty died of whooping cough on New Year's Day.

Park Mead School headmistress Miss Margaret Thornton was concerned that shelters were still not available, and recorded that whooping cough and snow-covered roads had depleted attendance at the commencement of the new term. Wintery weather conditions, tribulations of wartime farming and a not-guilty plea for a parking obstruction in Lewes, the magistrate probably declared Monday 13th January another unfavourable day for 'Arch' Piper of Starnash Farm, when he dispensed a ten shilling fine.

Edna Blackwell and Phyllis Flowers of Upper Dicker were summoned at Hailsham Petty Sessions for riding bicycles without compulsory lighting at Magham Down on 25th January. Miss Flowers told Special Constable Saunders that water had caused her lamp to fail (case dismissed), whereas Miss Blackwell was fined five shillings. Too much illumination from unauthorized car sidelights were the reason Sidney Dinnis of Park Wood Farm was fined fifteen shillings. Cases brought before Hailsham Petty Sessions, prompted the chairman to state that a captured German airman had referred to the assistance they received from lights showing when flying over the country.

Although the threat of invasion had receded, preparations of the defence of Britain continued well into 1941. The drone of enemy bombers over Sussex were monitored as night attacks on London and other targets continued. Dicker's Home Guard and fire guard auxiliaries kept effective nightly vigil against impending danger. The nearby coastal towns of Eastbourne and Seaford were subject to sporadic bombing and machine gun strafing: on 24th March, Eastbourne's Churchdale Road and Willoughby Crescent areas were bombed by a lone Dornier 17, which returned a few minutes later and machine gunned the town; three died and twenty five were injured from the bombing. The previous day two HE bomb explosions had been heard; PC Max Soffner reported the incident which had occurred at Old Glen Farm, Horam, a constant reminder that enemy planes could strike anywhere. In common with many rural parishes, Arlington parish went relatively unscathed from enemy action in 1941. Only two aircraft crashed within the proximity of Dicker, one north of Wilmington's pre-war aerodrome and the other at Stream Farm, Chiddingly. The ever-present dangers from bombing and other falling debris is today hard to reconcile with our peaceful existence! Even though there had been a decrease in the enemy's daylight raids, Park Mead School had yet to receive adequate shelters, three years would pass before shelters were made available.

Wartime fund-raising schemes united a community in a common cause; every opportunity to raise money for public war funds were grasped. As with other towns and villages, Upper Dicker's whist drives, dances and other enterprises contributed much towards 'War Weapon Week' and other worthy causes. By way of variety entertainment on Thursday 8th May 1941, the Twinkling Stars concert troupe raised money for the comfort fund for HM forces; during the summer the Women's Institute members despatched hand knitted socks, mittens and scarves to the servicemen's Comforts Depot. Proceeds raised from whist drives and dances were donated to the Red Cross fund and 'Aid for Russia' fund. Easy access to liquid refreshment made the Old Oak Inn at Arlington a favoured venue for weekly whist drives.

In addition to daily newspapers, although wartime censorship and paper shortage restricted content, the *Sussex Express* kept the village abreast of local news. On Friday 23rd May, no prayers would have saved the Reverend F Potts of Arlington from the media's attention, after failing to immobilise his car in Hailsham's High Street the previous week. The same Hailsham and Heathfield edition reported on the mysterious fire at Wickens Mill, Golden Cross.

Extract from the *Sussex Express*, dated 23rd May 1941:

"At about 1am on Saturday, the Hailsham Fire Brigade received a call to Dicker Mill, Golden Cross, where they found corrugated iron and timber outbuildings used as a store and garage well alight. The local squad of the A.F.S. were already on the scene, and they and other helpers had prevented the flames spreading to an adjoining house, where the owner of the property Mr E E Wickens resides. A good supply of water from a nearby pond, but it was impossible to save the two buildings."

The reality of war was felt when it was reported that Denis Coleman (at one time a member of Upper Dicker Scout Troop) was missing and presumed killed in action as a result of the sinking of HMS *Hood*, and an increase in the 'Killed on Active Service' column in the *Sussex Express* gave cause for reflection. The Reverend Filler's sermons were listened to with rapt attention, mirrored by

Military camp behind Upper Dicker church

thoughts of husbands and sons in the armed forces, each name spoken in the Intercession. To mark the first anniversary of the Home Guard's formation, members of No 20 (Dicker) platoon mustered at Page's Mill on Sunday 8th June and marched to the church service.

Even though Germany's military overtures had turned towards Russia, increased military presence in the village resulted in a nissan hut camp being constructed on land behind the church. Built by the Royal Canadian Engineers, mystery still surrounds the underground bunker in Park Wood at Upper Dicker. No evidence appears in Stuart Angel's book *Secret Sussex Resistance*. Park Wood commanded a good view of the surrounding area and would have allowed monitoring of troop movements on the roads from Cuckmere Haven. It should be recorded that for farmer Stanley Dinnis of Park Wood Farm, like his brother Tom, some of his wartime duties were of a secretive nature, and may have been linked to organised secret resistance.

By 1942, most people in Dicker had become accustomed to the routine of war. Hitler was blamed for all manner of things that went wrong. The government's pledge to honour ration coupons failed to register with old 'Shackles' Akehurst: perplexed by stringent food rationing and refused his request for extra sugar, he retorted, "Don't buggering want none"! As under-the-counter sales had been known in some shops, when John Dunk retired as shopkeeper in 1938 he felt it unlikely he would suffer from problems of wartime rationing. Park Mead's schoolchildren had resigned themselves to the regular gas mask drills but were delighted when blackberry picking excursions substituted for classroom boredom. Away from Home Guard duties, dances and dart matches brought a welcome diversion.

Extracts from the *Sussex Express*, dated 26th December 1941:
"HOME GUARD DANCE
Arranged by the local Upper Dicker Platoon, a dance took place last Thursday at the

Village Hall which had been decorated for the occasion. There was a company of nearly 70, the M C duties were shared by Sergeant W Peerless and Volunteer L Page; Fred Baker and his accordion band from Selmeston provided the music. The proceeds amounted to £3 and was donated to the Princess Alice Hospital."

"DARTS MATCH
Last week a darts match was played at the Plough Inn, between teams representing the Local Home Guard and the Civil Defence Services. The latter winning 6 games to 4, and became the first holders of a Challenge Trophy, (a tailfin of a German incendiary bomb suitably mounted, which had been dropped in a field near the village)."

Dicker's inhabitants settled themselves into another year of uncertainty, with a calm and cheerful fatalism at the beginning of 1942: helpers of the WVS canteen and friends enjoyed a party held in the Parish Room, and the village children were entertained again by Mr and Mrs Kent to a belated Christmas party, to which Bob Coleman conducted three hearty cheers for their benevolent hosts. Meantime, the local Home Guard members organised a dance on the 26th February in the Village Hall with music provided by a Services dance band. Billeted in the area, Gunner Spike Milligan's talents on trumpet and saxophone, as a member of a services dance band, evoked memories of playing at Robin Post near Hailsham and Upper Dicker Village Hall. After his military service Spike Milligan was known for "The Goon Show" on radio and as author of "Adolf Hitler, My part in his downfall".

After a lull of several months, explosions were heard on 28th April, when bombs were dropped in the Horam area. Six days later Eastboune suffered a

Military convey shatter the tranquility of Upper Dicker village

'tip and run' raid by nine enemy planes, resulting in 5 people killed and 36 reported injured. The town would undergo further raids during 1942.

Dicker again witnessed an increased military presence, when detachments of Canadian Signals and Engineers were quartered at Crossways House and Michelham Priory. Troops were also bivouacked in nearby Mill Wood and Hylands Wood. The sudden abundance of eligible young men caused mothers to keep an attentive eye on their daughters.

A total of eleven aircraft crashed in the Hailsham District in 1942, presenting local boys with opportunities to extend the unlawful pastime of collecting war-related souvenirs. The Spitfire which crashed on 5th May at Englewick Farm, Arlington may have provided such an opportunity.

The government's scheme to collect at least 40,000 tons of scrap iron in 1942 to aid the war effort, led to the forfeiture of ornate railings fronting houses in the village built by Bottomley. But because of an exceptional display of rambling roses, those that fronted 3 Crossways Cottages were saved. The village's own effort to collect scrap extended to waste paper collections overseen by the Women's Institute, stored ready for collection in the old Brickyard's cart-lodge. The redundant Dicker Pottery buildings requisitioned by the military had also been used as a scrap metal and waste paper depot.

When collecting their new ration books on 28th July from the Village Hall, the residents of Upper Dicker immediately became aware of a new points scheme which now included sweets and chocolate (only half a pound a person every four weeks). During August the villagers donated nearly £15 in a house-to-house collection to the East Sussex Hospital; further amounts were raised from whist drives and a dance organised by Mrs May Shier for the Red Cross and St Johns funds.

Military traffic was noticeable day and night in the village. On the 19th August Canadian soldiers based at Michelham Priory and detachments of the Calgary Regiment camped at Hylands Wood took part in the ill-fated Dieppe Raid when 907 were killed and 1,874 made prisoners of war. Members of Dicker's No 20 Home Guard platoon continued their nightly vigilance and weekend training in battle tactics; the *Sussex Express* reported on 10th April 1942,

"IF INVASION COMES

Everything possible to safeguard the public in case of invasion has been carefully and systematically carried out. Proper and sufficient means of informing the public of these arrangements at the proper time are in being and there is no need for scaremongering.

One final point needs stressing. Not everyone may have a job to do when the enemy is near, and those whose services are not required when the battle is on, must stay put in their homes."

October, saw both Park Wood and Hackhurst Farms sold, the latter purchased by Tex McLeod who had starred in a number of Hollywood cowboy films. Park Mead School had been given custodial rights to some rabbits and chickens and the children were still subject to gas mask drills, features of wartime curriculum! On the 15th November, church bells, silent since June 1940, rang out to celebrate the victory at El Alamein; whether Holy Trinity's single bell contributed to the celebration, remains uncertain!

With the dispersement of Slate Club funds at the Plough Inn on Saturday 12th December and a dance at the Village Hall the following week, war or not, Dicker families endeavoured to enjoy another wartime Christmas.

During 1943, policing of the Dicker area was applied more to civil disturbance than enemy attack. Planes were frequently observed over the Hailsham district, and both Polegate and Hailsham were Luftwaffe targets in early 1943. On 10th February, a lone German bomber dropped two HE bombs on Hailsham, one after shedding its tail fins on impact bounced 300 yards over the town to explode near St Mary's Church, destroying the town's newly constructed fire station. Eastbourne's ordeal continued with numerous hit-and-run raids on the town, and on 3rd April the town suffered it's worst ever casualty numbers for a single raid when thirty-five people were killed and ninety-nine injured. German raids were a constant threat to towns and villages, and reports in the *Sussex Express* headlined "South East Villages Attacked" and "Town Gunned", highlighted the dangers. In 1943 retiling was being carried out on the roof of 14 The Croft, Lower Dicker, when alerted by machine gun fire from aerial combat, Ernie Pitcher and his co-workers escaped unscathed as bullets seemed destined to undermine their work on 'Squeaker' Scrace's house. After a three-month lull in daylight raids, explosions were heard on 17th October when two bombs were dropped at Grovelands Farm, Hailsham. Parish Clerk Mr R Wigg complained to Hailsham Rural District Council about the considerable damage to several roads by military vehicles, but Arlington parish was relatively unscathed!

The Reverend Filler was gladdened by the ban on the ringing of church bells being lifted in time for Eastertide services. By July in response to the Holy Trinity Church's centenary fund, a satisfactory £75 had been donated. Response to Hailsham district's endeavour to raise £125,000 to meet the cost of 25 Typhoo fighter airplanes, Mr J Duncan reported Upper Dicker residents had raised £456 17s. 11d towards the Wings for Victory campaign.

Police Constable Edgar Heard's over-zealous not-on-my-patch attitude was to cost Matthew Moran two shillings for allowing two pigs to stray on the highway, and War Ag tractor driver Fred Medhurst was summonsed for wasting fuel and failing to have a road fund licence.

As the war went on, the morale of No 20 (Dicker) platoon was boosted when every member laid claim to a 303 Lee Enfield rifle. Through a weekend training camp in Hylands Wood, musketry competitions at Chiddingly and spigot motor training on Milton Hide, Dicker platoon felt they were every bit of a fighting force. In October Lieutenant W Peerless relinquished command of the Dicker platoon to Lieutenant E H Rose MC, with Sergeant Frank Page as Second in Command. At a recent Home Guard social evening in the Village Hall, a silver challenge cup and two other prizes donated by Private Fred Page for a rifle shooting competition were presented. The cup was won by Corporal Charlie Harmer, with second and third prizes won by Lt Wilfred Peerless and Private Cyril Shier.

Surveyed during 1942, Deanland near Golden Cross, had one of the Advance Landing Grounds built for the projected allied invasion of Europe. It also became a safe haven on 6th September 1943 for nineteen returning B17 Flying Fortress bombers, crippled or short of fuel after a raid on Stuttgart. Local boys who wanted a piece of the action, cycled from Dicker to see the B17 that overshot the runway and came to rest near Forty Foot Lane, any thoughts of a souvenir were dashed by the presence of the authorities!

There was a war of words with the object of getting a main water supply to houses along the Lower Dicker between the junction of Coldharbour Road and The Croft. At that time the Government deemed it could not release pipes for such an extension if it did not help the war effort. Such constraints never befell the Women's Institute ladies when holding their 'Make do and Mend' classes in the Parish Room!

In the run up to Christmas 1943, the Twinkling Stars concert party presented a variety entertainment at the Village Hall to raise funds for the Children's Christmas party. The cast comprised Messers S Page and O Lavender, Mrs K Levett, Eileen Mills, Rose Houghton, Leslie Medhurst, Barbara and Dora Shier, Violet Knight, John and Peter Langridge, Margaret, Christine and Alan Levett, Bob Coleman, Maurice Pelling, Christine Farley, Theresa Fletcher and Melba Blake. Donations from Upper Dicker residents, the WVS canteen volunteers and proceeds from whist drives enabled a Christmas gift to be sent to those in the armed forces from the village. The pre-Christmas dance in the Village Hall on 17th December and the party given by Mrs Kent on Boxing Day for members of ATS and Women's Land Army billeted in the Dicker area showed that the war had failed to blight the village's festive spirit.

By 1944 the rigours of war had become an inherent part of village life. Prior to the allied landings in Normandy, Sussex became a training and holding area for thousands of troops. The detachment of North Staffordshires billeted in the Nissan hutted camp behind Upper Dicker church increased village inhabitants to an unprecedented level, demand for cigarettes from Tom Henty's shop untenable!

Military vehicles continued to damage grass verges and roads in the area, and there were numerous complaints to the Parish Council which necessitated further constabulary investigation by Arthur Page whose only thought was, "don't they know there was a war on?" Farmer H Marchant of Wick Street Farm certainly was not amused and hoped for compensation after an army lorry backed through one of his hedges, knowing that the military had already paid for damage caused to Sessingham footbridge.

In an effort to confuse the Germans if they had invaded, the removal of Dicker's signposts probably brought trepidation to it's new acquired populace of evacuees, land girls and soldiers. Total acquisition by the military of Michelham Priory forced the owners, Mr and Mrs R B Wright, to move to Scotland; since 1939 the seeming catalogue of change had been endless. Wall art showing a map of the Dieppe raid and graffiti are still evidence of the military's wartime presence at Michelham.

Even with decreased enemy bomber activity over Sussex, much to the cost of Mrs Winnifred Beals, blackout restrictions remained until 20th April 1945.

Extract from the *Sussex Express*, dated 17th March 1944:

"LIGHTS IN BLACKOUT

Mrs Winifred Beals was summonsed in respect of a light at 8.30pm on February 10th at Old Forge Cottage, Upper Dicker, and also for wasting electricity, she pleaded guilty on both summonses. Special Constable D Martin stated he saw a light from a bedroom window. Receiving no reply to his knocking, he found a neighbour who knew where the key was hidden, they went into the house and turned the light off. (Constituted a fine of 10 shillings on each summons, with costs of 2s. 9d.)"

Upper Dicker's response to 'Salute the Soldier' week was a fund-raising programme on Saturday 27th May with a social evening in the Village Hall. Other events included children's sports, a tug of war competition between the local Home Guard and an army team, and a stoolball match on the Recreation Ground. The week concluded with a dance on Friday 2nd June, the total raised being £1,204.

Discarded war ordnance and souvenir collecting brought untold dangers to young boys whose ambition was to retain a war-related memento, sometimes with unfortunate injurious consequences. One such instance with what was believed to be an anti-tank grenade, was an explosion seriously injuring Michael Piper (age 12) and four others at Starnash Farm, Upper Dicker.

The allied invasion in June 1944 for the liberation of Europe brought stern resolve that at last Germany's military aspirations were nearer to being terminated. Memories of air raid siren warnings and enemy planes overhead were surpassed by one of the most traumatic periods of the war, the flying bomb offensive. Defence against Hitler's much-vaunted pilotless aircraft

Cool courage of a Spitfire pilot of 41 squadron diverts a 'doodlebug' from its course over Upper Dicker by tipping the flying bomb's wing.

(christened 'doodlebug') were anti-aircraft guns and fighter aircraft that sought to blast the missiles out of the sky before they reached London.

At 4.30am on Friday 16th June, the local Civil Defence room recorded two PAC (Pilotless Aircraft) had crashed north of Hailsham; at 5am the first PAC was observed to pass over the Dicker in a northerly direction, the prelude to a hectic two months when the Hailsham and Battle areas were rarely out of the action. The once-heard-never-forgotten sound of a doodlebug continued until the engine cut out. Then it fell silently to earth, followed by the ear-shattering explosion of its 850 kg warhead. The *Daily Telegraph* reported on 21st June, "fewer pilotless planes reached Southern England yesterday"; two days later, the Civil Defence incident book records that sixteen doodlebugs were shot down in the Hailsham area. One caused damage to a farmhouse at Upper Dicker, and many more were observed rumbling towards London. On the 24th June, a doodlebug shot down on farmland between Arlington and Upper Dicker damaged Park Mead School and Holy Trinity Church; later in the day an unexploded cannon shell crashed through Pensons Grove farmhouse roof at Lower Dicker. Flying bombs became a feature of daily life, and explosions were frequently heard. On 7th July, Mrs Daziel lost her life at Placketts Corner, Arlington, when her house was demolished by a doodlebug;

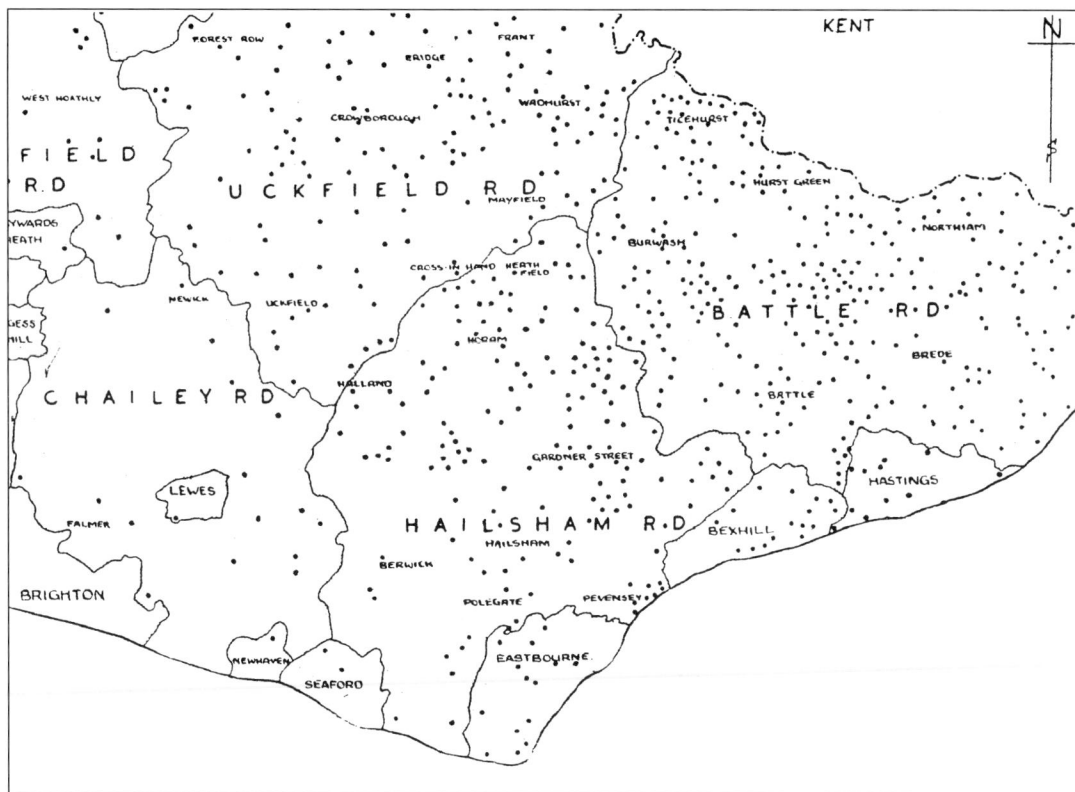

Where the 'doodlebug' flying bombs came down

damage occurred to another property and one family made homeless. Three days later, a man and a woman were killed at Mullbrooks Farm, Hailsham. Fatalities occurred on Sunday 23rd July in an incident when Spitfire IX fighters (based at Deanland) shot down a doodlebug, which struck trees and exploded, completely wrecking Camberlot farmhouse, and killing Mrs Saunders and another person. Forty houses were damaged at Lower Dicker.

Extract from the *Sussex Express*, dated 28th July 1944:
"FLYING BOMB WRECKS FARMHOUSE

Six casualties, two of them fatal, were caused when a flying bomb was shot down by fighter planes over Southern England early on Sunday morning, struck some trees at the side of the road and exploded. A farmhouse was completely wrecked, the front and side walls being blown away, and the building partially collapsed. The six occupants, the farmer and his wife, daughter and three cousins who were on a visit, were in bed at the time. The farmer's wife and a visitor were killed. The others conveyed to hospital.

The farm buildings were extensively damaged. Trees over a wide area were stripped of leaves and those in close proximity of the explosion were torn down. The various Civil Defence services were quickly on the scene and did splendid work."

Church Parade at Michelham Priory, Upper Dicker *3rd September 1944*

With the danger posed by the doodlebugs and later the V2 rocket, news was received during July that Park Mead School would receive three Morrison shelters. At the same time notices were received concerning the evacuation of children whose parents wished them to be moved to a safer area. By September, Kent and East Sussex became known as Doodlebug Alley: 880 flying bombs had fallen in Sussex, of which 159 in Hailsham Rural District; That was when the Vergeltungswaffe (doodlebug) bombardment petered out.

Extract from the *Sussex Express*, dated 8th September 1944:

"HOME GUARD AT MICHELHAM PRIORY

In connection with the National Day of Prayer on Sunday, a drumhead service was held. It was attended by members of E Company 20th Home Guard Battalion, Hailsham Army Cadets and contingent of ATS. A parade of about 200 assembled at the Plough Inn, headed by a band and marched to Michelham Priory where the service was held."

By October 1944, all threats of invasion had disappeared, and the government decided that there was no longer an active role for the Home Guard, so the force was ordered to stand down. In accordance with this decision, parades were to be held throughout the country. On Sunday 3rd

December, members of No 20 (Dicker) platoon joined the rest of the battalion for the Stand Down parade, passing cheering crowds in Hailsham. A few days later Park Mead schoolteacher, Mrs Farrant, secured the return of village children evacuated to South Wales during the flying bomb ordeal, in time for their Christmas party in the Village Hall. Some were perplexed by the attendance of two Father Christmases (Messers Owen Lavender and Stanley Page).

With the defeat of Germany in Europe imminent, Hailsham's siren sounded the All Clear for the last time. The parishes of Arlington, Chiddingly and Hellingly had been the targets for 160 high explosive bombs and 1,665 incendiary bombs; in total 7,609 HE bombs were dropped in East Sussex by enemy aircraft. The Dicker area was divested of military presence; years of war-related uncertainty had finished, Victory in Europe was declared on May 8th 1945. Upper Dicker's lone church bell joined other parishes in celebration; on Sunday Morning (13th May) Reverend Sinnett-Davis conducted a Thanksgiving Service at Holy Trinity Church, followed by a parade of military units and members of the Home Guard. One choirboy (who would years later write a definitive history of The Dicker), recalled, "every pew was taken to the extent people stood in the aisle, the volume of singing was loud enough to raise the roof of the village church".

Extract from the *Sussex Express*, dated 17th August 1945:
"TWO DAYS REJOICING FOR FINAL PEACE
Soldiers stationed at Hellingly and Upper Dicker making an effort to arouse the immediate neighbourhood, gave the first indication the war was over to many residents who had gone to bed before the news was broadcast at midnight on Tuesday. In their lorries, drove round Hailsham and adjoining districts, singing, shouting and banging petrol cans."

The surrender of Japan on Tuesday 14th August effectively brought an end to the war, the next day Mr E N Petch and Mr B Wise carried out an impromptu programme of sports on the Recreation Ground for the children of Upper Dicker. Without hesitation the village cast aside the mantle of war-related hardships and set plans into motion for the forthcoming Peace Celebrations.

Extract from the *Sussex Express*, dated 31st August 1945:
"DANCE
The Peace Celebrations Fund target of £100 is almost in sight, proceeds from a dance held on Monday in the Village Hall, Upper Dicker, brought the total to nearly £89. Enjoyed by a company of nearly a 100 Mr John Davies provided the music. Prices for "spot" dances were secured by Private Osborne and Miss A Shier, Mrs E Jenner and Private Stewart, Mrs B Manser and Mr Hafekost."

People were keen to move on and in July 1945 Hailsham were making efforts to have tank blocks and other defence works removed. No longer warning of approaching German planes, the wail of the town's air-raid siren would now summon Hailsham's Fire Brigade to civil duties. Some beaches were now reportedly open to the public, but in view of the possible dangers from stranded or drifting mines, Eastbourne's seafront may well have remained out of bounds. Upper Dicker inhabitants were about to move into the realms of a new modern era, when it was reported that as a result of the Parish Council's efforts, the military authorities had consented to the two standpipes being made available to the residents! In all their wisdom, the Council resolved that cows and other stock could be grazed on the Cricket Ground; cow-pats would surely be detrimental to next season's averages.

Extract from the *Sussex Express*, dates 14th June 1946:

"UPPER DICKER – VICTORY CELEBRATIONS

In about six months during the latter part of the war, £106 4s. was raised at Upper Dicker by means of entertainments and other social functions so that peace could be fittingly celebrated. The festivities took place on Saturday and despite the inclement weather, the arranged programme was carried out. A large marquee was erected on the Recreation Ground in which there was a fancy dress parade for children and grown-ups. The judges had a difficult task, for many of the costumes displayed considerable ingenuity.

A programme of sports for children and adults was held on the Recreation Ground, where there were donkey rides for the youngsters. The events for the grown-ups included a football match in which the players were in sacks and it caused much amusement. Tea for everyone was served in the marquee. Later in the evening, there was a social held in the Village Hall, where games and dancing were enjoyed. Mrs L Hunneysett was MC and the music was provided by Mr Davies. When it was dark, a bonfire was lit on the Recreation Ground. There was one disappointment as it was impossible to obtain any fireworks, but it was hoped to have a display on November 5th."

FOOTNOTE – Purchased with part of the Peace Celebration Fund, a new bible was presented to the Holy Trinity Church and was dedicated on Sunday 4th August 1946, replacing the bible donated in 1897 by Horatio Bottomley.

Hardly had the excitement and tumult of Victory celebrations faded away, than the human cost of war emerged of the supreme sacrifice made by John Softley, killed in action in 1942 and Leslie Barton also from Lower Dicker, killed in Italy on 21st September 1944. With hostilities over, it was ironic that 20 year old Sergeant air gunner John Peckham had tragically died on 29th September 1945 when his Lancaster bomber crashed on route back from Italy.

For Fred Hearsey, the war would have a happy ending. Decorated with the Distinguished Flying Medal for his adeptness as the bomber's rear gunner, he had also survived baling out of a crippled bomber to return after being a prisoner of war. Demobilised, most would look forward and cast aside images of war, but Sergeant Vena Davies of Lower Dicker had been keen to retain his steel helmet which bore testimony to his active service. It was inscribed with a record of the places he had served in: France, North Africa and Italy.

For the men and women from Lower and Upper Dicker who served their country during World War Two, every effort has been made to include all their names on a Roll of Honour.

ROLL OF HONOUR 1939-1945
No 20 (Upper Dicker) Platoon. Home Guard

Herbert Arron
Phillip Colman
Bert Dudley
Sidney Finch
Fred Hider
Pat Jessop
Fred Messenger*
Stanley Pelling
Leslie Page
Wilfred Peerless
Cyril Shier

John Clark
William Colman*
Fred Evenden
Percy Guy
Charlie Harmer
K Kane*
G Owen*
Nelson Pelling
Nelson Pettitt
E H Rose MC
Sidney Smith
George Townsend

William Colman (Stud House)
John Delaney
Gerald French
Michael Hayes
Arthur Hunt*
Fred Medhurst*
Laurie Parker*
Frank Page
Fred Page
William Saunders*
Fred Tatnall

*signifies they served with No 7 (Horsebridge/Hellingly) Platoon.

THOSE WHO SERVED IN THE ARMED FORCES

Jack Allcorn
Ernest Baker
Thomas Barton
Donald Case
Doris Cleeve
James Cleeve
Alfred Dadswell
Ivor Davis
Raymond Dinnis
Reginald Evenden
David Fletcher
Jack Fowlie
Thomas French
Bertram Guy
R Harding
Alfred Hills
Charles Lambert
Martin Manley
George Miles
John Peckham
Geoffrey Sanders
B Siggs
John Softley
Frank Westley

Ronald Ashford
Ernest Barton
A W Brett
Leonard Cottington
Evelyn Cleeve
Percival Cleeve
Aubrey Dann
Vena Davis M.I.D.
Bert Dudley
Frank Finch
James Flowers
Ronald Fowie
Alan Funnell
Ernest Guy
Margaret Hayes
Frederick Hearsey DFM
Edward Lancaster
Frederick Messenger
Leslie Page
Nelson Pelling
P Sanders
Frederick Smith
Edward Turnerìí
Leslie Winchester
Eric Wisbey

Ebenezer Ashdown
Leslie Barton
Frederick Cane
David Cleeve
Harry Cleeve
John Crittenden
Maurice Dann
Kathleen Dinnis
Frederick Evenden
Sidney Finch
Phyllis Flowers
Dennis French
Harold Griffin
Sidney Guy
Stanley Henty
T G Lade
Gordon Manley
Frank Messenger
Henry Peach
Robert Pratt
Alfred Shilton
Thomas Smith
Bernard Verall
Roy Winchester

Chapter 12

CONTINUITY AND CHANGE IN DICKER

So far in this book I have endeavoured to set down, at some length, the history of these two villages up until the end of World War II. It is only right that the last chapter should portray the changes which pushed Lower and Upper Dicker into the 21st century.

Though the war was over, rationing continued to be the villain of peacetime. Shopkeepers Tom Henty, Maurice Austen and Reuben Langridge cursed the ever present hindrance of ration book coupons. The absence of military personnel in the village, saw the return of Michelham Priory, Crossways House and Camberlot Hall to private ownership; at the same time, Frederick George Handel Elvey moved into the empty vicarage, becoming the last vicar to reside there.

After nearly six years of wartime constraints, there was an urgent need to get back to normal, and eventually one political party would inform us "we have never had it so good"! Partly as a spin-off from the government's wartime Dig for Victory campaign, Upper Dicker held their first Produce Association show in August 1946. Formed in the same year, was a youth club which met on Wednesday evenings at the Vicarage, giving us youngsters the opportunity to play table tennis and billiards. Those who walked home after one such evening in April 1950, observed an aircraft flying towards Chiddingly on fire.

Extract from the *Sussex Express*, dated 26th May 1950:
"PLANE DISINTEGRATED AT 1000 FEET
RESUMED INQUEST ON CHIDDINGLY CRASH VICTIMS
The Royal Air Force Wellington twin engine bomber which crashed in East Knowle Wood, Chiddingly, at 10pm on April 5th, got out of control through some unknown reason, went into a dive and broke up in the air at about 1,000 feet. The bomber had taken off from RAF Middleton, near Darlington, Co Durham, at 6.45pm for a night exercise."

Although the inquiry failed to support that a fire had occurred while the bomber was in flight, both John Chilton of Bugh Hill Farm, Chiddingly; and Arthur Braidon of Horam, claimed the aircraft was on fire before it crashed.

The avenue of tall trees was a constant bane to roadman Jack Morris's broom in autumn, with Upper Dicker remaining far removed from the bustle of the outside world. As car ownership in the village was minimal, most still

1952

Coronation seat
From left: Sheila Tatnall, Ann Parker, Iris Shier, Bert Shilton, Richard Wise, Les Smith,
Peter Peach, Pat Mitchell

relied on the green Southdown 92a bus (later the 198) for journeys into Hailsham. The traffic on this road contrasted greatly with Lower Dicker's increased main road traffic, which caused many fatal accidents in the 1950s.

With television now in almost every home, the days are gone when my generation's favoured meeting place was by the village telephone kiosk or the porch of Crossways House, debating whether it was a night at the flicks or just playing a prank on someone! Octogenarian Mrs Guy of Crossways Cottages expressed that the younger generation had, "far too much pleasure, lipstick and flirting nowadays"!

Designed to dispel postwar austerities, and create a sense of fun, fantasy and colour, the Festival of Britain in 1951 attracted many visitors from the Dicker area; the Dome of Discovery, pavilions and concourses were awe-inspiring to one 17-year-old lad. But in the main, Upper Dicker would remain cocooned in events of its own making.

Extract from the *Sussex Express*, dated 4th July 1952:
"FIRST BEETLE DRIVE
The first beetle drive held at Upper Dicker took place on Monday in the Village Hall,

organised by John Hanson, with Gordon Manley as MC. The prize winners were
Nora Bishop, Janet Kilkenny and Mrs E Verall for most completed beetles. The
proceeds were for the Village Hall."

The fine mansion and grounds, formerly the home of Horatio Bottomley, in August 1956 were lent by Mr Peter Pickard for a village fete to raise funds for repairs to the Holy Trinity Church. Even the inclement weather failed to deter the people who were attracted to view the mansion for the first time. In the continuous drive for church funds, a performance of a new style of music played by the Meteor Skiffle Group took place at a function in the Village Hall.

The fifties had witnessed The Vicarage sold as a private residence and Mr Scott granted permission to use the outbuildings for light engineering workshops. Represenations by the Parish Council to higher authorities, had seen "Slow – Major Road Ahead" signs erected at Camberlot and Michelham roads at Upper Dicker crossroads. It had been suggested that the signpost should read Golden Cross or London, not Camberlot Road. There is little wonder confusion reigned when a lorry driver, totally nonplussed with Dicker's byways, even more bamboozled after 'Chub' Hollobon's directions of "first right, then right and right again", found himself back in Upper Dicker!

Another anecdote conveyed to me was of the near demise of Sharrards Cottage, which was derelict and uninhabited in the early 1950s. A bullock strayed into the house and ascended the narrow staircase into a bedroom. A great deal of blasphemy was required to extract the beast and in an unguarded moment of unrelenting rage, Mus Piper threatened to demolish the old dwelling. It was saved and is now renovated and renamed Knights Acre.

Throughout the 1950s, peacetime conscription, regularised by the National Service Act of 1947, whisked young men into the armed forces for eighteen months, extended later to two years. Many would experience the realities of conflict in war-torn places such as Korea, Malaya, Cyprus, Egypt and Borneo. Some would pay the supreme sacrifice. On Tuesday 23rd October 1951, a telegram arrived to inform Mr and Mrs Pelling of Brickyard Cottages, Upper Dicker, that their 19-year-old son Maurice had been killed in action while serving with the Royal West Kents in Malaya. In what was claimed as bravery of the highest order, in which men of No 11 Platoon were not found wanting, Maurice and nine other soldiers were killed in a terrorist ambush, with ten other ranks wounded. The village lost a promising cricketer and footballer, and for many, a friend.

Dicker's immediate post-war years is best remembered at the time when the recreation ground became the hub of the 1953 Coronation festivities. The programme included a fancy dress parade, comic cricket match, children's and adults' sports, and a bonfire and firework display in the evening. In 1958 Mrs R H Hotblack purchased Michelham Priory from Mrs Storey with the express purpose of preserving the priory for posterity. Later she donated the priory to the Sussex Archaeological Society.

Recalling the fifties, when a new Ford Prefect cost only £560, Dicker Cricket Club's financial status plummeted in 1958 when they went for broke and purchased a gang mower for £80! Farmers complained bitterly about the loss of revenue because their cows gave less and chickens laid from undisclosed heights due to sonic booms of jet aircraft. Wallace Allenby Sinden's speed was far slower when apprehended by the local constabulary for being drunk again while in charge of a bicycle along the Lower Dicker road. While motorists were coming to terms in the 1960s with Hailsham's new one-way traffic system, Upper and Lower Dicker were endeavouring to combat its own highway problems. The increased traffic along the A22 main road, with an estimated 7,000 vehicles daily, peaked to 11,000. Little wonder that Gomer Jones of Knights Farm was fined 30

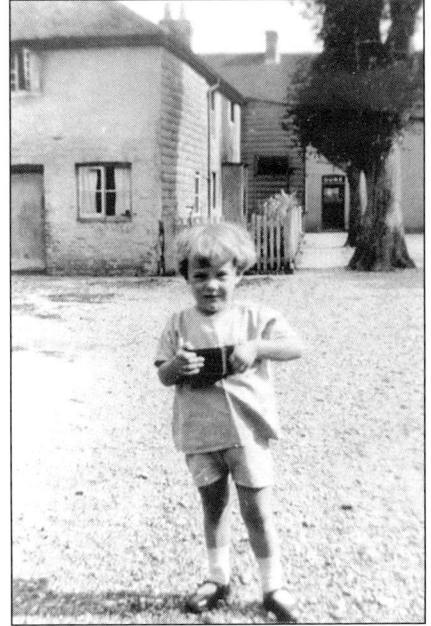

Shop Lane, Upper Dicker 1920s
Cowpers Cottages on the left

shillings for allowing cattle to stray on the highway, or had someone left the gate open? The advent of a main water supply to Upper Dicker, brought in its

Snowbound Upper Dicker 1963

wake another problem in 1960. The village had plenty of piped water, but with flushing toilets and baths, where would the additional water go? The building of new private houses such as Wedgewood, Fairlands, Oaklands, Shermans Oak, Pippins and Carrick House in the 1960s, would obviously have added to that problem. But not so, the much needed council housing and a residential caravan park between Mansers Lane and Coldharbour Road, where permission to build was refused on several occasions by the rural district council, a development that would have satisfied the housing needs of those on lower incomes.

Mistaken orthography had led Cowpers Cottages (owned by William Cowper in the 1840s), to be called Coopers Cottages. These 2-up and 2-down dwellings sharing a common wash house, with outside thunder boxes (privvies) were pulled down and replaced in the 1960s.

In common with the rest of southern England, Upper Dicker became isolated by the worst weather conditions since 1881 in January and February 1963. Gigantic snowdrifts blocked rural roads for days. Lower Dicker fared little better as snow ploughs struggled to clear drifting snow from the A22 road. The snowbound village made Sid Smith curse and spit as he struggled to deliver the milk. The ensuing weeks of snow clearance cost the East Sussex County Council £240,000 and Dicker residents a great deal of vexatious moments!

Following the advent of television, Dicker residents became aware of the detector van in 1967 touring the village seeking out the licence dodgers. BBC's popular *Z-Cars* programme was blamed for poor attendance at an Arlington Parish Council meeting. Probably it was television that forced Hailsham's cinema to close. But the village saw the revival of Upper Dicker's annual horticultural show in 1962. The same sense of community spirit that made the annual summer carnival so successful, in 1968 launched the popular Dicker Day. It progressed into a two-day event, with decorated carnival floats, gymkhana, entertainment, and a tug-of-war competition and the Miss Dicker competition keenly contested. One dubious entrant had been Ted Spiers, surprising the judge when he jokingly dressed in female attire, but his hairy legs gave the game away!

Extract from the *Sussex Express*, dated 11th September 1970:

"DICKER DAY ANOTHER BIG SUCCESS

Dicker Day the once-a-year day in a tiny village just outside Hailsham, leaped its way to another great success on Saturday, providing the crowds with plenty of entertainment food and dancing.

It was the third Dicker Day, an eve of event dance, when scores rocked the evening away to the music provided by Charade.

The horse show and gymkhana was a much improved feature. The number of stalls were well patronised Tug of war being truly revived in the villages, attracting a large

Carnival spirit at the annual Dicker Day *1970s*

Members of Dickers Tug of War with trophies won in their first season *1969*
From left, standing: Lawrence Holt, 'Arch' Piper, John Gutsell, Trevor Smith, Ernest Newnham, Edward Spires, Derek Turner, David Prodger, Andrew Gottleib. In front 'Skip' Maskell, Barrie Ransom, Geoff Davies.

New children's slide erected on Recreation Ground   *1970s*

Celebrations of the tercentenary of cricket played on the Dicker   *1977*
From left: David Hawkins, Terry Brown, Ernest Smith, John Page, Leslie Page

A gusting wind causes problems

DICKER DAYS 1988

Dicker Day six-mile fun run attracts over 400 runners

Christmas revellers pose for the camera, before the Boxing Day pram race

entry and big crowds. In the marquee, the Miss Dicker 1970 was won by Miss Caroline Hamper."

To combat the dreaded death-watch beetle in the church timbers, events were held in 1964 to raise funds. "Beatles" music and a Beetle Drive were deemed as appropriate for one such fund raising event! A year earlier had seen ladies affiliated to Eastbourne's Liberal Association hold a meeting at Livingstone Villa in Upper Dicker. So some ladies of the village had become politically inclined, rather than concerned over the loss of a bus service to Hailsham's shops!

No longer cost-effective, the Southdown Bus Company's withdrawal of a service to Upper Dicker in 1971, left a public transport vacuum until filled by the new Cuckmere Community Bus. It linked rural villages with Hailsham, particularly for people wanting to visit the new Vicarage Field shopping precinct. For those who wished to dine out, both the Old Orchard Restaurant at Lower Dicker and Camberlot Hall, offered good food in pleasant surroundings.

The Dicker area still remains predominantly agricultural, although no longer being the major source of employment. An aerial photograph taken of Coldharbour Mill in 1966, clearly shows vast structural changes had taken place to incorporate the increase in animal feed production. Plans to knock down the old Dicker Pottery buildings, and replace them with car showrooms and a filling station, were thwarted in 1970 at a local planning enquiry. However, plans were passed for the extensive building work which transformed the seventeenth century Boship farmhouse, into a new spacious country hotel in 1974, with 28 bedrooms in a new wing, and a further eight ground-floor suites. The new proprietors, Roland Pratt, Doug and Patricia Cox offered accommodation from £3 per person per night. The clubroom and restaurant, built by the local firm of Fradd and Lancaster, were used for corporate and other functions. The Northfields and Hackhurst Lane industrial parks at Lower Dicker, along with the factories occupied by Abbott Joinery and Shep Plastic, have been integral to modern day employment, albeit most coming from outside the area.

Throughout the 1970s, the Village Hall committee's calendar of events was full, hardly a day went by without something happening on the social scene. Cheese and wine parties to a badminton club, keep fit classes for the ladies to a disco evening for the younger generation. Robert Gardner gave a local history talk in the village hall in 1977, understood to be the first of its kind. A national tabloid newspaper, the *Sun*, was bought by nearly everyone in Dicker when it became known the centre pages conveyed news and pictures of Dicker's fame in the cricketing world, the sport having been played here since 1677.

By the close of the 1970s more houses had been built, Alvisia, Cherrylea and The Pines in 1976; Long House and Winchmore, which obscured the older Pollards and Plough Cottages. Cuckmere Cottages occupied land at the bottom of Shop Lane, in Upper Dicker. The new phase of house construction in the village seemed to have coincided with a disturbing increase in house prices. A new bungalow under construction in 1972 on the outskirts of the village, was placed on the market for £12,850.

No-one today would remember the sweeping changes made when Horatio Bottomley's mansion, The Dicker, became a dominant feature. Bottomley's grand scheme was to pull down older dwellings and to build new red-brick houses that totally changed the character of the village. Residents at that time must have disapproved of the man's sheer audacity, even though many would become housed and employed by him.

After Bottomley's death in 1933, Crossways House saw a change of ownership. Mr Peter Pickard purchased the property in 1939 for £4,000, and in the 1950s it was owned by Admiral Ronald Oldham. Sometime later it was occupied by the Downs and Weald Society. It was purchased in 1978 by St Bedes for use as a private school, which two years later also bought Nos 1 and 2 Crossways Cottages in Camberlot Road, the first of seventeen houses purchased over the ensuing two decades. Further property acquisitions followed in 1981 and 1983 with Camberlot Hall and the Dicker Stud, mirroring the changes of the Bottomley era.

Instinctively alarm bells rang as residents of Upper Dicker endeavoured to come to terms with the rapid growth of St Bedes property holdings. Many feared the village character would change. The parish council discussed at some length their concerns at a meeting in December 1981. It was acknowledged that "the School has brought to Upper Dicker a sense of purpose, more employment and trade." However a note of caution was struck regarding the extent the school might expand and dominate the life of the village and its rural character, notably the acquisition of farm land for playing fields and the possible further building of school premises.

St Bedes' plans to expand continued to be a bone of contention at parish council meetings. Many believed events were out of control, when the school trust purchased the village shop and post office in 1991, and the adjacent Providence House. There were those who believed the purchase of Stud Cottages to be the last straw, not only a loss of six dwellings to the village but converted into student accommodation. Local protests were supported by the Council for the Protection of Rural England, who called the expansion as, "being of detriment to the village". Following the purchase of Malvern House in 1999, one councillor said, "the village is fast disappearing, there is nothing else but school buildings!" Forge Cottages which had been vacant for many years were purchased in 2001, along with Wise's garage site. Perhaps in jest, someone said, "why not change the name of the village to St Bedes?" Contention rumbled on, when it was felt the school owned half the village, but important factors have emerged. After 25 years and with over 600 pupils, St Bedes has become one of the county's leading independent schools. Through the school the village has been able to retain its shop and post office. The school has welcomed the use of its facilities by the village. Following twenty three years as headteacher and founder, Roger Perrin retired in August 2001, and was succeeded by Stephen Cole from New Zealand. Although St Bedes presence in Upper Dicker has not always been seen as favourable, future generations may view this as a storm in a teacup. But there is no doubting the school's impact on the village in a short space of time.

Many of us look back nostalgically to the ideal village we once lived in. The older residents such as Ben Wise, and 'Dorrie' Page, whose father was the village baker for many years, have passed on. Change has always been the order of the day, we now have television, most families own a motorcar and travel longer distances to their work. The needs of the motorist have been satisfied by a new service station, motel and restaurant at Lower Dicker, built in 1990. Public pressure in more recent years has seen heavy lorries banned from using

Upper Dicker after the wrath of the 1987 hurricane

Wartime spirit of camaraderie prevails as residents endeavour to extricate a fallen pine tree following the 1987 hurricane

Park Mead School pupils planting saplings in the new Dicker Copse

Upper Dicker as a 'rat run', and a 40 miles an hour speed limit has also been introduced.

Most of us can recall the hurricane that threatened to lift the roofs of houses and flatten every tree in southern England. During the early hours of Friday 16th October 1987, Dicker's landscape was transformed in the space of a few hours. At daybreak everyone was confronted by a scene of unbelievable devastation. Gusting wind of deafening ferocity, had damaged houses and made Upper Dicker's roads impassable by a tangle of fallen trees. Downed power lines would deny me that first cuppa on that memorable day. The hurricane's destructive power revealed this was no ordinary gusting wind. Storm damage even brought Michelham Priory's visitor season to a premature end. It was certainly evident a hurricane had passed through the Dicker area! The avenue of trees which owed something to earlier memories, were gone forever.

In embarking on the history of the Dicker, a knowledge of parish and manorial boundaries has always been important. The revision of parish boundaries in 1983 extended Arlington's boundary, encompassing Coldharbour and Camberlot road areas. The Smith's ancestral home (Lambert's Farm) since 1907 was no longer part of Hellingly parish but in Arlington.

The rural area I once lived in has seen a growth in house construction, and by contrast nearly everyone is now a stranger. The redundant village slaughterhouse in Shop Lane had been pulled down to make way for Meadowbank to be built, with a further eight detached dwellings built in 1990 on land fronting Camberlot Road in the village. The razing of the derelict Coldharbour Mill in 1999 made way for an estate of 24 dwellings at Lower Dicker, transcending any previous house construction during the post war era.

On Saturday 17th March 1990, when the Potters Arms was being refurbished to cater for the hungry traveller, a band of intrepid divers led by Bill Crittenden were searching the murky pond waters at Clifton Farm in the vain hope of finding fragments of Bottomley's legendary submarine. My recent guided tour of Park Mead School by Mrs J Munns, made me aware today's world is never still. Two new classrooms had been built since my days there, with plans in place for a school hall. Although the use of the school's older classrooms has changed since the war years, memories returned of my time under the teacher's watchful eye, of Mrs Farrant and Mrs Robinson. The Dicker where I grew up and lived until 1957, over the years has remained my spiritual home. Villages continue to be shaped by new generations with a sense of community spirit. The outsider will probably see these two Sussex villages as mere dots on a map, whereas others will recall that this is where the notorious Horatio Bottomley once lived. Incarcerated in 1922 for fraud, having induced the public to invest 20 million pounds in wildcat investments.

While absorbing and appreciating the changes that have taken place in and around these two rural villages, it is hoped this book has conveyed a fragment of local history to the reader.

BIBLIOGRAPHY

Chapter 1: The Dicker

An Historic Atlas of Sussex.   (Phillimore)   1999.
A History of Sussex.   by J R Armstrong   1984.
The Lost Villages of Sussex.   by John Vigar   1994.
Hailsham and its Environs.   by C A Robertson   1982.
The Concise Dictionary of English Place-names.   by E Ekwell   1991.
The Place-names of Sussex part 2.   by A Mawer and F M Stenton   1930.
History of Hailsham.   by L F Salzmann.
Michelham Priory (guide brochures).   1957-2000.
Arlington Parish Council Minute Books
Sussex Express   (East Sussex Record Office)
East Sussex Record Office   (Tithe maps and schedules – Arlington and Hellingly)
(Court Rolls – AMS 5909/5, ADA 167, ACC2327-1-4-7 and 1-4-8)
(Indenture ACC 2327 1-4-33/3)
(Common land awards ACC 2327 1-4-31)
(Warneford Collection XA37/2)
(Land Tax LLT-Hellingly, Arlington XA31/1)

Chapter 2: Church of the Holy Trinity

Diocese of Chichester
The Dicker Parish – First Hundred Years   by Rev Filler   1943
Kelly's Directories
Sussex Express   (East Sussex Record Office)
Previous Offences   by W H Johnson   1997

Chapter 3: Non-conformity and the Chapels

The Chronicle of Britain   1992
Further History of the Gospel Vol 2   by S F Paul
Recollections of John Grace
The Strict Baptist Chapels of England   by R F Chambers
East Sussex Record Office
Sussex Express   (East Sussex Record Office)
SFM Vol 11 (Records discovered at Hellingly)
Kelly's Directories (1855)
Huge Cheese Company
Arlington 1843 Tithe Map   (East Sussex Record Office)
1875 and 1899 OS maps   (East Sussex Record Office)

Chapter 4: Roads and Transport

East Sussex Milestones   by B Austin and J Upton
ESCC Roads and Bridges Committee Minutes   í(East Sussex Record Office)
On Your Bicycle   by James McGurn   1987
The Country Bus   by John Hibbs   1986
The Golden Days on Heavy Haulage   by Bob Tuck   1992
The Old Roads of England   by W Addison   1980
The Turnpike Road System in England   by W Albert
Arlington Parish Council Minute Books
Sussex Express   (East Sussex Record Office)

Chapter 5: The Village School

Park Mead School Logs
Kelly's Directories
Sussex Express   (East Sussex Record Office)
Arlington Parish Council Minute Books

Chapter 6: Welfare in the Parish

The Chronicle of Britain   1992
An Historical Atlas of Sussex (Phillimore)   1999
Hailsham and its Environs   by C Robertson   1982
Arlington 1843 Tithe Map and Schedule
Sussex Express   (East Sussex Record Office)
Park Mead School Logs

Chapter 7: Commerce and Employment

Farming (Sources for Local Historians)   by Peter Edwards   1991
Rural Life   by Peter Edwards   1993
A Social History of England   by Asa Briggs   1994
English Villagers   by Valerie Porter   1992
A History of Hellingly   by R R Creasey   1980
Steam in the Village   by R A Whitehead   1977
Tractors at Work   by Stuart Gibbard   1994
Sussex Express   (East Sussex Record Office)
Seasons of Change   by Sadie Ward   1982
The Village Blacksmith   by Joycelyn Bailey   1977
Water Mills of Sussex Vol 1   by D Stiddert and C Smith   1997
The Windmills of Sussex   by M Brunnaruis   1979
An Historical Atlas of Sussex (Phillimore)   1999
Kelly's Directories
Brickmaking in Sussex   by Molly Beswick

Chapter 8: Bare Necessities

Seasons of Change   by Sadie Ward   1982
The Shopkeepers World   by Michael J Winstanley   1983

Kelly's Directories
Sussex Express   (East Sussex Record Office)
Arlington Parish Council Minute Books

Chapter 9: Recreation and Sport

Sussex Express   (East Sussex Record Office)
Arlington Parish Council Minute Books
Womens Institute records
Boy Scout Association
Guide and Brownie Association
Dicker Newsletters 1977-1989
A History of Cricket   by Benny Green   1988
Village Cricket   by Gerald Howat   1980
Dicker Cricket Club – Commemorative Booklet   by Jack Cocks   1977
Cycle Speedway in South (booklet) Kent and Sussex   by Robin Richardson   1946-56

Chapter 10: The Bottomley Era

The Real Horatio Bottomley   by Henry Houston
The Rise and Fall of Horatio Bottomley   by Alan Hyman
Horatio Bottomley – His Book
Sussex Express   (East Sussex Record Office)
Arlington Parish Council Minute Books

Chapter 11: A Village in Wartime

Action Stations – Airfields of Sussex
The War in East Sussex   by Sussex Express   1985
War in the Countryside   by Sadie Ward
The Secret Sussex Resistance   by Stuart Angel   1996
Battle over Sussex 1940   by P Burgess and A Saunders   1990
Blitz over Sussex 1941-42   by P Burgess and A Saunders   1994
Bombers over Sussex 1943-45   by P Burgess and A Saunders   1995
Eastbourne 1939-1945
Sussex Home Guard   by Paul Crook   1998
Hailsham at War   by George Farebrother
The Blitz – Then and Now   Vols 1, 2 and 3   1990
Military Aviation Museum, Tangmere
Sussex Express   (East Sussex Record Office)

Chapter 12: Continuity and Change in Dicker

Sussex Express (East Sussex Record Office)
In the Wake of the Hurricane Bob Ogley 1988
Dicker Newsletter   1978-1989

INDEX